Our Brilliant Heritage

containing

Grow Up Into Him

As He Walked

If You Will Be Perfect

Disciples Indeed

Our Brilliant Heritage

containing

Grow Up Into Him

As He Walked

If You Will Be Perfect

Disciples Indeed

Oswald Chambers

Books, music, and videos that feed the soul with the Word of God

Box 3566 Grand Rapids, MI 49501

Our Brilliant Heritage
© 1929 Oswald Chambers Publications Association
Grow Up Into Him
© 1931 Oswald Chambers Publications Association
As He Walked
© 1930 Oswald Chambers Publications Association
If You Will Be Perfect
(originally, *If Thou Wilt Be Perfect*)
© 1939 Oswald Chambers Publications Association
Disciples Indeed
© 1955 Oswald Chambers Publications Association

This edition © 1998 Oswald Chambers
Publications Association Limited. All rights reserved.

Discovery House Publishers is affiliated with RBC Ministries,
Grand Rapids, Michigan 49512

Discovery House books are distributed to the trade exclusively by
Barbour Publishing, Inc., Uhrichsville, Ohio 44683

Unless indicated otherwise, Scripture is taken from the New King James
Version. © 1979, 1980, 1982, Thomas Nelson Publishers, Inc.

Chambers, Oswald, 1874–1917.
    [Selections. 1998]
    Our brilliant heritage ; and, If you will be perfect ; with, Disciples
indeed / by Oswald Chambers.
        p.   cm.
    ISBN 1-57293-042-X
    1. Christian life. I. Title.
BV4501.2.C4742   1998
248.4—dc21   98-26759
                                                                    CIP

Printed in the United States of America

98 00 02 03 01 99
CHG
1 3 5 7 9 10 8 6 4 2

Contents

Disciples Indeed

Foreword to *If You Will Be Perfect*

On Tauler and *Theologia Germanica*

Two names are mentioned in this book, one is a man, Tauler, and the other a volume, *Theologia Germanica.* Quotations are made from them. Both belong to pre-Reformation times. John Tauler was born in Strasbourg about 1300. He was a Dominican monk and had already achieved honor and reputation as a preacher when a great change occurred in his spiritual outlook. An unknown layperson, after hearing him preach, was moved to tell him that he was allowing himself to be "killed by the letter" and was yet in darkness and had not tasted the sweetness of the Holy Spirit. The preacher took the words in a spirit of meekness and was ready to receive helpful counsel from his unknown friend. "You must," he said, "take up your cross and follow our Lord Jesus Christ and His example in utter sincerity, humility, and patience and must let go all your proud reasoning." He advised him to cease his preaching for a while and in quiet contemplation examine his life in the mirror of our Lord's. Tauler was nearly fifty, but he took the place of abasement and self-surrender and for nearly two years was a seeker of God's way, praying that God's life might be brought forth in him. His former friends thought him demented. When the clear light came and he knew the time had come to bear his witness in public, he found it not easy to begin, but soon wisdom and grace from the Holy Spirit were bestowed in abundant measure. So began years of wonderful work for God. In those days when salvation by simple faith in Jesus Christ was so largely hidden beneath ceremonial worship, he taught many that the way to God was by a new birth that brought people into a vital relation to the living God. His sermons greatly influenced Luther. They have ministered to many in many countries. A volume of his sermons has been published in English under the title, The Following of Christ.

The book *Theologia Germanica* belongs to the same period. Its author is unknown. It also prepared for the Reformation, as it lays stress on the Holy Spirit's application of Christ's work to the heart of a believer. God never leaves Himself without a witness, and in that dim period these lights were shining and have been shining ever since. John Wesley complained to William Law that when he was an earnest inquirer he had been directed to the mystic writers and so had missed the basic truth of salvation by faith in Jesus Christ. We all need to know the initial experience of Christ as the propitiation for our sins and as the One who has brought to a world of sinners the abundance of grace and the *gift* of righteousness. Afterwards we may find, as Wesley did, much light in such writers as the above upon how God works in us to will and to do for His good pleasure and how we can work out our own salvation (see Philippians 2:12–13). The quotations made by Oswald Chambers are themselves of great value, and the expository words that follow are full of luminous and practical teaching for us today.

David Lambert

Foreword to *Disciples Indeed*

Oswald Chambers was above all else a teacher of spiritual truth. Our ascended Lord's promise was to give His church "some to be . . . teachers, for the equipping of the saints" (Ephesians 4:11–12). This book contains messages spoken by such a teacher, full of wisdom and instruction in righteousness. Teachers call for learners. Some of us who heard the spoken word became humble and eager learners. Many who never saw or heard the speaker are learning from him now. In a recent letter the writer says, "It is not generally known how these books came into being, and the time seems favorable for revealing God's providence in it all." Oswald Chambers received his Home-call in 1917 when working with the YMCA among the troops in Egypt. It seemed like the end of a fruitful ministry. Then it was that Mrs. Chambers realized that her custom of taking down in shorthand her husband's lectures and addresses for her own profit had left her with a great store of spiritual wisdom that could be shared with the wider world by the printed page. So began a remarkable ministry of spreading in book form the original spoken words. As the writer of the above-mentioned letter says, "The whole matter is a sheer miracle, especially as the only planning has been God's."

Disciples Indeed, the latest book to be issued, speaks for itself. Other volumes show by the outlines and headings given what careful preparation was made for every spoken message. But often the spontaneous word of a Spirit-filled man, whether the subject was Christian doctrine, psychology, biblical ethics, or homiletics, would be added and appear in the shorthand notes. Many of these not included in the earlier publications are printed here. They touch a wide range of subjects and take us to the heart of Oswald Chambers's message. They make this book a kind of *vade mecum* of sainthood.

David Lambert

Our Brilliant Heritage

The Mystery of Sanctification

And without controversy great is the mystery of godliness: God was manifest in the flesh. 1 Timothy 3:16

By the word mystery we mean something known only to the initiated; therefore if we are going to understand the gospel mystery of sanctification and fully experience it, we must belong to the initiated, that is, we must be born from above by the Spirit of God. Robert Murray McCheyne said, and I would like his words engraved on my own heart, "The greatest need for my people is my personal holiness." Minister of the Gospel, say that of your congregation: "The greatest need for my people is my personal holiness." Teacher, say that of your class: "The greatest need for my Sunday school class is my personal holiness."

Am I born again of the Spirit of God? What is the relation of my heart to holiness? Our Lord said, "Every tree is known by its own fruit" (Luke 6:44), and I know whether I am born of the Spirit by the desires of my heart. Do I desire holiness more keenly than I desire any other thing? Do I desire that my motives, my heart, my life, everything in me, should be as pure as God wants it to be? If so, it is a strong witness to the fact that I am amongst the initiated; I am in the place where I can understand the mystery of sanctification sufficiently to enter into it.

The Awakening of Desires

Be transformed by the renewing of your mind. Romans 12:2

When we are born again of the Spirit of God, the Word of God awakens great desires in us, and in times of prayer the

Spirit of God renews our minds; in times of meeting with God's people the gracious sense of God's quickening comes until we know that the great desire of our hearts before God is to be as holy as God desires us to be. We do want to be baptized with the Holy Spirit so that we bear a strong family likeness to Jesus Christ. These deep desires are strong in the heart of everyone who is born from above. Paul says he speaks the mystery of God to all such, because they have the Spirit of God to enable them to understand it. We must watch and note whether these are our desires. The candi- dates for sanctification are those who have the firstfruits of sanctification in the initial work of grace, those who are rightly adjusted to God through the atonement of the Lord Jesus Christ and who hunger and thirst after holiness and desire to do all God's will.

Do we long for holiness? Are the deepest desires of our hearts Godward? Do we know, first of all, that we are recon- ciled to God? Do we know that our sins are forgiven, that God has put the life of His Spirit into us, and are we learning how to walk in the light, and are we gaining victories by the power of the Spirit? Do we realize that as we rely on God we have strength to perform our duties in accordance with God's will? All this is grand, ordinary, Christian experience in its elementary stages. All who are born again of the Spirit of God experience these things; they are the initiated, the ones who can understand the mystery of sanctification and, God grant, may enter into the experience of it.

There is a type of Christian who says, "Yes, I have the desire for holiness, I am reading God's Word, I am trying to be holy and to draw on the resurrection life of Jesus." Never will the mystery of sanctification dawn in that way, it is not God's way. Sin is a step *aside;* being born of the Spirit of God is a step *inside,* and sanctification is being built into all the perfect character of Jesus Christ *by a gift.*

Another type of Christian says, "Well, I have tried and striven and prayed, but I find it so hard to cut off my right arm, to poke out my right eye, that I have come to the conclusion that I am unworthy of this great blessing from God, I am not one of these special people who can be holy." I believe there are numbers of Christians who have laid themselves on one side, as it were, and come to the conclusion that sanctification is not meant for them, the reason being that they have tried to work sanctification out in their own ways instead of in God's way, and have failed.

There are others who by strange penances, fastings and prayers, and afflictions to their bodies are trying to work out sanctification. They, too, have tried to penetrate the mystery in a way other than God's appointed way.

Are you trying to work out sanctification in any of these ways? You know that salvation is a sovereign work of grace, but, you say, sanctification is worked out by degree. God grant that the Spirit of God may put His quiet check on you and enable you to understand the first great lesson in the mystery of sanctification, which is Christ Jesus, who of God is made to us sanctification.

Impartation, Not Imitation

Sanctification does not put us into the place that Adam was in and require us to fulfill the will of God as He makes it known to us; sanctification is something infinitely more than that. In Jesus Christ is perfect holiness, perfect patience, perfect love, perfect power over all the power of the Enemy, perfect power over everything that is not of God, and sanctification means that all that is ours in Him. The writer to the Hebrews does not tell us to imitate Jesus when we are tempted; he says, Come to Jesus, and He will succor you in the nick of time. That is, all *His* perfect overcoming of temptation is ours in Him.

We have heard it put in this way so often: When faced with difficulties, we do not try to brace ourselves up by prayer to meet them, but by the power of the grace of God we let the perfections of Jesus Christ be manifested in us. Jesus Christ does not give us power to work up a patience like His own. *His* patience is manifested if we will let His life dwell in us. So many have the idea that in sanctification we draw from Jesus the power to be holy. We draw from Jesus the holiness that was manifested in Him, and He manifests it in us. This is the mystery of sanctification.

Sanctification does not mean that the Lord gives us the ability to produce by a slow, steady process a holiness like His; it is *His* holiness in us. By sanctification we understand experimentally what Paul says in 1 Corinthians 1:30: "Of Him you are in Christ Jesus, who became for us . . . sanctification." Whenever Paul speaks of sanctification, he speaks of it as an impartation, never as an imitation. Imitation comes in on a different line. Paul does not say, nor does the Spirit of God say anywhere, that after we are born again of the Spirit of God, Jesus Christ is put before us as an example and we make ourselves holy by drawing from Him. Never! Sanctification is Christ formed in us—not the Christ-life, but Christ Himself. In Jesus Christ is the perfection of everything, and the mystery of sanctification is that we may have in Jesus Christ not the start of holiness but the holiness of Jesus Christ. All the perfections of Jesus Christ are at our disposal if we have been initiated into the mystery of sanctification. No wonder people cannot explain this mystery for the joy and the rapture and the marvel of it all, and no wonder people see it when it is there, for it works out everywhere.

The Mystery of Fellowship

We will come to him and make Our home with him. John 14:23

The nuggets of gold spoken by our Lord in the Gospels are beaten out by the apostles in the Epistles. Jesus states that the relationship between the Father and the Son is to be the relationship between the Father and the Son and the sanctified soul. Talk about "nothing between"! There is no possible room for anything between, unless the soul steps aside. As long as souls realize in the simplicity of faith that all that Jesus was and is is theirs, then the very life, the very faith, the very holiness of Jesus is imparted to them.

Think what the fellowship of our Lord Jesus Christ with His Father was when He was here: "I know that You always hear Me"; "I always do those things that please Him" (John 11:42; 8:29). This is not an example for us—it is infinitely more. It means that this fellowship is exactly what is made ours in sanctification. Jesus said, "In that day . . . , I do not say to you, that I shall pray the Father for you; for the Father Himself loves you" (16:26–27). In what day? The day when we are brought into that union of fellowship with the Father and all the perfections of Jesus are made ours, so that we can say with Paul: "It is no longer I who live, but Christ lives in me" (Galatians 2:20).

Those of you who are hungering and thirsting after holiness, think what it would mean to you to go out tonight knowing that you may step boldly into the heritage that is yours if you are born of the Spirit and realize that the perfections of Jesus are yours by His sovereign gift in such a way that you can prove it experimentally!

The Mystical Union

I am the vine, you are the branches. John 15:5

He who is joined to the Lord is one spirit with Him. 1 Corinthians 6:17

The New Testament exhausts itself in trying to expound the closeness of this union. The Spirit of God conveys to the initiated, to those who are born again, what a marvelous thing sanctification is. The perfections of Jesus—ours by the sheer gift of God; God does not give us power to imitate Him, He gives us His very self.

This is what sanctification means for you and me. Do you say it is too much? Do you know what it comes down to? It comes down to *faith;* our word is *confidence.* If we are born again of God by the Spirit, we have not the slightest doubt in our minds of Jesus Christ; we have absolute confidence in Him. But draw nearer still—have we confidence to let the Spirit of God explain to us what sanctification means and lead us into the experience? If so, instead of it being painful to follow the ways of wisdom, we will find that "her ways are ways of pleasantness, and all her paths are peace" (Proverbs 3:17).

The Mystery of the Incarnation

> Therefore, also, that Holy One who is to be born will be called the Son of God. Luke 1:35

There are three big mysteries: the mystery of the triune God—Father, Son and Holy Spirit; the mystery of our Lord Jesus Christ, who is both human and divine; and the mystery we are dealing with—the mystery that I, a sinner, can be made into the image of Jesus Christ by the great work of His atonement in my life.

Have you ever noticed how our Lord's death is explained and applied by the Spirit of God in the apostle Paul's teaching? For instance, "Therefore we were buried with Him through baptism into death, that just as Christ was raised from the dead by the glory of the Father, even so we also should walk in newness of life" (Romans 6:4) means that all that our Lord's death is stated to mean in the New Testament can be made real in our experience. We can go through iden-tification with the death of Jesus until we are alive only to the things that He was alive to. Jesus Christ does not give us power to put the "old man" to death in ourselves: "our old man was crucified with Him" (verse 6); we can be identified with His death and know that this is true. We are not merely put into a state of innocence before God; by identification with our Lord's death we are delivered from sin in every bit of its power and every bit of its presence.

God never removes from us the power of stepping aside—we can step aside any moment we like. Read 1 John: *If anyone steps aside* (see 2:1). John's thought is surely that it is a rare thing for someone to step aside. Our attitude seems to be that it is a rare thing to keep in the light!

"And raised us up together, and made us sit together in heavenly places"—like Christ Jesus? No, *"in* Christ Jesus" (Ephesians 2:6, emphasis added). The very Spirit that ruled Jesus in His life now rules us. How has it come about? Read Romans 8:10: "And if Christ is in you, the body is dead because of sin, but the Spirit is life because of righteousness." John the Baptist said of Jesus: "He will baptize you with the Holy Spirit and fire" (Luke 3:16). The Spirit of God who wrought out that marvelous life in the Incarnation will bap-tize us into the very same life—not into a life like it—but into His life, until the very holiness of Jesus is gifted to us. It is not something we work out in Him, it is *in Him,* and He man-ifests it through us while we abide in Him. This explains why in the initial stages of sanctification we sometimes see mar-velous exhibitions of Christlike life and patience. All that was wrought out in the life of Jesus was wrought out by the Holy Spirit whom our Lord has poured out by His ascended right, and by the baptism of the Holy Spirit the perfections of Jesus are made ours. We are not put into the place where we can imitate Jesus; the baptism of the Holy Spirit puts us into the very life of Jesus. Are you hungering after sanctification? Have you such confidence in Jesus that you can pray this prayer, the prayer of a child: "Father, in the name of Jesus, baptize me with the Holy Spirit and fire until sanctification is made real in my life"?

The Gospel of the Grace of God

To me, who am less than the least of all the saints, this grace was given, that I should preach among the Gentiles the unsearchable riches of Christ. Ephesians 3:8

To them God willed to make known what are the riches of the glory of this mystery among the Gentiles: which is Christ in you, the hope of glory. Colossians 1:27

The mystery of sanctification is that the perfections of Jesus Christ are imparted to us, not gradually, but instantly, when by faith we enter into the realization that Christ is made to us sanctification. Sanctification does not mean anything less than the holiness of Jesus Christ being made ours manifestly, and faith is the instrument given us to use in order to work out this unspeakable mystery in our lives. There are two means: the Gospel of the grace of God and faith, which enable the life and liberty and power and marvel of the holiness of Jesus Christ to be wrought in us.

The Instrument of Faith

Do we know anything about this mystical union whereby the unsearchable riches of Jesus Christ are made ours? If we have been born from above of the Spirit of God, the deep craving of our hearts is to be as holy as Jesus Christ, and just as we took the first step in salvation by faith, so we take the next step by faith. We are invited, we are commanded and pleaded with, to believe the Gospel of the grace of God, which is, "Christ in you, the hope of glory."

The one marvelous secret of a holy life is not in imitating Jesus but in letting the perfections of Jesus manifest themselves in our mortal flesh. Do we believe that? Do we believe it with the same simple trust and confidence we had when we first trusted Jesus to save us? The way to believe it is to listen first. "So then faith comes by hearing, and hearing by the word of God" (Romans 10:17). Have we listened? Have we ever listened with the ears of our spirits to this wonderful statement, "Christ in you"? Do we hear that? If we are born of the Spirit of God, we do hear it; we hear it more eagerly, more passionately, more longingly than anything else that can be told. We are invited and commanded by God to believe that we can be made one with Jesus as He is one with God, so that His patience, His holiness, His purity, His gentleness, His prayerfulness are made ours. The way the gift of faith works in us and makes this real is by hearing. We first hear, and then we begin to trust. It is so simple that most of us miss the way. The way to have faith in the Gospel of God's grace, in its deepest profundity as well as in its first working, is by listening to it. How many of us have brought the ears of our spirits straight down to the Gospel of God's grace?

Our ideas of faith have a good deal to do with the harmful way faith is often spoken of. Faith is looked upon as an attitude of mind whereby we assent to a testimony on the authority of the one who testifies. We say that because Jesus says these things, we believe in Him. The faith of the New Testament is infinitely more than that; it is the means by which sanctification is manifested, the means of introducing the life of God into us—not the effect of our understanding only. In Romans 3:24–25, Paul speaks about faith in the blood of Jesus, and faith is the instrument the Spirit of God uses. Faith is more than an attitude of the mind; faith is the complete, passionate, earnest trust of the whole nature in the Gospel of God's grace as it is presented in the life and death and resurrection of our Lord Jesus Christ.

Implicit Trust in Jesus

Some of us have never allowed God to make us understand how hopeless we are without Jesus Christ. It was my experience of the Tempter and my knowledge of my own heart under his assaults that made me a preacher of Paul's gospel. It was my own exceeding sinfulness of heart that ever more and more taught and compelled me to preach Jesus Christ alone, His blood and His righteousness. Everyone who is born again of the Spirit of God knows that there is no good thing outside the Lord Jesus Christ. It is no use looking for sanctification through prayer or obedience; sanctification must be the direct gift of God by means of this instrument of faith—not a half-hearted faith but the most earnest, intense, and personal faith.

Sanctification is "Christ in you." Is anything we hear in testimonies to sanctification untrue of Jesus Christ? It is *His* wonderful life that is imparted to us in sanctification, and it is imparted by faith. It will never be imparted as long as we cling to the idea that we can get it by obedience, by doing this and that. We have to come back to one thing, faith alone, and after having been put right with God by sanctification, it is still a life of faith all through. Those who are in the experience of sanctification know that it means that the holiness of Jesus is imparted as a sovereign gift of God's grace. We cannot earn it, we cannot pray it down, but, thank God, we can take it by faith: "by His blood, through faith " (Romans 3:25).

When we have become rightly related to God, it is the trial of our faith that is precious (see 1 Peter 1:7). Satan tries to come in and make the saint disbelieve that sanctification is only by faith in God; he comes in with his cinematography show and says, "You must have this, and you must do that." The Spirit of God keeps us steadily to one line—faith in Jesus and the trial of our faith, until the perfections of Jesus Christ are lived over again in our lives.

Identification with Jesus

God says that He will give us the desires of our hearts. What are our desires? What do we desire more than anything else on earth? If we are born again of the Spirit of God, our one desire is a hunger and thirst after nothing less than holiness, the holiness of Jesus, and He will satisfy it.

"Whoever eats My flesh and drinks My blood has eternal life" (John 6:54). Just as we take food into our bodies and assimilate it, so, Jesus says, we must take Him into our souls. Faith is not seeing food and drink on the table; faith is taking it. So many say, "Oh, yes, I have faith that the Lord Jesus will save me." If we have faith that the Lord Jesus will save us, we *are* saved, and we know it. When, by the Spirit of God, Jesus is made real to us, His presence makes everything as natural as breathing. His presence is the reality.

What do we do to earn a gift? Nothing; we take it. If we have the slightest remnant of thinking we can earn it, we will never take it; if we are quite certain we do not deserve it, we will take it. We come with the sense of abject unworthiness, knowing that "in me (that is, in my flesh) nothing good dwells" (Romans 7:18); if ever I am to be holy, I must be made holy by God's sovereign grace. That is the Gospel. We receive it by faith, and the Spirit of God is the One who makes the simple act of faith the supernatural work of God. To those outside Christian experience it sounds foolish; to those inside it is wonderfully real. As soon as we stretch out the instrument of faith with implicit trust, the Spirit of God imparts to us the holiness of Jesus Christ and all that means, and it is on this line alone we live. Obedience is the means whereby we show the earnestness of our desire to do God's will. We receive this perfect adjustment to God as a gift and then begin to manifest the life of Jesus Christ in our mortal flesh.

Those of you who have never had this experience of sanctification, think! The perfections of Jesus Christ made yours entirely! The Lord showing His love, His purity, His holiness through you! "It is no longer I who live, but Christ lives in me" (Galatians 2:20). It is not power to live like Jesus; it is Christ living in us, and it is His life that is seen, but it is only seen as, by faith, we walk in the light.

What does Paul say? "My little children, for whom I labor in birth again until Christ is formed in you" (4:19); and again, "We are His workmanship, created in Christ Jesus for good works" (Ephesians 2:10). How many of us can look up into God's face by simple faith, trusting entirely in the great Gospel of His grace, and say, "Lord, make the sanctification in me as real as the sanctification revealed in Your Word"? Are we willing for Him to do it? Then we must turn from every other thing and trust in Him. Jesus Christ re-creates us by His marvelous life until we are new creations in Him, and "all things are from God" (1 Corinthians 11:12). The life is lived naturally as we lived the old life. Consciously? No, infinitely deeper; it is lived moment by moment by the faith of the Son of God; only in rare moments are we conscious of it. When we come up against a crisis, for a moment we hesitate and wonder how we are going to meet the difficulty, then we find that it is the perfections of Jesus Christ imparted into us that meet it, and slowly and surely we begin to live lives of ineffable order and sanity and holiness, kept by the power of God. No wonder the apostle Paul says, "When He comes . . . to be glorified in His saints and to be admired among all those who believe" (2 Thessalonians 1:10)!

Have you any doubt about the Gospel of the grace of God? None whatever, you say. Then launch out in simple faith and say, "My God, make the sanctification of the New Testament mine, make the unsearchable riches of Jesus Christ mine till my Lord and I are one"—so much one that it never consciously occurs to you to be anything else, and in all the circumstances of life you will find that you have the perfections of Jesus Christ—at the back of you? No, dwelling in you! No wonder the apostle John is so eager that we should walk in the light!

Unrealized Truths of Sanctification

Therefore, if anyone is in Christ, he is a new creation; old things have passed away; behold, all things have become new. Now all things are of God, who has reconciled us to Himself by Jesus Christ, and has given to us the ministry of reconciliation. 2 Corinthians 5:17–18

I want to deal with some of the unrealized truths of sanctification, the things we do not readily notice, from the standpoint of the new creation in Christ Jesus. As we have seen, the idea of sanctification is not that God gives us a new spirit of life and then puts Jesus Christ in front of us as a copy and says, Do your best and I will help you; but God imparts to us the perfections of Jesus Christ. By the perfections of Jesus we do not mean His attributes as Son of God. What is imparted to us is the holiness of Jesus, not a principle of life that enables us to imitate Him, but the holiness of Jesus as it meets life in Him.

Creation through Christ

For by Him all things were created that are in heaven and that are on earth, visible and invisible, whether thrones or dominions or principalities or powers. All things were created through Him and for Him. Colossians 1:16

And to the angel of the church of the Laodiceans write, "These things says the Amen, the Faithful and True Witness, the beginning of the creation of God." Revelation 3:14

These verses are chosen out of a number in the Bible that reveal that God almighty created the world and everything that was created through the eternal Son. Some people tell us that Revelation 3:14 means that the Son was the first creation of God almighty. The Bible does not say so. The Bible says, "He is before all things, and in Him all things consist" (Colossians 1:17). Jesus Christ was introduced into the world in this way: the Spirit of God took hold of a part of that creation, of which the Son of God was Himself the Creator, in the Virgin Mary and formed in her the Son of God: "Therefore, also, that Holy One who is to be born will be called the Son of God" (Luke 1:35). That is the last reach of the creation of God. The Son of God was the One whom we know as Jesus Christ, and in the life of Jesus we have the pattern life of all God desires humanity to be, and also the pattern life of sanctification.

Creation in Christ

> All things were made through Him, and without Him nothing was made that was made. In Him was life, and the life was the light of men. John 1:3–4

By creation we are the children of God; we are not the sons and daughters of God by creation; Jesus Christ makes us sons and daughters of God by regeneration (see John 1:12). The idea of the fatherhood of Jesus is revealed in the Bible, though rarely mentioned. "Everlasting Father" (Isaiah 9:6) refers to the Being we know as the Son of God. Paul, in talking to the Athenians, said, "We are the offspring of God" (Acts 17:29). But the creator-power in Jesus Christ is vested in a more marvelous way even than when God created the world through Him, for He has that in Himself whereby He can create His own image. God created the world and everything that was made through the Son, and "in Him was life"; therefore just as God created the world through Him, the Son is able to create His own image in anyone and everyone. Have we ever thought of Jesus as the marvelous Being who can create in us His own image? "Therefore, if anyone is in Christ, he is a new creation."

We do not sufficiently realize the wonder of it. Those of us who are in the experience of God's mighty salvation do not give ourselves half enough prayerful time and wondering time and studying time to allow the Spirit of God to bring this marvelous truth home to us. "Most assuredly, I say to you, he who believes in Me has everlasting life" (John 6:47). The very life that was in Jesus is the life of the soul who believes in Him, because it is created in that soul by Jesus. This life is only in Jesus Christ, it is not in anyone else, and we cannot get it by obeying or by praying, by vowing or by sacrificing. "Do not marvel that I said to you, 'You must be born again'" (John 3:7). We must have the image of God in our spirits, and Jesus will create His image in us by His sovereign right. The fullest and most gracious meaning of regeneration and sanctification is that in Christ Jesus we can be made new creations. Sanctification is not being given a new start, not that God wipes out the past and says it is forgiven, but something inconceivably grander, namely, that Jesus Christ has the power to create in us the image of God as it was in Himself. Paul says, "My little children, for whom I labor in birth again"—every strand of my spirit and soul and body aches—"until Christ is formed in you" (Galatians 4:19). "I fear," he says, "lest somehow . . . your minds may be corrupted from the simplicity that is in Christ" (2 Corinthians 11:3). "Beware lest anyone cheat you through philosophy" (Colossians 2:8). We have already dealt with this along the line of faith; we have to receive Jesus Christ in implicit confidence and let Him do His work in us. Creation in Christ means that Jesus Christ is able to create us into His own image, not merely recreate us, because what we get in Jesus Christ is something that Adam never had. Adam was created a "son of God," an innocent being with all the possibilities of development before him; God intended him to take part in that development by a series of moral choices whereby the natural life was to be sacrificed to the will of God and turned into a spiritual life. Adam failed to do this. Jesus Christ creates in us not what was in Adam, He creates in us what He was and is. "Christ Jesus, who became for us . . . sanctification" (1 Corinthians 1:30). This is the meaning of the grand old evangelical hymn:

> My hope is built on nothing less
> Than Jesus' blood and righteousness.

Creation like Christ

As He is, so are we in this world. 1 John 4:17

Those of us who are God's children ought to stand in determined reverence before this verse. It can mean only one thing, and that is that the image and character and holiness of Jesus Christ is ours by the sovereign right of His creation. Sanctification means that we are taken into a mystical union that language cannot define (compare 1 John 3:2). It is Jesus Christ's holiness that is granted to us—not something pumped up by prayer and obedience and discipline but something created in us by Jesus Christ. No wonder the New Testament puts Jesus Christ upon the throne! No wonder Jesus said that the Holy Spirit would glorify Him! And no wonder this talk is called "*Unrealized* Truths of Sanctification"!

We are potentially sons and daughters of God through God's claim upon us in Christ, but we are only sons and daughters of God *in reality* through our wills. Do we will not to imitate Jesus but to hand ourselves over to God until His claim is realized in us? Paul says, "We are ambassadors for Christ, as though God were pleading through us: we implore you on Christ's behalf, be reconciled to God" (2 Corinthians 5:20). It is one thing to realize in speechless wonder, when the heart is attuned to an impulse of worship, what the claim of God is, and another thing to tell God that we want Him to realize His claim in us. "My God, I am Yours by creation, I am Jesus Christ's through His atonement, and I choose that Your claim shall be realized in me."

"Therefore if anyone is in Christ, he is a new creation." *Anyone* means us—people of no account. Our Lord never taught individualism; He taught the value of the individual, a very different thing. Does Paul mean that I, an ordinary person with no particular education, with ordinary, commonplace work, surrounded by commonplace people, can be made a new creation in Christ Jesus? He does, because he says "anyone," and you must come in there. Will you choose to be one of the ordinary, common rut—the "anyone"—and let God get hold of you? You are part of the creation of God—then let Jesus Christ make His creation good in you.

Jesus Christ does not make us original characters, He makes our characters replicas of His own; consequently, argues the Spirit of God, when people see us, they will not say, What wonderful, original, extraordinary characters. No, none of that rubbish! They will say, How marvelous God must be to take poor pieces of human stuff like those people and turn them into the image of Jesus Christ—"things which angels desire to look into" (1 Peter 1:12). We are too free from wonder nowadays, too easy with the Word of God; we do not use it with the breathless amazement Paul does. Think what sanctification means—*Christ in me; made like Christ; as He is, so are we.*

The Transient Life

Old things have passed away . . .

By "old things" Paul does not mean sin and the "old man" only, he means everything that was our lives as natural people before we were re-created in spirit by Christ. That means a great deal more than some of us mean. The "old things" means not only things that are wrong—any fool will give up wrong things who can—but things that are right. Watch the life of Jesus and you will get Paul's meaning. Our Lord lived a natural life as we do; it was not a sin for Him to eat, but it would have been a sin for Him to eat during those forty days in the wilderness, because during that time His Father's will for Him was otherwise, and He sacrificed His natural life to the will of God. That is the way the "old things" pass away.

In 2 Corinthians, Paul uses as an illustration of this the glory that came from Moses. It was a real glory, but it was a glory that was "passing away" (3:7), and the writer to the Hebrews writes of a covenant that was doomed "to vanish away" (8:13). The natural human life is a real creation of God, but it is meant to pass away into a spiritual life in Jesus Christ's way. Watch Paul's argument in the epistle to the Romans: "But you are not in the flesh but in the Spirit" (8:9). Paul was talking to flesh-and-blood women and men, not to disembodied spirits, and he means that the old order is passed. You used to look at things differently from Jesus Christ, he says, but now that you have turned to the Lord (God grant you may if you have not), the veil is taken away, and "where the Spirit of the Lord is, there is liberty" (2 Corinthians 3:17).

The Transfigured Life

Behold, all things have become new . . .

Have those of us who are in the experience of sanctification learned the practical, insistent habit of realizing that the old things have passed away and that all things have become new? In their testimonies people put it in this way: "God alters the thing that matters; it used to matter to me what certain people thought, now it does not matter at all." Old things have passed away, not only sin and the old disposition, but the whole old order of things, and behold, all things have become new.

Paul is trying to get us to an amazed state of mind: "Therefore if anyone is in Christ, he is a new creation"! Some of us talk about sanctification as if we were talking of a new book or an article in the newspaper. With Paul, the wonder never ceased; however often he talked about it, each time he was more full of wonder than the last.

The great, mighty work of God's grace in sanctification is a divine work. Do we choose to walk in God's way and let Him make it real in us? Then let the things that have passed *be* passed, and when the circumstances come again that tempt us to self-pity, remember that the old things have passed away. Do we choose never to let things affect us that never affected Jesus Christ? As soon as we do, we will find it is possible because the perfections of Jesus Christ are made ours by the sovereign right of His creation. No wonder Paul talks of "the unsearchable riches of Christ" (Ephesians 3:8)! No wonder the marvel of the revelation breaks through his language and escapes, until those who are not sanctified think him mad, and John is called an old man in "the sere and yellow leaf" who talked vaguely about the possibility of living without sin! Those who talk in this way have never entered into the wonderful experience of sanctification, but, thank God, it is for "anyone."

The Truest Life of All

> . . . All things are of God.

"Therefore be imitators"—of good principles? of holiness? of the life Jesus lived on earth? No! "Therefore be imitators of God" (Ephesians 5:1).

"Therefore you shall be perfect, just as your Father in heaven is perfect" (Matthew 5:48). God by sanctification creates us into the image of His Son. Do we choose to walk in the light of that life? Never make excuses, never turn to the right hand nor to the left. Keep the life concentrated on this marvelous gift of God, "Christ Jesus, who became for us . . . sanctification."

In Heavenly Places

And raised us up together, and made us sit together in heavenly places in Christ Jesus. Ephesians 2:6

Sanctification is the impartation to us of the holy qualities of Jesus Christ. It is His patience, His love, His holiness, His faith, His purity, His godliness that are manifested in and through every sanctified soul. The presentation that God by sanctification plants within us His Spirit and then, setting Jesus Christ before us, says, There is your Example; follow Him and I will help you, but you must do your best to follow Him and do what He did—is an error. It is not true to experience, and, thank God, it is not true to the wonderful Gospel of the grace of God. The mystery of sanctification is "Christ in you, the hope of glory" (Colossians 1:27). "Without Him nothing was made that was made. In Him was life" (John 1:3–4); that is, Jesus Christ can create in us the image of God even as it was in Himself.

The Impartial Power of God

And raised us up . . .

Who are the "us" He has raised up? We have pointed out the "anyone" aspect, and it needs pointing out because we often hear someone say: "Well, it cannot mean me, I'm not a true, fine-spirited person; my past life has been very sordid; I have not had the advantages of other people, and it cannot mean me; God cannot mean that by His marvelous grace He can raise *me* up." Yes, He can, and it is just such people He does mean. God stoops down to the very lowest, to the very weakest, to the disobedient, the children of wrath, and raises them right up. In this particular instance Paul is driving home the impartiality of God with more than usual insistence; he is talking to Gentiles and he says that God by the cross of Jesus Christ makes no distinction between Jew and Gentile in the matter of personal salvation. Thank God for the impartiality of His grace!

Anyone, everyone, we ourselves, may partake of this marvelous raising up whereby God puts us into the wonderful life of His Son, and the very qualities of Jesus Christ are imparted to us. There is plenty of room to grow in the heavenly places; room for the head to grow, for the heart to grow, for the bodily relationships to grow, for the spirit to grow—plenty of room for every phase of us to grow into the realization of what a marvelous Being our Lord Jesus Christ is.

"God . . . made us alive together with Christ" (Ephesians 2:4–5). The illustration Paul uses is that as God raised the dead body of Jesus, so He has made alive those who were dead in trespasses and sins and has raised them up with Jesus. It means that there is a participation now in all the wonderful perfections of Jesus Christ and that ultimately "we shall be like Him, for we shall see Him as He is" (1 John 3:2).

The Inviolable Place of God

... heavenly places in Christ Jesus.

That is where God raises us. We do not get there by climbing, by aspiring, by struggling, by consecration, or by vows; God lifts us right straight up out of sin, inability and weakness, lust and disobedience, wrath and self-seeking—lifts us right up out of all this, "up, up to the whiter than snow shine," to the heavenly places where Jesus Christ lived when He was on earth and where He lives to this hour in the fullness of the plenitude of His power. May God never relieve us from the wonder of it. We are lifted up into that inviolable place that cannot be defiled, and Paul states that

God can raise us up there *now,* and that the wonder of sitting in the heavenly places in Christ Jesus is to be manifested in our lives while we are here on earth.

"And made us sit together." Sit? But I have to earn my living! Sit? But I am in the midst of the wild turmoil of city life! Sit? But I have my calling in life and my ambitions to fulfill! Paul says that God has raised us up and made us *sit* together in heavenly places in Christ Jesus. We must have in our minds that by "heavenly places" is meant all that Jesus Christ was when He was down here and all that He is revealed to be now by the Word, and God raises us up to sit together with Him there. There is ample time and ample room to grow in the heavenly places.

The Symbols in the Heavenly Places

Have you ever noticed the kind of pictures God gives to the saints? They are always pictures of creation, never pictures of people. God speaks of the unfailing stars and the upholding of the "worm Jacob" (Isaiah 41:14). He talks about the marvels of creation and makes His people forget the rush of business ideas that stamp the kingdoms of this world. The Spirit of God says, Do not take your pattern and print from those; the God who holds you is the God who made the world—take your pattern from Him. The marvelous characteristic of the Spirit of God in you and me when we are raised up to the heavenly places in Christ Jesus is that we look to the Creator and see that the marvelous Being who made the world and upholds all things by the word of His power is the One who keeps us in every particular.

Our Lord always took His illustrations from His Father's handiwork. In illustrating the spiritual life, our tendency is to catch the tricks of the world, to watch the energy of the business realm and to apply these methods to God's work. Jesus Christ tells us to take the lessons of our lives from the things people never look at: "Look at the birds of the air. . . . Consider the lilies" (Matthew 6:26, 28). How often do we look at clouds or grass, at sparrows or flowers? Why, we have no time to look at them, we are in the rush of things—it is absurd to sit dreaming about sparrows and trees and clouds! Thank God, when He raises us to the heavenly places, He manifests in us the very mind that was in Christ Jesus, unhasting and unresting, calm, steady, and strong.

The Safety of the Heavenlies

My peace I give to you. John 14:27

For you died, and your life is hidden with Christ in God. Colossians 3:3

We are familiar with these verses, but has God ever struck the marvel out of them, until we are lost in wonder, love, and praise as they are applied to us as sanctified souls? "My peace I give to you." We talk about the peace of Jesus, but have we ever realized what that peace was like? Read the story of His life, the thirty years of quiet submission at Nazareth, the three years of service, the slander and spite, backbiting and hatred He endured—all unfathomably worse than anything we shall ever have to go through—and His peace was undisturbed, it could not be violated. It is that peace that God will exhibit in us in the heavenly places—not a peace like it, but that peace. In all the rush of life, in working for our living, in all conditions of bodily life, wherever God engineers our circumstances: "My peace"; the imperturbable, inviolable peace of Jesus imparted to us in every detail of our lives. "Your life is hidden with Christ in God." Have we allowed the wonder of it to enwrap us round and soak us through, until we begin to realize the ample room there is to grow there? "The secret place of the Most High" (Psalm 91:1), absolutely secure and safe.

As we go on in life and grow in grace, we realize more and more wonderingly what the peace of Jesus means. Watch the saint who is sanctified, "in tumults," Paul says— tribulation, turmoil, trouble, afflictions all around every' where, yet the peace of Jesus is gifted and manifests itself, and the life grows as the lily spiritually. Tolstoy made the blunder of applying the teaching of Jesus to people who were not born again of the Holy Spirit, and with what result? They found it impossible to carry it out. But when we are born again from above, made alive and raised up by God, we find it is possible to consider the lilies because we have not only the peace of God, but the very peace that characterized Jesus Christ; we are seated in heavenly places in Christ Jesus, absolutely safe, the mind imperturbably ensphered in Christ. "For you died," says Paul; that is, the old way of looking at things, the old way of doing things, the old fuss and fume are dead, and you are a new creation in Christ Jesus, and in that new creation is manifested the very peace that was mani' fested in Jesus Christ.

The Strength in the Heavenlies

Every spiritual blessing in the heavenly places in Christ. Ephe- sians 1:3

The unsearchable riches of Christ. Ephesians 3:8

God is able to make all grace abound toward you. 2 Corinthians 9:8

These verses mean that just as the overflowing, omnipo' tent power of God was exhibited in and through our Lord, so it will be exhibited in and through us when we are raised up into the heavenly places. Get into the habit of saying, "Lord Jesus, prove Yourself sufficient in me for this thing now." Do not say, "Oh, Lord, show me what to do"; let Him do it and it will be done. It is *His* perfections, not ours: His patience, His love, His holiness, His strength; "every spiritual blessing . . . in Christ." How blind we are! There is a danger with the children of God of getting too familiar with sublime things. We talk so much about these wonderful realities and forget that we have to exhibit them in our lives. It is perilously possible to mistake the exposition of the truth for the truth; to run away with the idea that because we are able to expound these things we are living them too. Paul's warning comes home to us: "lest, when I have preached to others, I myself should become disqualified" (1 Corinthians 9:27).

The Sight in the Heavenlies

Blessed are the pure in heart. Matthew 5:8

What do we mean by "pure in heart"? We mean nothing less and nothing else than what the Son of God was and is. When God raises us up into the heavenly places, He imparts to us the very purity that is Jesus Christ's. That is what the sanctified life means—the undisturbable range of His peace, the unshakable, indefatigable power of His strength, and the unfathomable, crystalline purity of His holiness. There is plenty of room in the heavenly places to grow into the realization of the unfathomable depths of the purity of Christ's heart.

"Blessed are the pure in heart, for they shall see God." When the Son of God "walked this earth with naked feet, and wove with human hands the creed of creeds," He understood the revealed counsels of His Father to Him because His heart was pure, and to the sanctified soul God says, Friend, come up higher. Jesus warns disciples never to be afraid of the contempt of the world when they possess spiritual discernment. Those who are in the heavenly places see God's counsels in what, to the wisdom of the world, is arrogant stupidity. We can never stand for one second in the heavenly places in a secular mood. Jesus never had secular moods, His heart was never defiled by secular thinking or by secular ways. What do we mean by secular ways? Secularity has to do with what we desire within, not with what happens to our bodies. What do we desire most? What the heart of Jesus wanted most was God's glory, and sanctification means that that same desire is imparted to us. The wonder of a pure heart is that it is as pure as Jesus Christ's heart. Sanctification does not mean that a purity like Jesus Christ's is gifted to us but that *His* purity is gifted to us. Our Lord was wonderfully sensitive to the things of God, and He says: "all things that I have heard from My Father I have made known to you" (John 15:15). His Father distinctly revealed things to Him. The sanctified soul realizes with growing amazement what we are trying feebly to put into words, that all these things are ours if we are willing for God to realize His claim in us. "All things are yours. . . . And you are Christ's, and Christ is God's" (1 Corinthians 3:21, 23).

To be "in Christ Jesus" means that we are initiated into the position of sons and daughters. Do you know how God speaks to His sons and daughters? He softly breathes His stern messages in the heavenly places—with what result? There is never any panic in His sons and daughters. The Son of God had preintimations of what was to happen, and as we walk with the mind stayed where God places it by sanctification, in that way steadfastly keeping our garments white, we will find that nothing strikes us with surprise or with panic. God never allows it to, He keeps us in perfect peace while He whispers His secrets and reveals His counsels. We are struck with panic whenever we turn out of the way, when we forget to "grow up in all things into Him" (Ephesians 4:15), when we forget to keep the childlike weakness that never dreams it can look at things in the way Jesus does apart from His Spirit.

"Bringing every thought into captivity to the obedience of Christ" (2 Corinthians 10:5). Our Lord never pried into His Father's secrets, neither will the saint. Some have made the blunder of trying to wrest God's secrets from Him. That was never Jesus Christ's way, nor is it communicated by the Spirit of God. God always gifted His intimations to His Son. How many of us have allowed God to reveal His counsels to us in this way, and how many of us are being humiliated by realizing that we have been trying to probe into God's secrets some other way? When we are raised up into the heavenly places, it is a life of joy unspeakable and full of glory.

One word of warning—we must guard the life where the Spirit of God warns we should guard it, and the first thing to be guarded against is inordinate curiosity. Remember what Jesus said of Himself and of the Holy Spirit: "I do nothing of Myself; but as My Father taught me, I speak these things" (John 8:28). "The Spirit of truth . . . will not speak on His own authority, but whatever He hears He will speak" (16:13). When our minds are stayed on God, and we are growing in the realization of the purity of Christ's heart and His wonderful strength and power, we will find that that same characteristic is being worked out in us—there is no mental or intellectual insubordination, but a complete subordination to Jesus Christ, even as He was subordinated to His Father. The same thing is true of our wills; just as Jesus brought His will into subjection to His Father and said, "I do not seek My own will but the will of the Father who sent Me" (5:30), when we are raised up to the heavenly places in Christ Jesus, we will manifest the same.

Whenever a decline comes, whenever there is a tendency to turn aside, we will find God is a consuming fire; He will hold and hurt cruelly, and we may cry out to Him to let us go, but He will not let us go. God loves us too much to let us go, and He will burn and burn until there is nothing left but the purity that is as pure as He is—unless we determine to side with the impure and become as reprobate silver. People are apt to cry to God to stop; "If only God would leave me alone!" God never will. His passionate, inexorable love never allows Him to leave people alone, and with His children He will shake everything that can be shaken till there is nothing that can be shaken anymore; then will abide the consuming fire of God until the life is changed into the same image from glory to glory, and people see that strong family likeness to Jesus that can never be mistaken.

The Inheritance of the Saints

Giving thanks to the Father who has qualified us to be partakers
of the inheritance of the saints in the light. Colossians 1:12.

Sanctification means the impartation to us and through us of
the Lord Jesus Christ, His patience, His purity, His holiness.
It is not that Jesus Christ enables us to imitate Him, not that
the power of God is in us and we try our best and fail and try
again, but that the very virtues of Jesus Christ are manifested
in our mortal flesh.

The Possession of Light

The inheritance of the saints in the light.

How often God's book refers to God as light, to Jesus
Christ as light, to the Spirit of God as light, and to the saints
as light! By sanctification God places us in the light that He is
in, the light in which our Lord Jesus lived His life. "The life
was the light of men" (John 1:4). Our inheritance in the light
means that we manifest in our mortal flesh the life of the
Lord Jesus Christ. The light means the very things He exhibited, a life full of approach to God, full of understanding of
God and of humanity.

"He who follows Me shall not walk in darkness, but have
the light of life" (8:12). Supposing you are walking over a
moor at night; you know there is a path but it is too dark and
obscure for you to see, then the moon struggles through the
clouds and you see the path, a clear strip of white, straight
across the hill; in a little while all is obscure again, but you

have seen the path and you know the way to go. There are times in our experiences when life is just like that. We do not see the path though we know it is there, then the light shines and we see it, and when darkness comes again we can step boldly. Sometimes the light is as the moonlight or the dawn, or it comes as a terrifying flash of lightning, when all of a sudden we see the way we should go. "While you have the light, believe in the light, that you may become sons of light" (12:36). Have we believed in the light we have had? Can we recall the time when the light of God in the face of Jesus Christ was clearer to us than anything else has ever been, when we saw perfectly clearly and understood exactly what the Lord wanted? Did we believe in that light, and have we walked up to the light? Can we say tonight, "I was not disobedient to the heavenly vision" (Acts 26:19)? So many of us see the light, we see the way across the moor; by a sudden lightning flash of God's revealing grace we see the way to go—but we do not take it. We say, "Oh, yes, I did receive the Spirit of God, and I thought that it would be like this and that, but it has not been." The reason is that we did not believe in the light when it was given. You say, "I am a Christian, I have been born of the Spirit of God; I understand that sanctification is the qualities of the Lord Jesus being exhibited in me; only two weeks ago I had a wonderful time of communion with the Lord in the heavenly places; I saw the way so clearly, and I knew exactly what I should do in the circumstances I was in, but I failed to do it."

"While you have the light, believe in the light," and slowly and surely we shall find what our Lord said is true: "He who follows Me shall not walk in darkness, but have the light of life."

If we have entered into the heavenly places in Christ Jesus, the light has shone, and, this is the marvelous thing, as we begin to do what we know the Lord would have us do, we find He does not enable *us* to do it, He simply puts through us all His power, and the thing is done in His way. Thank God for everyone who has seen the light, who has understood how the Lord Jesus Christ clears away the darkness and brings the light by showing His own characteristics through us.

Did I believe the light when I had it? Is there someone who had the light a year ago? last week? You saw clearly what God wanted; did you obey the light? You answer, "No, I did not." Well, tell Him so, and thank God there is another opportunity, and those who have obeyed the light and have been going on, ask God to confirm you in the way that you may be partakers of the inheritance of the saints in the light.

One remarkable thing about our Lord's life is that He always understood that His Father was right. I wonder if we always do? There is much that is obscure, much we cannot understand, but are we certain that our Father understands? Have we let Jesus Christ so manifest Himself in us that we know that the Father always does things well? When we come across a dark trial such as war or a trial more personal and peculiarly our own, something that is a distress and a pain and a wildness with no light or liberty, the danger is that we begin to say, "Why should this happen to me? Why should I be plunged into this darkness?" But if we remember our possession of light, the Son of God in all His understanding of the Father takes possession of us absolutely, and we see in our hearts just as Jesus Christ saw. That is the marvel of sanctification. At the threshold of every new experience, of every new phase of the truth of God, there is a margin of darkness where we have this glorious test—will I let the Son of God manifest Himself in my mortal flesh in this thing, and will I possess the light that God has given me? If so, we shall see just as Jesus Christ saw.

Partakers of Light

There is a difference between this inheritance and an earthly inheritance. When we partake in an earthly inheritance it becomes a particular possession of our own that no one else can have, and not only so but by taking it we may impoverish someone else. The marvelous thing about the inheritance of the saints in the light is that when we take our part of the inheritance, everyone else is blessed in the taking, but if we refuse to be partakers of the inheritance of the saints in the light, we rob others of its glory and its wonder.

There is another thing about the possession of light in Jesus Christ: my possession of light is quite different from yours. Each of us has a particular possession of light that no one else can have, and if we refuse to take our possession, everyone else will suffer. In every saint's life there is a particular, personal edition of the possession of light, and until that is partaken of with full-hearted confidence, all the others suffer. The difficulty is that the round person wants to be in the square hole—this shows how we become deflected from the light that is in Christ. There is a possession of light that the Spirit distributes to each one according to the perfect wisdom of God. It is Satan, not God, who makes someone say everyone must be just as he is or as she is. As we participate in the light and the Son of God is manifested in us in our particular setting, there will be marvelous blessing to all the people round about. The test for apostles and teachers is not that they talk wonderful stuff, not that they are able to expound God's Word, but that they edify the saints (see Ephesians 4:12). No individual can develop a holy life with God without benefiting all other saints. I wonder if we have been obedient to the heavenly vision, or have we been hankering after being like others?

One of the greatest dangers of Satan when he comes as an angel of light is that he tries to persuade the saints of God that they must let go the possession of what God wants them to have and take possessions belonging to others. If some have a special gift for preaching God's truth, Satan will try to persuade them that preaching the Gospel of Jesus Christ is not what God has called them to do but that they have been called to live quiet lives with God in secret. Always remember that the tiniest deflection of the eye or the heart away from God in light and from Jesus Christ in light and from obeying the light when it is given will mean a deflection for a long while, much sorrow and much distress. Thank God He does not leave His children alone; there is much pain and distress, but He will always bring them back.

I wonder if we have seen Jesus Christ as a possession of light—in our circumstances, in our businesses, in our home relations, or in whatever it may be? Have we seen clearly what God wants us to do, and have we done it? As surely as we begin to put ourselves into the path of obedience, the perfections of the Son of God are manifested through us with such a great brilliancy of light that we will never think of taking credit to ourselves for it. One step in the right direction in obedience to the light, and the manifestation of the Son of God in your mortal flesh is as certain as that God is on His throne. When once God's light has come to us through Jesus Christ, we must never hang back, but obey, and we shall not walk in darkness but will have the light of life.

"As He is, so are we" (1 John 4:17). The sanctified life is a life that bears a strong family likeness to Jesus Christ, a life that exhibits His virtues, His patience, His love, His holiness. Slowly and surely we learn the great secret of eternal life, which is to know God.

Every bit of knowledge that we have of God fills us with ineffable joy. Remember what Jesus said to His disciples:

"That My joy may remain in you" (John 15:11). What was the joy of Jesus? That He understood the Father. Do we understand God on any one point? If we do, we will know something of the joy that Jesus had. It is a wonderful possession, it is the very characteristic of Jesus. To understand the tiniest bit of truth about God is to love it with all the heart and soul and mind; all that lies dark and obscure just now is one day going to be as clear, as radiantly and joyously clear, as the bit we have seen. No wonder God counsels us to be patient. Little by little, everything will be brought into the light, until we understand as Jesus Christ understood. The whole of eternity will be taken up with understanding and knowing God, and, thank God, we may begin to know Him down here. The sanctified life means that we begin to understand God and to manifest the life of the Son of God in our mortal flesh.

Before we get hold of the Spirit of God and the Spirit of God gets hold of us, we are apt to be taken up with the outside of things; we cling to them and mistake them for the essential reality, until slowly they begin to dwindle from us and to turn to ashes and disappointment. But when we are made partakers of light we are wedded to God's realities behind the things that are seen, and we remain absolutely true to Him.

Light Indwelling

> Now you are light in the Lord. Walk as children of light. Ephesians 5:8

What we have in the kingdom of light, we give. That is always the characteristic. If we try to picture to others the glory of communion with God without being in close contact with God ourselves, we will paralyze the imagination of those we talk to. George MacDonald, in his poem "The Disciple," pictures the sense of dreary disappointment that came

to a boy when he heard it said that godly people were as pil-
lars in the temple of God:

> Straightway my heart is like a clod,
> My spirit wrapt in doubt:—
> A pillar in the house of God,
> And never more go out!

That will always be the result when we try to portray a
truth of God without being partakers of the light, without
being lifted into the inheritance.

As we partake of this possession of light, it is as if the
Son of God lifted the veil from the way God created things.
He lifts our eyes up to the stars and says, Do you see those?
Every one of them is known to your Father in heaven—and
something we cannot state in words gets hold of our souls
and it means this: God is so full of light that He knows us
down to the tiniest detail of our lives. Then another time He
shows us the makeup of a daisy and He says, That was God's
thought when He created a daisy, and slowly the Spirit of
God makes our lives into exactly God's idea of what we
ought to be.

By sanctification we are placed in the will of God. We
have not to ask what the will of God is, we *are* the will of
God, and as we keep in the light as He is in the light, the decisions of the mind and the natural progress of the life go on
like a law, and when the decision is likely to be wrong the
Spirit checks. Whenever there is the tiniest inward check,
we must stop, and we will find that the Lord Jesus Christ
and His perfections will be there to meet every emergency.

In prayer, have we learned the wonderful power of that
phrase "boldness to enter the Holiest by the blood of Jesus"
(Hebrews 10:19)? It means that we can talk to God as Jesus
Christ did, but only through the right of His atonement. We

must never allow the idea that because we have been obedient, because our needs are great, because we long for it, therefore God will hear us. There is only one way into the Holiest, and that is by the blood of Jesus. Being made partakers of the light means that we are taken into the fellowship Jesus referred to when He said, "the Father Himself loves you" (John 16:27).

As we are made partakers of the inheritance of the saints in the light, we begin to understand that there is no division into sacred and secular, it is all one great, glorious life with God, as the Son of God is manifested in our mortal flesh. Paul puts it in this way: "When it pleased God . . . to reveal His Son in me" (Galatians 1:15–16). You in your shop, you in your office, you in your home, say that in your own heart, "The Son of God revealed in me!" That is sanctification.

Placed in the Light

He has . . . conveyed us into the kingdom of the Son of His love.
Colossians 1:13

Just as the stars are poised by God almighty, so, the apostle says, the great power of the Father lifts the saints into the light that He and His Son are in and poises them there, as eternally established as the stars. Have we ever allowed our imaginations to be kindled by the light of God? God is light, and He lifts us up in Himself, no matter who we are, and poises us as surely as He established the stars, in the very light that He is in. He makes us meet to be partakers of that wonderful inheritance, and slowly and surely the marvel of the life of the Son of God is manifested in our mortal flesh. No wonder Paul says, "Giving thanks to the Father" (Colossians 1:12)!

It was never from His right to Himself that our Lord Jesus Christ spoke, He never thought from His right to Himself; that is, He never thought or spoke from His bodily conditions or the condition of His circumstances. We do talk from our right to ourselves, from the conditions of our bodies, from our personal possessions; these are the things we all reason from naturally. They are the things the Son of God never reasoned from, He thought and spoke always from His Father; that is, He expressed the thought of God in light. When we are sanctified, the Spirit of God will enable us to do the same. As we go on with God we shall find that we see things in quite a different way—we see them with the eyes of Jesus Christ.

When we shut ourselves in alone with God at night, with the stars and the great quietness round about, it is so easy and so wonderful to talk to Him, but do we walk in the light of the talk we had, when the morning comes? Do I allow the Son of God to manifest Himself in my walk and conversation, or do I forget and begin to work from myself, and at the end of the day do I have to say to God, "I am sorry, Lord, but I made a tremendous blunder, I forgot to step back and let You manifest Yourself"?

Remember, God wants to lift us up and poise us in the light that He is in, and everything that is dark just now will one day be as clear to us as it is to Him. Think of all the things that are dark just now. Jesus said, "There is nothing covered that will not be revealed" (Matthew 10:26). Things are dark and obscure to us because we are not in a right condition to understand them. Thank God for all that we have understood, for every bit of truth that is so full of light and liberty and wonder that it fills us with joy. Step-by-step, as we walk in that light and allow the Son of God to meet every circumstance by His virtues, by His power, and by His presence, we shall understand more and more with a knowledge "which passes knowledge" (Ephesians 3:19).

How many of us know anything about this gospel mystery of sanctification? Are we allowing the life and liberty and power and marvel of the holiness of Jesus Christ to be wrought out in us? Do we know what it is to be made new creatures in Christ Jesus? Have we let God raise us up to the heavenly places in Christ Jesus, and are we learning to walk in the light as God is in the light ?

> For this is the will of God, your sanctification. 1 Thessalonians 4:3

> Of Him you are in Christ Jesus, who became for us . . . sanctification. 1 Corinthians 1:30

Grow Up Into Him

Take the Initiative

Add to your faith virtue. 2 Peter 1:5

> This love requires nothing of us but innocent and
> regular manners and behaviour. It would only have
> us do all those things for the sake of God which rea-
> son bids us practise. The thing required is not to
> add to the good actions we have already done, but
> only to do that out of love to God which people of
> reputation and virtuous lives do from a principle of
> honour and regard of themselves. We are not only
> to lop off evil. That we must do if we were guided
> by no other principle than right reason. But for
> everything else leave it in the order God has estab-
> lished in the world. Let us do all the same honest
> and virtuous actions, but let us do them for the sake
> of Him Who made us and to Whom we owe our
> all. (Fenelon)

The question of forming habits on the basis of the grace of
God is a very vital one. God regenerates us and puts us in
contact with all His divine resources, but He cannot make us
walk according to His will; the practicing is ours, not God's.
We have to take the initiative and add to our faith virtue. To
take the initiative means to make a beginning, and all of us
must do it for ourselves: We have to acquaint ourselves with
the way we have to go and beware of the tendency of asking
the way when we know it perfectly well.

To "add" means to acquire the habit of doing things, and
it is difficult in the initial stages. We are in danger of forgetting that we cannot do what God does and that God will not

do what we can do. We cannot save ourselves or sanctify ourselves—only God can do that—but God does not give us good habits, He does not give us character, He does not make us walk aright; we must do all that. We have to work out what God has worked in (see Philippians 2:12–13). Many of us lose out spiritually not because the devil attacks us but because we are stupidly ignorant of the way God has made us. Remember, the devil did not make the human body; he may have tampered with it, but the human body was created by God, and its constitution after we are saved remains the same as before. For instance, we are not born with a ready-made habit of dressing ourselves, we have to form that habit. Apply it spiritually—when we are born again, God does not give us a fully fledged series of holy habits, we have to make them; and the forming of habits on the basis of God's supernatural work in our souls is the education of our spiritual lives.

Many of us refuse to do it; we are lazy and we frustrate the grace of God.

Stop Hesitating

A double-minded man [is] unstable in all his ways. James 1:8

We have to stop hesitating and take the first step, and the first step is to stop hesitating! "How long will you falter between two opinions?" (1 Kings 18:21). There are times when we wish that God would kick us right over the line and *make* us do the thing, but the remarkable thing about God's patience is that He waits until we stop hesitating. Some of us hesitate so long that we become like spiritual storks—we look elegant only as long as we stand on one leg; when we stand on two we look very ungraceful. Or we have stood so long on the verge of a promise of God's that we have grown like monuments on its edge, and if we were asked to go over the edge in the way of giving our testimonies or doing something for God, we should feel very awkward. It would be a good thing for us if we could be pushed over, no matter how we sprawled. If God tells us to do something and we hesitate over obeying, we endanger our standing in grace.

"A double-minded man," that is, a discreet individual, diplomatic and wise—is "unstable in all his ways." Those who do not put God first in their calculations are always double minded. *If I do, supposing,* and *but*—these are all in the vocabulary of the double minded. If we begin to weigh things, we let in that subtle enemy against God, namely, insinuation. When God speaks, we have to be resolute and act immediately in faith on what He says. When Peter walked on the water, he did not wait for someone to take his hand, he stepped straight out, in recognition of Jesus, and walked on the water.

Never revise decisions. If you have made a wrong decision, then face the music and stand up to it; do not whimper and say, "I won't do that again." Take the initiative, take the step with your will now, burn your bridges behind you: "I *will* write that letter"; "I *will* pay that debt"; make it impossible to go back on the decision. Sentimentality always begins when we refuse to obey, when we refuse to take some stand God has told us to because of an insinuation that has come in from somewhere. If we hesitate, insinuations are sure to come.

Start Hearkening

Whoever . . . hears My sayings and does them. Luke 6:47

Whether we are Christians or not, we must all build; the point is that a Christian builds on a different basis. If we build to please ourselves, we are building on the sand; if we build for the love of God, we are building on the rock. Do we listen to what Jesus has to say? All we build will end in disaster unless it is built on the sayings of Jesus. "He who has ears to hear, let him hear" (Matthew 11:15). Before we can hear certain things, we must be trained. One's disposition determines what one listens for, and when Jesus alters the disposition, He gives us the power to hear as He hears (compare John 12:29–30). If, when no one is watching us, we are building ourselves up in the Word of God, then when a crisis comes, we shall stand; but if we are not building on the Word of God, when a crisis comes we shall go down, no matter what our wills are like. Have we learned the habit of listening to what God says? Have we added this resolute hearing in our practical lives? We may be able to give testimonies as to what God has done for us, but do the lives we live evidence that we are not listening now, but living only in the memory of what we once heard? We have to keep our ears trained to detect God's voice, to be continually renewed in the spirit of the mind. If when a crisis comes we instinctively turn to God, we know that the habit of hearkening has been formed. At the beginning there is the noisy clamor of our own misgivings, we are so taken up with what we have heard that we cannot hear any more. We have to hearken to that which we have not listened to before, and to do it we must be insulated on the inside.

"He awakens My ear to hear as the learned" (Isaiah 50:4). Once a week at least read the Sermon on the Mount and see how much you have hearkened to it: "Love your enemies, bless those who curse you" (Matthew 5:44); we do not listen to it because we do not want to. We have to learn to hearken to Jesus in everything, to get into the habit of finding out what He says. We cannot apply the teachings of Jesus unless we are regenerated, and we cannot apply all His teachings at once. The Holy Spirit will bring to remembrance a certain word of our Lord's and apply it to the particular circumstances we are in; the point is—are we going to obey it? "Whoever . . . hears My sayings, and *does* them." When Jesus Christ brings a word home, never shirk it.

Stand Heroically

Having done all, to stand. Ephesians 6:13

It is a great deal easier to fight than to stand, but spiritu-ally our conflict is not so much a fight as a standing on guard: "having done all, to stand." When we are in a frenzy, we attack; when we are strong, we stand to overcome. Today in Christian work we are suffering from a phase of spiritual dyspepsia that emphasizes *doing*. The great thing *to do* is *to be* a believer in Jesus. With Jesus it is never, *Do, do,* but, *Be, be,* and I will do through you. "To stand" means to work on the level of the heroic. It would be a terrible thing to lose the sense of the heroic, because the sense of duty is only realized by the sense of the heroic. Our Lord calls us to joyful, heroic lives, and we must never relax. "Put on the whole armor of God" (Ephesians 6:11). If we try to put on the armor without a right relationship to God we shall be like David in Saul's armor, but when we are right with God we find that the armor fits us exactly, because it is God's own nature that is the armor. The armor God gives us is not the armor of prayer but the armor of Himself—the armor *of God.* "That you may be able to stand against the wiles of the devil." The devil is a bully, but when we stand in the armor of God, he cannot harm us; if we tackle him in our own strength we are soon done for, but if we stand with the strength and courage of God, he cannot gain one inch. Some of us run away instead of standing; when there is a fresh onslaught of the wiles of the devil we lose heart instantly, and instead of standing we scuttle, and others have to stand until we are sufficiently ashamed to come back again. We have to take the initiative in standing against panic. One strong, moral man or woman will form a nucleus around whom others will gather, and spiritually, if we put on the armor of God and stand true to Him, a whole army of weak-kneed Christians will be strengthened. Remember, we have to take the initiative where we are, not where we are not.

You Won't Reach It on Tiptoe!

Add . . . to godliness brotherly kindness. 2 Peter 1:5, 7

Love, to most of us, is an indefinite thing; we do not know what we mean when we speak of love. The love Paul mentions in 1 Corinthians 13 means the sovereign preference of my person for another person, and everything depends on who the other person is. Jesus demands that the sovereign preference be for Him. We cannot love to order, and yet His word stands: "If anyone comes to Me and does not hate his father and mother, wife and children, brothers and sisters, yes, and his own life also, [that is, a hatred of every loyalty that would divide the heart from loyalty to Jesus] he cannot be My disciple" (Luke 14:26). Devotion to a person is the only thing that tells, and none on earth have the love that Jesus demands, unless it has been imparted to them. We may admire Jesus Christ, we may respect Him and reverence Him, but, apart from the Holy Spirit, we do not love Him. The only Lover of the Lord Jesus Christ is the Holy Spirit. In Romans 5:5, Paul says that "the love of God"—not the power to love God, but the love of God— "has been poured out in our hearts by the Holy Spirit who was given to us." The Holy Spirit is the gift of the ascended Christ. "Have I received the Holy Spirit?" Not, "Do I believe in Him?" but, "Have I received Him?" Something must come into me (see Luke 11:13). When by a willing acceptance I receive the Holy Spirit, He will pour out the love of God in my heart, and on the basis of that love I have to practice the working out of the things that Peter mentions here and Paul mentions in 1 Corinthians 13. We cannot reach it on tiptoe; some of us tried to once, for seven days, then we got tired! The springs of love are in God, not in us. It is absurd to look for the love of God in our natural hearts—the love of God is only there when it has been poured out by the Holy Spirit.

Love Where You Cannot Respect

> But God demonstrates His own love toward us, in that while we were still sinners, Christ died for us. Romans 5:8

The revelation of God's love is that He loved us when He could not possibly respect us—He loved us "while we were still sinners," when we were enemies. When we receive the nature of God into us, the first thing that happens is that God takes away all pretense and pious pose, and He does it by revealing that He loved us not because we were lovable but because it is His nature to love. "God is love" (1 John 4:8). The surest evidence that the nature of God has come into me is that I know I am a sinner: "I know that in me (that is, in my flesh) nothing good dwells" (Romans 7:18). When God has made me know what I am really like in His sight, it is no longer possible for me to be annoyed at what others may tell me I am capable of, God has revealed it to me already. When once we have had a dose of the plague of our own hearts, we will never want to vindicate ourselves. The worst things that are said about us may be literally untrue, but we know that whatever is said is not so bad as what is really true of us in the sight of God.

Never try to prevent people feeling real disgust at what they are like in God's sight. The first thing the Holy Spirit does when He comes in is to convict, not to comfort, because He has to let us know what we are like in God's sight; then He brings the revelation that God will fill us with His own nature if we will let Him. The curious thing about the love of God is that it is the cruelest thing on earth to everything that is not of Him. God hurts desperately when I am far away from Him, but when I am close to Him He is unutterably tender. Paul says that "God demonstrates His own love to us." God's love seems so strange to our natural conceptions that it has to be demonstrated to us before we see anything in it. It is only when we have been awakened by conviction to the sin and anarchy of our hearts against God that we realize the measure of His love toward us, even "while we were still sinners."

"The Son of God, who loved me and gave Himself for me" (Galatians 2:20)—Paul never lost the wonder of that love.

The Lord "suffers long and is kind." If I watch God's dealings with me, I shall find that He gives me a revelation of my own pride and bad motives toward Him, and the realization that He loved me when He could not begin to respect me will send me forth into the world to love others as He loved me. God's love for me is inexhaustible, and His love for me is the basis of my love for others. We have to love where we cannot respect and where we must not respect, and this can only be done on the basis of God's love for us. "This is My commandment, that you love one another as I have loved you" (John 15:12).

Love means deliberate self-limitation, we deliberately identify ourselves with the interests of our Lord in everything. "Having loved His own who were in the world, He loved them to the end" (13:1). The revelation comes home to me that God has loved me to the end of all my meanness and my sin, my self-seeking and my wrong motives, and now this is the corresponding revelation—that I have to love others as God has loved me. God will bring around me any number of people I cannot respect, and I have to exhibit the love of God to them as He has exhibited it to me. Have we ever realized the glorious opportunity we have of laying down our lives for Jesus Christ? Jesus does not ask us to die for Him but to lay down our lives for Him. Our Lord did not sacrifice Himself for death, He sacrificed His *life,* and God wants our lives, not our deaths. "I beseech you," says Paul, "present your bodies a living sacrifice" (Romans 12:1).

The greatest love of anyone is love for friends (see John 15:13), the greatest love of God is His love for His enemies (see Romans 5:8–10), the highest Christian love is to lay down one's life for one's Friend, the Lord Jesus Christ: "I have called you friends" (John 15:15). Our Lord here connects the highest human love with the highest divine love, and the connection is in the disciple, not in our Lord. The emphasis is laid on the deliberate laying down of the life, not in one tragic crisis such as death, but in the gray face of actual facts illumined by no romance, obscured by the mist of the utterly commonplace—expending the life deliberately day by day because of my love for my Friend. This is the love that never fails, and it is neither human nor divine love alone but the at-one-ment of both being made manifest in the life of the disciple. The supreme moment of the Cross in actual history is but the concentrated essence of the very nature of the divine love. God lays down His life for the very creation that people utilize for their own selfish ends. The self-expenditure of the love of God, exhibited in the life and death of our Lord, becomes a bridge over the gulf of sin, whereby human love can be imbued by divine love, the love that never fails.

Love Where You Are Not Respected

> But when you do good and suffer, if you take it patiently, this is commendable before God. For to this you were called, because Christ also suffered for us, leaving us an example, that you should follow His steps. 1 Peter 2:20–21

We shall not always be respected if we are disciples of Jesus. Our Lord said: "These things I have spoken to you, that you should not be made to stumble. They will put you out of the synagogues; yes, the time is coming that whoever kills you will think that he offers God service" (John 16:1–2), and that will be so again. "A disciple is not above his teacher, nor a servant above his master" (Matthew 10:24). How much respect did Jesus Christ receive when He was on this earth? A Nazarene carpenter, despised, rejected, and crucified. "We e'en must love the highest when we see it" is not true, for when the religious people of our Lord's day saw the Highest incarnate before them, they hated Him and crucified Him. "Remember the word that I said to you, 'A servant is not greater than his master.' If they have persecuted Me, they will also persecute you" (John 15:20). We are apt to think of a Christian merely as a civilized individual; a Christian is one who is identified with Jesus, one who has learned the lesson that the servant is not greater than the Lord.

If we are despised because we have extraordinary notions, we are apt to be uplifted by that—it suits our natural pride—but Jesus said, "Blessed are you, when men hate you, and when they exclude you, and revile you, and cast out your name as evil, for the Son of Man's sake" (Luke 6:22). If you want a good time in this world, do not become a disciple of Jesus. "If anyone desires to come after Me, let him deny himself" (Matthew 16:24), that is, give up his right to himself to Me. There is always an IF in connection with discipleship, and it implies that we need not unless we like. There is never any compulsion, Jesus does not coerce us. There is only one way of being a disciple, and that is by being devoted to Jesus.

Love Wherever Redemption Reaches

Whoever believes in Him should not perish but have everlasting life. John 3:16

What has God redeemed? Everything that sin and Satan have touched and blighted, God has redeemed—redemption is complete. We are not working *for* the redemption of the world, we are working *on* the redemption, which is a very different thing. Jesus Christ's last command to His disciples was not to go and save the world—the saving is done. He told them to go and make disciples. Our work is to "open their eyes, in order to turn them from darkness to light, and from the power of Satan to God, that they may receive forgiveness of sins" (Acts 26:18), that is, that they may receive the redemption that is complete but that is incredible to people until they do receive it. "I do not doubt that God saves people, nor do I doubt that He can do all the Bible says He can, but it is ridiculous to suppose it includes me!" We have to beware of making the need the call; the redemption is the call, the need is the opportunity, and the opportunity is in our own homes, in our work, just wherever we are, not simply in meetings. Naturally we always want to go somewhere else, but the love of God works just where we are, and His love works irrespective of persons.

Are we banking in unshaken faith on the redemption of Jesus Christ? Is it our conviction amongst people that everyone can be presented perfect in Christ Jesus? Are we filling up "what is lacking in the afflictions of Christ, for the sake of His body" (Colossians 1:24)? That means we have to be so identified with our Lord that His love is being poured out all the time, we have to be prepared to be nothing at all so that He can pour His sweetness through us. Neither natural love nor divine love will remain unless it is cultivated. We must form the habit of love until it is the practice of our lives.

Make a Habit of Having No Habits

For if these are yours and abound, you will be neither barren nor unfruitful in the knowledge of our Lord Jesus Christ. 2 Peter 1:8

When we are forming a habit we are conscious of it, but in the real Christian life, habits do not appear, because by practice we do the thing unconsciously. As Christians, we have to learn the habit of waiting upon God as He comes to us through the moments and to see that we do not make common sense our guide—we do until we have seen the Lord. When we realize that God's order comes to us in the haphazard, our lives will manifest themselves in the way our Lord indicates in the Sermon on the Mount. The illustrations our Lord uses there are the fowls of the air, the lilies of the field. Birds and flowers obey the law of their lives in the setting in which they are placed, they have no consciousness of being conscious, it is not their own thought that makes them what they are, but the thought of the Father in heaven. If our child-like trust in God is giving place to self-consciousness and self-depreciation, it is a sign that there is something wrong, and the cure for it is to reach the place where every habit is so practiced that there is no conscious habit at all. Watch how God will upset our programs if we are in danger of making our little Christian habits our gods. Whenever we begin to worship the habit of prayer or of Bible reading, God will break up that time. We say, "I cannot do this, I am praying, it is my hour with God." No, it is an hour with a habit; we pray to a habit of prayer.

Exercising Habits until Each Habit Is Lost

For if these are yours and abound . . .

Are they existing in us? There are times when we are conscious of becoming virtuous and patient and godly, but they are only stages; if we stop there we get the strut of the "pi" person. Pi people are those who do their level best to be what they would like to be but know they are not. Our Christian lives continually resolve themselves into consciousness and introspection because there are some qualities we have not added yet. Ultimately, the relationship is to be a completely simple one.

Consciousness of a defect is a disease spiritually, yet it is produced by the finger of God because we have neglected to add some quality. We must acknowledge the defect and then look out for the opportunity of exercising ourselves along the line of the quality to be added—patience, godliness, love. We have to exercise the quality until the habit is merged in the simplicity of a child's life.

We have to beware of singling out one quality only. Peter says "For if these," faith, virtue, knowledge, temperance, patience, godliness, brotherly kindness, charity, "are yours and abound." Our Lord is the type of all Christian experience, and He cannot be summed up in terms of natural virtues but only in terms of the supernatural. "Come to Me," says Jesus, "and I will give you rest" (Matthew 11:28), the rest of perfection of activity that is never conscious of itself. This perfection of activity can be illustrated by the spinning of a colored top: If the top spins quickly, all the colors merge and a musical sound is heard, but if it spins slowly, it wobbles and sighs and every color is conspicuous. If we are conscious of a defect it is because the Lord is pointing out that there is a quality to be added, and until it is added we are conscious of a black streak here and a colored streak there. But when the particular quality has been added we are no longer conscious of the defect, all the qualities are merged and the whole life is at rest in the perfection of activity.

The dominant thing about a saint is not self-realization but the Lord Himself, consequently a saint can always be ignored because to the majority of eyes our Lord is no more noticeable in the life of a saint than He was to people in the days of His flesh. But when a crisis comes the saint is the one to whom people turn, and the life that seemed colorless is seen to be the white light of God.

Expressing Holiness until Conscious Holiness Is Lost

you will be neither barren nor unfruitful . . .

It is an utter mistake to fix our eyes on our own whiteness, for all we are conscious of then is a passionate longing for a holy relationship to God. We have to come to the place where conscious holiness ceases to be, because of the presence of the One who is holiness. When we have been made partakers of the divine nature, we are taken up into God's consciousness, we do not take God into our consciousness. If we are consciously holy we are far from simple in certain relationships, for there will be certain things we imagine we cannot do, whereas in reality we are the only ones who ought to be able to do those things. Once we come into simple relationship with God, He can put us where He pleases and we are not even conscious of where He puts us. All we are conscious of is an amazing simplicity of life that seems to be a haphazard life externally. The only supernatural life ever lived on earth was the life of our Lord, and He was at home with God anywhere. Wherever we are not at home with God, there is a quality to be added. We have to let God press through us in that particular until we gain Him, and life becomes the simple life of a child in which the vital concern is putting God first.

Experiencing Knowledge until Knowledge Is Lost

. . . in the knowledge of our Lord Jesus Christ.

"Then I shall know just as I also am known" (1 Corinthians 13:12)—love abides, and knowledge is merged. Knowledge is faith perfected, and faith in turn passes into sight. We experience knowledge until knowledge is swallowed up in the fact of God's presence—"Why, He is here!" Knowledge is an expression of the nature of God and is the practical outcome of the life of God in us, but if we isolate knowledge we are in danger of criticizing God. We look for God to manifest Himself *to* His children; God only manifests Himself *in* His children, consequently others see the manifestation, the child of God does not. You say, "I am not conscious of God's blessing now"—thank God! "I am not conscious now of the touches of God"—thank God! "I am not conscious now that God is answering my prayers"—thank God! If you are conscious of these things it means you have put yourself outside God. "That the life of Jesus also may be manifested in our mortal flesh" (2 Corinthians 4:11).

"I am not conscious that His life is being manifested," you say, but if you are a saint it surely is. When a little child becomes conscious of being a little child, the childlikeness is gone, and when a saint becomes conscious of being a saint, something has gone wrong. "Oh, but I'm not good enough." You never will be good enough! That is why the Lord had to come and save you. Go to your own funeral and ever after let God be all in all, and life will become the simple life of a child in which God's order comes moment by moment.

Never live on memories. Do not remember in your testimony what you once were, let the Word of God be always living and active in you, and give the best you have every time and all the time.

The Habit of a Good Conscience

Having a good conscience. 1 Peter 3:16

We hear it said that conscience is the voice of God, but logically that is easily proved to be absurd. Paul said, "Indeed, I myself thought I must do many things contrary to the name of Jesus of Nazareth" (Acts 26:9); Paul was obeying his conscience when he hated Jesus Christ and put His followers to death; our Lord said that "whoever kills you will think that he offers God service" (John 16:2). If conscience were the voice of God it would be the most contradictory voice human ears ever listened to. Conscience is the eye of the soul, and how it records depends entirely upon the light thrown upon God. The God whom Saul of Tarsus knew had the light of Judaism upon Him, and Saul's conscience, recording in that light, brought him to the conclusion that he should hate Jesus and persecute His followers.

As soon as the white light of our Lord was thrown upon God, Saul's conscience recorded differently: "So he, trembling and astonished, said, 'Lord, what do You want me to do?'" (Acts 9:6). Saul had not another conscience, but it recorded differently, and the result was a tremendous disturbance in his life. Conscience is the faculty of the spirit that fits itself on to the highest a person knows, whether the person is an agnostic or a Christian; everyone has a conscience, although everyone does not know God.

The Sensitive Conscience

I myself always strive to have a conscience without offense toward God and men. Acts 24:16

73

If I am in the habit of steadily and persistently facing myself with God, my conscience will always introduce God's perfect law to me; the question then is will I do what my conscience makes me understand clearly I should do? When conscience has been enlightened by the Son of God being formed in me, I have to make an effort to keep my conscience so sensitive that I obey that which I perceive to be God's will. I have to be so keen in the scent of the Lord, so sensitive to the tiniest touch of His Spirit that I know what I should do. If I keep my soul inwardly open to God, then when I come in contact with the affairs of life outside, I know immediately what I should do; if I do not, I am to blame. I should be living in such perfect sensitivity to God, in such perfect sympathy with His Son that in every circumstance I am in, the spirit of my mind is renewed, and I prove, that is, make out, what is God's will, the thing that is good and acceptable and perfect.

We avoid forming sensitive consciences when we say, "Oh, well, God cannot expect me to do this thing, He has not told me to do it." How do we expect God to tell us? The word is "not in heaven. . . . Nor is it beyond the sea. . . . But the word is very near you, in your mouth and in your heart, that you may do it" (Deuteronomy 30:12–14). If we are Christians, that is where the Word of God is—in our hearts. In the engineering of our circumstances, God gives us opportunities to form sensitive consciences, and in this way He educates us down to the scruple. When we come to a crisis it is easy to get direction, but it is a different matter to live in such perfect oneness with God that in the ordinary occurrences of life we always do the right thing. Is my conscience so sensitive that it needs neither terrible crime nor sublime holiness to awaken it, but the ordinary occurrences of life will awaken it? "Do not grieve the Holy Spirit" (Ephesians 4:30). He does not come with a voice of thunder but with a voice so gentle that it is easy to ignore it. The one thing that keeps the conscience sensitive is the continual habit of seeing that I am open to God within. Whenever there is debate, quit. "Why shouldn't I do this?" You are on the wrong track. When conscience speaks, there must be no debate whatever. In a crisis, human nature is put on the strain, and we usually know what to do, but the sensitive conscience of the Christian is realized in the ordinary things of life, the humdrum things. We are apt to think of conscience only in connection with something outrageous. The sensitivity of conscience is maintained by the habit of always being open toward God. At the peril of your soul, you allow one thing to obscure your inner communion with God. Drop it, whatever it is, and see that you keep your inner vision clear.

The Seared Conscience

Having their own conscience seared with a hot iron. 1 Timothy 4:2

The conscience referred to here has been damaged by some terrific iron cramp [a device for holding or fastening things together; metaphorically, anything that confines or hampers]. Conscience is the eye of the soul recording what it looks at, but if what Ruskin calls "the innocence of the eye" is lost, then the recording of conscience may be distorted. If I continually twist the organ of my soul's recording, it will become perverted. If I do a wrong thing often enough, I cease to realize the wrong in it. Bad people can be perfectly happy in their badness. That is what a seared conscience means.

Our critical faculties are given us for the purpose of self-examination, and the way to examine ourselves under the control of the Spirit of God is to ask ourselves, "Am I less sensitive than I used to be to the indications of God's will, less sensitive regarding purity, uprightness, goodness, honesty and truth?" If I realize that I am, I may be perfectly certain that something I have done (not something done to me) has seared my conscience. It has given me, so to speak, a bloodshot eye of the soul and I cannot see aright.

Conscience may be seared by means of a desperate crime, as in the case of Herod. Herod ordered the voice of God to be silent in his life (see Mark 6:16–28), and when Jesus Christ stood before him we read that Jesus "answered him nothing" (Luke 23:9).

The human eye may be damaged by gazing too much on intense whiteness, as in the case of snow blindness, when people remain blind for months. And conscience may be damaged by tampering with the occult side of things, giving too much time to speculation—then when we turn to human life we are as blind as bats. It may be all right for angels to spend their time in visions and meditation, but if I am a Christian I find God in the ordinary occurrences of my life. The special times of prayer are of a different order. If I sequester myself and press my mind on one line of things and forget my relation to human life, when I do turn to human affairs I am morally blind. Am I trying to embrace a sensation of God spiritually for myself? When God has saved and sanctified us, there is a danger that we are unwilling to let the vision fade, we refuse to take up our ordinary work, and soon we will be completely at a loss because we have hugged an experience to our souls instead of maintaining a right relationship to God who gave us the experience.

My mortal flesh does not come in contact with God, it comes in contact with other mortal flesh, with earthly things, and I have to manifest the Son of God there by putting on the "new man" in connection with all these things. Am I doing it? Have I formed the habit of keeping my conscience sensitive to God on the inside and equally sensitive to people on the outside, by always working out what God works in? God engineers our circumstances and He brings across our paths some extraordinary people, namely, embodiments of ourselves in so many forms, and it is part of the humor of the situations that we recognize ourselves. Now, God says, exhibit the attitude to them that I showed to you. This is the one way of keeping a conscience void of offense toward God and toward other people.

The Saintly Conscience

> Having our hearts sprinkled from an evil conscience. Hebrews 10:22

Can God readjust a seared conscience and make it sensitive again? He can, and it is done by the vicarious atonement of our Lord. "How much more shall the blood of Christ . . . cleanse your conscience from dead works to serve the living God?" (Hebrews 9:14). When the Holy Spirit comes into me, my whole nature is in a desperate turmoil because as soon as I see Jesus and understand who He is, that instant I am criticized and self-condemned. If the Holy Spirit is obeyed, He will make the atonement of the Lord efficacious in me so that the blood of Christ cleanses my conscience from dead works, and I become readjusted to God. The experimental element that works this transforming mystery of the Atonement becoming my vital life is repentance wrought in me by the Holy Spirit. The deepest repentance is not in the sinner but in the saint. Repentance means not only sorrow for sin, it involves the possession of a new disposition that will never do the thing again. The only truly repentant individual is the holy individual. "If we confess our sins, He is faithful and just to forgive us our sins and to cleanse us from all unrighteousness" (1 John 1:9). To *admit* instead of *confess* is to trample the blood of the Son of God underfoot, but as soon as we allow the Holy Spirit to give us the gift of repentance, the shed blood of Christ will purge our consciences from dead works and send us into heart-spending service for God with a passionate devotion.

If I allow the saintly conscience to have way in me, it will mean that I keep my own life steadfastly open toward God and keep steadfastly related to Him on the line of intercessory prayer for others. The clearinghouse for the guilty conscience is that by our intercession Jesus repairs the damage done to other lives, and the consolation to the conscience is amazing. The saintly conscience means that I maintain an open scrutiny before God and that I carry out the sensitivity gained there all through my life.

The Habit of Enjoying
the Disagreeable

For he who lacks these things is shortsighted, even to blindness, and has forgotten that he was cleansed from his old sins. 2 Peter 1:9

In order to express what God's grace has done in us, we have to form habits, until all habits are merged in the perfect relationship of love. It is the relationship of a child, wherein we realize that everything that God tells us to do we must do and not debate. God's commands are made to the life of His Son in us, not to our human nature, consequently all that God tells us to do is always humanly difficult, but it becomes divinely easy as soon as we obey, because our obedience has behind it all the omnipotent power of the grace of God.

The meaning of sanctification is that the Son of God is formed in us (see Galatians 4:19), then our human nature has to be transfigured by His indwelling life, and this is where our actions come in. We have to put on the "new man" in accordance with the life of the Son of God in us. If we refuse to be sanctified, there is no possibility of the Son of God being manifested in us, because we have prevented our lives being turned into a Bethlehem; we have not allowed the Spirit of God to bring forth the Son of God in us. Are we putting on the new man, in accordance with the Son of God, or are we choking His life in us? If we allow things that do not spring from the Son of God, we will put His life in us to death. The historic life of our Lord is the type of the life that will be produced in us if we take care to work out what God works in. Human nature is meant for the Son of God to manifest Himself in, and this brings us to the margin of human responsibility. Scriptural language may seem to destroy individual responsibility, but in reality it increases it a hundredfold. For example, to say with Paul, "I have been crucified with Christ; it is no longer I who live, but Christ lives in me; and the life which I now live in the flesh I live by faith in the Son of God, who loved me and gave Himself for me" (Galatians 2:20), does not mean that I am without responsibility; it means that I have the responsibility now of seeing that the Son of God works through me all the time. I have to see that the outer courts in which He lives are kept in perfect trim for Him to work through. I must not allow them to be choked up with prejudices or notions of my own.

By Keeping Yourself Fit

He who lacks these things is shortsighted . . .

When Christ is formed in us we have to see that our human nature acts in perfect obedience to all that the Son of God reveals. God does not supply us with character; He gives us the life of His Son and we can either ignore Him and refuse to obey Him, or we can so obey Him, so bring every thought and imagination into captivity, that the life of Jesus is manifested in our mortal flesh. It is not a question of being saved from hell but of being saved in order to manifest the Son of God in our mortal flesh. Our responsibility is to keep ourselves fit to manifest Him.

Are we lacking in the things that Peter, through the Spirit of God, says we must add—the things that ought to mark the life of the saint? For instance, do we exhibit the virtue of self-control, the virtue of godliness, in the letters we write, in the conversations we hold? If not, then we not only give a wrong impression of the Son of God, but we hurt His life in us. If we are lacking in these things, it is because we have become shortsighted; we have forgotten that we have been cleansed from our old sins and are in imminent peril of being taken up with an experience and an illumination and of forgetting that the life of Jesus is to be manifested in our mortal flesh.

The only way to keep ourselves fit is by the discipline of the disagreeable. It is the disagreeable things that make us exhibit whether we are manifesting the life of the Son of God or living a life that is antagonistic to Him. When disagreeable things happen, do we manifest the essential sweetness of the Son of God, or the essential irritation of ourselves apart from Him? Whenever self comes into the ascendant, the life of the Son of God in us is perverted and twisted, there is irritation, and His life suffers. We have to beware of every element in human nature that clamors for attention first. Growth in grace stops the moment we get huffed. We get huffed because we have peculiar people to live with—just think of the disagreeable person you have been to God! Every disagreeable man or woman you ever met is an objective picture of what you were like in the sight of God. We have to learn to get in the first blow at the thing that is unlike God in ourselves. We can take in our human nature the blow that was meant for Him and so prevent the tramp of feet on Him. That is what Paul means when he speaks of filling up "what is lacking in the afflictions of Christ, for the sake of His body" (Colossians 1:24).

It is one thing to go into the disagreeable by God's engineering but another thing to go into it by choice. If God puts us there, He is amply sufficient. No matter how difficult the circumstances may be, if we will let Jesus Christ manifest Himself in them, they will prove to be new means of exhibiting the wonderful perfection and extraordinary purity of the Son of God. This keen enthusiasm of letting the Son of God manifest Himself in us is the only thing that will keep us enjoying the discipline of the disagreeable. "Let your light so shine before men" (Matthew 5:16). The light is to shine in the darkness—it is not needed in the light. It is on earth, in this condition of things, that we have to see that the life of the Son of God is manifested in us, and we must keep ourselves fit to do it.

By Keeping Your Sight Fit

even to blindness . . .

In human sight we soon lose the innocence of sight; we know what we see, but instead of trusting the innocence of sight we confuse it by trying to state what we ought to see. Jesus restores the spiritual innocence of sight: "Unless one is born again, he cannot see the kingdom of God" (John 3:3). Paul said that he was sent by God to "open their eyes" (Acts 26:18). If you are being trained as an art student you will first of all be taught to see things as a whole, in mass outline, and then in detail. The meaning of perspective is that we keep the view of the whole while paying attention to the detail.

What is the thing that is pressing just now so that you cannot see aright? The reason it presses is that you have forgotten the One who is far off to human sight but very near to spiritual sight—God Himself. "There we saw the giants . . . and we were like grasshoppers in our own sight, and so we were in their sight" (Numbers 13:33). When we see God, we see neither the obstacle nor ourselves, but, like Moses, we endure "as seeing Him who is invisible" (Hebrews 11:27). Can I see the Invisible One in the thing that is nearest to me—my food, my clothes, my money, my friendships? Can I see these in the light of God? Everything that came into the life of our Lord externally was transfigured because He saw always Him who is invisible: "I know that You always hear Me" (John 11:42); "I always do those things that please Him" (8:29).

I cannot keep my sight right if I give way to self-pity. "Why should this happen to me?" To talk in that way is a grief to Jesus because it is a deliberate refusal on my part to take His yoke upon me. He was meek toward His Father's dispensations for Him and never once murmured. The reason the thing has happened to you will only be seen when you are identified with Jesus in it; see that you remain in entire connection with Him. If you indulge in self-pity and the lux-ury of misery, it means that you have forgotten God, forgot-ten that you have been purged from your old sins, and that you have to put on the new man, in accordance with the life of the Son of God in you.

"While we do not look at the things which are seen, but at the things which are not seen" (2 Corinthians 4:18). The way to keep our sight fit is by looking at the things that are not seen, and external things become a glorious chance of enabling us to concentrate on the invisible things. Once we realize that God's order comes to us in the passing moments, then nothing is unimportant. Every disagreeable thing is a new way of bringing us to realize the wonderful manifesta-tion of the Son of God in that particular. What was the thing that obliterated God and you know it had no business to? You forget to take your heart to God and spill it. The thing that ought to make our hearts beat is a new way of manifest-ing the Son of God in us.

By Keeping Your Soul Fit

. . . and has forgotten that he was cleansed from his old sins.

Jesus says that someone must lose his or her soul in order to find it: "whoever loses his life [that is, soul] for My sake shall find it" (Matthew 16:25). Soul is "me," my personal spirit, manifesting itself in my body, my way of estimating things. The incoming of the Holy Spirit into my spirit enables me to construct a new way of reasoning and looking at things. "Let this mind be in you which was also in Christ Jesus" (Philippians 2:5). Our Lord's way of reasoning certainly is not ours naturally—we have to *form* His mind. We cannot form the mind of Christ without having His Spirit, but we may have the Spirit of Christ and refuse to form His mind. We cannot alter our reasoning until God calls us up short. We may have been going steadily on, not realizing that we had to readjust our views, and then the Holy Spirit brings to our conscious minds what we knew perfectly well but had never seen in that connection before. There must be instant obedience. The moment we obey the light the Spirit of God brings, the mind of Jesus is formed in us in that particular, and we begin to reason as He reasons, but if we debate and go back to our old ways of reasoning we grieve the Spirit of God. In new circumstances there are always readjustments to be made. No matter how disagreeable things may be, say, "Lord, I am delighted to obey You in this matter," and instantly the Son of God presses to the front, and in our human minds there is formed the way of reasoning that glorifies Jesus. We have to keep our souls fit to form the mind of Christ.

The Habit of Rising to the Occasion

Therefore, brethren, be even more diligent to make your call and election sure, for if you do these things you will never stumble.
2 Peter 1:10

In natural life our aims shift and alter as we develop, but development in the Christian life is an increasing manifesta-tion of Jesus Christ. Christian faith is nourished on dogma, and all young Christian life is uniform, but in the mature Christian life there are diversities. We must be careful that we do not remain children too long, but see that we "grow up in all things into Him" (Ephesians 4:15). We have to assimi-late truth until it becomes part of us and then begin to mani-fest the individual characteristics of the children of God. The life of God shows itself in different manifestations, but the aim ultimately is the manifestation of Jesus Christ. "Till we all come to the unity of the faith and of the knowledge of the Son of God, to a perfect man, to the measure of the stature of the fullness of Christ" (verse 13).

If Jesus Christ is not being manifested in my mortal flesh, I am to blame; it is because I am not eating His flesh and drinking His blood. Just as I take food into my body and assimilate it, so, says Jesus, I must take Him into my soul. "Whoever eats My flesh and drinks My blood has eternal life" (John 6:54). Food is not health, and truth is not holiness. Food has to be assimilated by a properly organized system before the result is health, and truth must be assimilated by the child of God before it can be manifested as holiness. We may be looking at the right doctrines and yet not assimilating the truths that the doctrines reveal. Beware of making a doctrinal statement of truth *the* truth: "I am . . . the truth," said Jesus (John 14:6). Doctrinal statement is our expression of that vital connection with Him.

If we divorce what Jesus says from Jesus Himself, it leads to secret self-indulgence spiritually, the soul is swayed by a form of doctrine that has never been assimilated, and the life is twisted away from the center, Jesus Christ.

The Habit of Ratifying Your Election

> Therefore, brethren, be even more diligent to make your call and election sure . . .

To *make sure* is to ratify. I have to form the habit of assuring myself of my election, to bend the whole energy of my Christian powers to realize my calling, and to do that I must remember what I am saved for, namely, that the Son of God might be manifested in my mortal flesh. How much attention have I given to the fact that my body is the temple of the Holy Spirit? When the Son of God is formed in me, is He able to exhibit His life in my mortal flesh, or am I a living contradiction of what my mouth professes? Am I working out what God works in, or have I become divorced from Jesus Christ? I become divorced from Him as soon as I receive anything apart from His indwelling. Have I a testimony to give that is not me? If my testimony is only a thrilling experience, it is nothing but a dead, metallic thing, it kills me and those who listen to me. But when I am in contact with Jesus Christ, every testimony of mine will reveal Him.

"That you may know what is the hope of His calling, what are the riches . . . of His inheritance in the saints" (Ephesians 1:18). That which is taken for humility to human sight is blasphemy before God. To say, "Oh, I'm no saint—I can't stand the folks who testify that they are sanctified," is acceptable with people, they will say it is true humility to talk in that way. But say this before God and, though it may sound humble, it is blasphemy because it means "God cannot make me a saint." The one whom people call proud is really unutterably humble before God: "Nothing in my hands I bring."

The Habit of Realizing Your Exercises

for if you do these things . . .

We cannot do anything for our salvation, but we must do something to manifest it—we must work it out. Am I working out my salvation with my tongue, with my brain, and with my nerves? We are all apt to say with Rip Van Winkle, "I won't count this time." We put off the realization that if we are going to "grow up in all things into Him," there are things that we must do. "If you know these things, blessed are you if you *do* them," said Jesus (John 13:17, emphasis added). Character is the way we have grown to act with our hands and our feet, our eyes and our tongues, and the characters we make always reveal the ruling disposition within. "If anyone is in Christ, he is a new creation" (2 Corinthians 5:17). Where is the new creation? If I am still the same miserable crosspatch, set on my own way, it is a lie to say that I am a new creation in Christ. Have I learned to submit my will to Jesus? When we are rightly related to God we have uncovered to us for the first time the power of our own wills. Our wills are infirm through sin, but when we are sanctified there is revealed to us the pure, pristine willpower with which God created us and which the Holy Spirit calls into action. Then we have to submit our wills to Jesus as He submitted His will to His Father. How was Jesus one with His Father when He was in this human frame? By complete obedience, complete dependence, and complete intercourse with Him all the time.

"If you do these things"—am I adding resolution to my faith, self-control to my knowledge, steadfastness to my piety? We ought to be infinitely more humble in exercising ourselves in these ways. God's order for the saint is trusting imperially and working humbly in the midst of things as they are, not thinking imperially and contemptuously ignoring things as they are. God knows where we are, and His order comes to us moment by moment. We are not called to manifest Jesus in heaven—we have to be the light in the darkness and the squalor of earth. Our place is in the demon-possessed valley, not on the Mount of Transfiguration. It is in the valley that we have to exercise these things.

God will never shield us from any requirements of a child of His. "Do not think it strange," says Peter, "concerning the fiery trial which is to try you" (1 Peter 4:12). God is the Master Engineer; He allows difficulties to come to see if we can vault over them properly. "By my God I can leap over a wall" (Psalm 18:29). *Do* the thing, it does not matter how it hurts so long as it gives God a chance to manifest Himself in our mortal flesh. May God not find the whine in us anymore, but may He find us full of spiritual pluck and athleticism, ready to face anything He brings and to exercise ourselves in order that the Son of God may be manifested in our mortal flesh. Remember, we go through nothing that God does not know about.

The Habit of Recognizing Your Expectations

. . . you will never stumble.

What do you expect? One way to detect inordinate imagination is to try and locate to yourself what you expect God to do. One expectation you cannot have, and that is the expectation of successful service. When the Lord sent out the disciples on their first evangelical tour, they came back hilarious over their success: "Lord, even the demons are subject to us in Your name" (Luke 10:17). That is all they thought about. Our Lord said, Don't rejoice in successful service, "but rather rejoice because your names are written in heaven" (verse 20). We are not called to success but to faithfulness.

The life of our Lord is given to us that we may know the way we have to go when we are made sons and daughters of God. We must be careful not to have the idea that we are put into God's showroom. God never has museums. We are to have only one aim in life, and that is that the Son of God may be manifested, then all dictation to God will vanish. Our Lord never dictated to His Father, and we are not to dictate to God; we are to submit our wills to Him so that He works through us what He wants. "I do not know why I should have to go through this"—the moment that thought is produced in us, no matter what our experiences may be, we are no longer saints. It is a thought that has neither part nor lot with the life of the Son of God in us, and it must be put away instantly. We are the only ones who should go through these things, though we need not unless we like. If we refuse to, the trample will go back on the Lord, and we will never hear Him complain. We will get off scot-free—"That was rather smart of me, that man thought he was going to put on me!"

"What is that mark on Your hand?"

That is the mark of the blow that should have been taken by you, but it came back on Me.

Always go the second mile with God. It is never our duty to do it, but if we make duty our god we cease to be Christians in that particular. It is never our duty to go the second mile, to turn the other cheek, but it is what we shall do if we are saints. The Lord is doing it with us just now, we compel Him to go the second mile—we won't do this and that, and He has to do it for us. Are you saying to God, "I shall not accept these circumstances"? God will not punish you, but you will punish yourself when you realize that He was giving you a glorious opportunity of filling up that which is lacking in the afflictions of Christ.

It is Peter, the man who denied his Lord and Master, who tells us that we "should follow His steps" (1 Peter 2:21). Peter had come to a recognition of himself by means of a strange and desperate fall: "Simon, Simon! Indeed, Satan has asked for you, that he may sift you as wheat. But I have prayed for you, that your faith should not fail; and when you have returned to Me, strengthen your brethren" (Luke 22:31–32). Peter understands these words of Jesus now by the indwelling Spirit bringing them back to his remembrance. Are we following in the steps of His unseen feet? Where did Jesus place His feet? He placed them by the sick and the sorrowful, by the dead, by the bad, by the twisted, and by the good. He placed His feet exactly where we have to place ours, either with or without Him, in the ordinary rough and tumble of human life as it is. "I will make the place of My feet glorious" (Isaiah 60:13). As we walk in these bodies according to the new life that has been imparted to us by the Holy Spirit, we shall find they are no longer mounting up in ecstasy, running and not being weary, but walking with an infinite, steady, uncrushable, indescribable patience, until people take knowledge that the Son of God is walking through us again.

The Habit of Wealth

So an entrance will be supplied to you abundantly into the ever-lasting kingdom of our Lord and Savior Jesus Christ. 2 Peter 1:11

Through the promises we are made "partakers of the divine nature" (2 Peter 1:4), then we have to manipulate the divine nature in our human nature by habits. Jesus prayed "that they may be one as We are" (John 17:11), and Paul urges, on the most practical lines, that we form in our actual lives the habits that are in perfect accordance with oneness with God. Our bodies are the temples of the Holy Spirit, in which Jesus Christ is to manifest His life, and He can only do it as we put on the "new man" and see to it that our external conduct springs from a right relationship to Him. Verses 3–4 of 2 Peter 1 describe the supernatural works of grace, then we have to form the habit of working out all that God has worked in. "Add to your faith virtue" (verse 5). "Add" means there is something we must do.

The Habit of Realizing the Provision

So an entrance will be supplied to you . . .

The entrance is "by a new and living way" (Hebrews 10:20), namely, our Lord Jesus Christ, and the outgoing is to God Himself: "filled with all the fullness of God" (Ephesians 3:19). We get impoverished spiritually because we will stop at the barrier of consciousness. We will believe only in what we consciously possess, consequently we never realize the provision. If the grace and majesty and life and power and energy of God are not being manifested in us to the glory of God (not to our consciousness), God holds us responsible, we are wrong somewhere. There is always a danger of placing experience and consciousness in the wrong place. If we want something conscious from God, it means there is a reserve, the will has not been surrendered; as soon as we do surrender, the tidal wave of the love of God carries us straight into all the fullness of God. "O foolish ones, and slow of heart to believe" (Luke 24:25)! We will believe only in what we have experienced. We never can *experience* Jesus Christ, that is, we can never hold Him within the compass of our own hearts. Jesus Christ must always be greater than our experiences of Him, but our experiences will be along the line of the faith we have in Him.

"If these are yours and abound" (2 Peter 1:8). Have we formed the habit of wealth spiritually, or are we gambling with what is not ours, hoodwinking ourselves with delusions? "These"—self-control, patience, love—are not in us if we are not born from above. Are we trying to persuade ourselves that we are right with God when we know we are not? Earthly inheritances are particular possessions of our own, and in taking them we may impoverish others; the marvelous thing about spiritual wealth is that when we take our part in that, everyone else is blessed, whereas if we refuse to be partakers, we hinder others from entering into the riches of God.

"To me . . . this grace was given, that I should preach . . . the unsearchable riches of Christ" (Ephesians 3:8). In the natural world it is ungovernably bad taste to talk about money; one of the worst lies is tucked up in the phrase we so often hear, "I can't afford it." The same idea has crept into the spiritual domain, and we have the idea that it is a sign of modesty to say at the close of the day, "Well, I have gotten through, but it has been a severe tussle!" And all the grace of God is ours without let or hindrance through the Lord Jesus, and He is ready to tax the last grain of sand and the remotest star to bless us! What does it matter if circumstances are hard? Why shouldn't they be! We are the ones who ought to be able to stand them.

It is a crime to allow external physical misery to make us sulky with God. There *are* desolating experiences, such as the psalmist describes in Psalms 42 and 43, and he says, "Then will I go . . . to God my exceeding joy" (43:4)—not *with* joy, but to God *who is my joy*. No calamity can touch that wealth. No sin is worse than self-pity, because it puts self-interest on the throne, it "makes the bastard self seem in the right"; it obliterates God and opens the mouth to spit out murmurings against God, and the life becomes impoverished and mean, there is nothing lovely or generous about it. Always beware of the conscious superiority that arises out of suffering—"I am so peculiarly constituted." If we indulge in the luxury of misery, we become isolated in the conception of our own sufferings, God's riches are banished, and self-pity, the deeply entrenched essence of Satanhood, is enthroned in the soul.

Rejoicing in the Privilege

abundantly into the everlasting kingdom . . .

Jesus said, "My kingdom is not of this world. If My kingdom were of this world, My servants would fight" (John 18:36), that is, they would do the same thing that every rational being does, but "My kingdom is not of this world"—it belongs to eternal realities. The idea of a kingdom that is not maintained by might is inconceivable to us, and the otherworldly aspect of Jesus Christ's kingdom is apt to be forgotten. Jesus Christ's kingdom is not built on principles that can be discerned naturally, but on otherworldliness, and we must never adapt principles that He did not adapt. If we have come to a dead stop spiritually, is it not because we have ceased to be otherworldly? Are we prepared to obey the scrutiny of the Holy Spirit when He brings the otherworldly standpoint of Jesus to bear upon our practical lives? If we are, we shall be considered fools from every standpoint but the standpoint of the Holy Spirit. We are to be *in* the world but not *of* it. Are we letting God's light break on us, as it did on Jesus? Are we showing in the prevailing bent of our lives the characteristics that were in Him? "The kingdom of God is within you" (Luke 17:21). Jesus Christ is the King *and* the kingdom. "This is eternal life, that they may know You" (John 17:3). Eternal life is God and God is eternal life, and the meaning of the Atonement is that Jesus produces that life in us. By sanctification we enter into the kingdom of perfect oneness with Jesus Christ; everything He is, we are by faith. He "became for us wisdom from God—and righteousness and sanctification and redemption" (1 Corinthians 1:30), we have nothing apart from Him. Have we formed the habit of rejoicing in this privilege?

Recognizing Him Personally

. . . of our Lord and Savior Jesus Christ.

Jesus Christ is *Savior* and *Lord* in experience, and *Lord* and *Savior* in discernment. "You call Me Teacher and Lord, and you say well, for so I am" (John 13:13)—but *is* He? The witness of the Holy Spirit is that we realize with growing amazement who Jesus is to us personally—our Lord and Teacher. The baptism of the Holy Spirit makes us witnesses to Jesus, not wonder-workers. The witness is not to what Jesus does but to what He is. "You shall be witnesses to Me" (Acts 1:8). We have had such an abundant entrance ministered to us into His kingdom, that is, into oneness with Him, that we are a delight to Him, and His heart is being satisfied with us. When God is beginning to be satisfied with us, He impoverishes every source of fictitious wealth. After sanctification God will wither up every other spring until we know that all our fresh springs are in Him. He will wither up natural virtues, He will break up all confidence in our own powers, until we learn by practical experience that we have no right to draw our lives from any other source than the tremendous reservoir of the unsearchable riches of Jesus Christ. Thank God if you are going through a drying-up experience! And beware of pumping up the dregs with the mud at the bottom of the well, when all the almighty power and grace of God is at your disposal. We have superabounding supplies, the unsearchable riches of Jesus Christ, and yet some of us talk as if our heavenly Father had cut us off with a shilling! What have we to spend this Christmastime? We ought to be going about like multimillionaires. Externally we may have next to nothing, but spiritually we have all the grace of God to spend on others.

"He who believes in Me, . . . out of his heart will flow rivers of living water" (John 7:38). If you turn away from the Source and look at the outflow, at what God is doing through you, the Source will dry up and you will sit down on the outskirts of the entrance and howl, "It is dreadfully hard to live the Christian life!" Turn round and enter into the kingdom, pay attention to the Source, our Lord Himself, and you will experience the hilarity of knowing that you see God. Never be surprised at what God does, but be so taken up with Him that He may continue to do surprising things through you.

Are you sulking before God? Are the corners of your mouth, morally and spiritually, getting down, and are you feeling sorry for yourself? You have turned your back on God and are marching away from Him. Get straight to God, be abundantly stamped with His grace, and His blessing will come through all the time, and when you get to heaven you will find that God has bound up the brokenhearted through you, has set at liberty the captives through you—but not if you have a murmur in your heart—"God is very hard." There is no self-pity left in the heart that has been bound up and succored by the Lord Jesus Christ.

As He Walked

The Next Best Thing to Do

Ask, and it will be given to you; seek, and you will find; knock, and it will be opened to you. Matthew 7:7

Experience is not what we think through but what we live through. The Bible is like life and deals with facts, not with principles, and life is not logical. Logic is simply a method of working the facts we know, but if we push the logical method to the facts we do not know and try to make God logical and other people logical, we shall find that the experience of life brings us to other conclusions. God sees that we are put to the test in the whole of life. We have to beware of selecting only the portions of life where we imagine we can live as saints and of cutting off any part of life because of the difficulty of being Christians there. Christian experience means that we go to the whole of life open-eyed, wearing no doctrinal or denominational "blinkers" that shut off whole areas of unwelcome fact. Our faith has to be applied in every domain of our lives.

Our Lord's teaching is so simple that the natural mind pays no attention to it, it is only moral perplexity that heeds. For instance, our Lord said: "Ask, and it will be given to you." These words have no meaning for us if we are wearing any kind of ecclesiastical blinkers and are refusing to see what we do not wish to see. "I can live beautifully in my own little religious bandbox." That is not Christian experience. We have to face the whole of life as it is, and to face it fearlessly. The difficulty of Christian experience is never in the initial stages. Experience is a gateway, not an end. There are definite stages of conscious experience, but never pin your faith to any experience; look to the Lord who gave you the experience. Be ruthless with yourself if you are given to talking about the experiences you have had. Your experiences are not worth anything unless they keep you at the Source, namely, Jesus Christ. It is tremendously strengthening to meet a mature saint, a man or a woman with a full-orbed experience, whose faith is built in strong, emphatic confidence in the One from whom the experience springs.

The next best thing to do is to ask if you have not received, to seek if you have not found, to knock if the door has not been opened to you.

Ask, and It Will Be Given to You

Nothing is more difficult than to ask. We long and desire and crave and suffer, but not until we are at the extreme limit will we *ask*. A sense of unreality makes us ask. We cannot bring ourselves up against spiritual reality when we like—all at once the staggering realization dawns that we are destitute of the Holy Spirit, ignorant of all that the Lord Jesus stands for. The first result of being brought up against reality is this realization of poverty, of the lack of wisdom, lack of the Holy Spirit, lack of power, lack of a grip of God. "If any of you lacks wisdom, let him ask of God" (James 1:5), but be sure you do lack wisdom. Have you ever asked out of the depths of moral and spiritual poverty?

If you realize you are lacking, it is because you have come in contact with spiritual reality. Don't put your reasonable blinkers on again—"Preach us the simple gospel."

"Don't tell me I have to be holy; that produces a sense of abject poverty, and it is not nice to feel abjectly poor."

Some people are poor enough to be interested in their poverty, and some of us are like that spiritually. "Ask" means *beg*. Paupers do not ask from any desire except the abject, panging condition of their poverty. Never deceive yourself by saying that if you do not ask you will not receive (compare Matthew 5:45), although you'll never receive from God until you have come to the stage of asking. Asking means that you have come into the relationship of a child of God, and you now realize, with moral appreciation and spiritual understanding, that "every good gift and every perfect gift is from above, and comes down from the Father of lights" (James 1:17).

"You ask and do not receive," says the apostle James, "because you ask amiss" (4:3). We ask amiss when we ask simply with the determination to outdo the patience of God until He gives us permission to do what we want to do. Such asking is mere sentimental unreality. And we ask amiss when we ask things from life and not from God, we are asking from the desire of self-realization, which is the antipodes of Christian experience. The more we realize ourselves the less will we ask of God. Are we asking things of God or of life? We shall never receive if we ask with an end in view; we are asking not out of our poverty but out of our lust.

Seek, and You Will Find

Get to work and seek, narrow your interests to this one thing. Have you ever really sought God, or have you only given a languid cry to Him after a twinge of moral neuralgia? "Seek," concentrate, and you will find. To concentrate is to fast from every other thing. "Ho! everyone who thirsts, come to the waters" (Isaiah 55:1)—are you thirsty, or are you smugly indifferent, so satisfied with your experience that you want nothing more of God? If you build your faith on your experience, the censorious, metallic note comes in at once.

You can never give other people what you have found, but you can make them homesick for the same thing. That is the meaning of these words of our Lord: "You shall be witnesses to Me" (Acts 1:8)—you will exhibit a oneness with

Jesus Christ while He carries out His will in your life in every detail.

Knock, and It Will Be Opened to You

"Draw near to God."—the door is closed, and you suffer from palpitation as you knock. "Cleanse your hands"—knock a bit louder, you begin to discover where you are dirty. "Purify your hearts, you double-minded"—this is more personal and interior still, you are desperately in earnest now, you will do anything. "Lament and mourn and weep!"—have you ever been afflicted before God at the state of your inner life? When you get there, there is no strand of self-pity left, only a heartbreaking affliction and amazement at finding the kind of person you are. "Humble yourselves in the sight of the Lord" (James 4:10). It is a humbling thing to knock at God's door—you have to knock with the crucified thief, with the cunning, crafty publican, but, "to him who knocks, it will be opened" (Matthew 7:8).

Not a Bit of It!

Therefore, if anyone is in Christ, he is a new creation; old things have passed away; behold, all things have become new. 2 Corinthians 5:17

Christian experience must be applied to the facts of life as they are, not to our fancies. We can live beautifully inside our own particular religious compartment as long as God does not disturb us, but God has a most uncomfortable way of stirring up our nests and of bringing in facts that have to be faced. It is actualities that produce the difficulty—the actual people we come in contact with, the actual circumstances of our lives, the actual things we discover in ourselves—and until we have been through the trial of faith in connection with actualities and have transfigured the actual into the real, we have no Christian experience. Experience is what is lived through.

The Experience of Useless Solemnity

Why do we and the Pharisees fast often, but Your disciples do not fast? Matthew 9:14

When the disciples of Jesus were criticized for not fasting and being solemn, Jesus did not apologize for them; all He said was, They are not in the mood to be gloomy. "Can the friends of the bridegroom mourn as long as the bridegroom is with them?" (Matthew 9:15). Our Lord was never careful not to offend the Pharisees nor careful to warn His disciples not to offend them, but our Lord never put a stumbling block in the way of anyone. The one thing about our Lord that the Pharisees found hard to understand was His gaiety in connection with the things over which they were appallingly solemn. And what puzzled the religious people of Paul's day was his uncrushable gaiety—he treated buoyantly everything that they treated most seriously. Paul was in earnest over one thing only, and that was his relationship to Jesus Christ. There he was in earnest, and there they were totally indifferent.

Reverence and *solemnity* are not the same. Solemnity is often nothing more than a religious dress on a worldly spirit. Solemnity that does not spring from reverence toward God is of no use whatever. The religious solemnity of the Pharisees was grossly offended at the social life of our Lord (see 11:19). Our Lord paid the scantiest attention to all their solemnity, but one thing our Lord was never lacking in, and that was reverence. The religion of Jesus Christ is the religion of a little child. There is no affectation about disciples of Jesus, they are as little children, amazingly simple but unfathomably deep. Many of us are not childlike enough, we are childish. Jesus said, "Unless you . . . become as little children" (18:3).

It is part of moral and spiritual education to watch how God deals with prejudices. We imagine that God has a special interest in our prejudices, and we magnify our conceptions and prejudices and put them on the throne. We are quite sure that God will never deal with our prejudices as we know He must deal with other people's. "God must deal very sternly with other people, but of course He knows that my prejudices are all right, they are from Him." We have to learn—not a bit of it! Instead of God being on the side of our prejudices, He deliberately wipes them out by ignoring them. God mortifies our prejudices, runs clean through them by His providence. God has no respect for anything we bring Him, He is after one thing only, and that is our unconditional surrender to Him.

The Experience of Useless Garments

No one puts a piece of unshrunk cloth on an old garment; for the patch pulls away from the garment, and the tear is made worse. Matthew 9:16

The way the Holy Spirit corrupts our natural virtues when He comes in is one of the most devastating experiences. He does not build up and transfigure what we possess in the way of virtue and goodness by natural heredity; it is corrupted to death, until we learn that we

> dare not trust the sweetest frame,
> But wholly lean on Jesus' name.

It is a deep instruction to watch how natural virtues break down. The Holy Spirit does not patch up our natural virtues, for the simple reason that no natural virtue can come anywhere near Jesus Christ's demands. God does not build up our natural virtues and transfigure them, He totally re-creates us on the inside. "And every virtue we possess is His alone." As we bring every bit of our nature into harmony with the new life that God puts in, what will be exhibited in us will be the virtues that were characteristic of the Lord Jesus, not our natural virtues. The supernatural is made natural. The life that God plants in us develops its own virtues, not the virtues of Adam but of Jesus Christ, and Jesus Christ can never be described in terms of the natural virtues. Beware of the hesitation of the natural against being turned into the spiritual—"I do not mind being a saint if I can remain natural and be a saint entirely on my own initiative, if I can instruct God in regard to my temperament, my affinities, and my upbringing." If we have a religious strut about us, some prejudice, some particular refinement, some possession of natural heredity, it is like putting a piece of new cloth into an old garment. All has to go. "Therefore, if anyone is in Christ, . . . old things have passed away." The Holy Spirit begins to work in us the manifestation of the new creation, until there comes a time when there is not a bit of the old order left. The old solemnity goes, the old attitude to things goes, the old confidence in natural virtues goes, and a totally new life begins to manifest itself, "now all things are of God" (2 Corinthians 5:18). It is time some of us had a new set of clothes! The outstanding characteristic of our Lord and His disciples is moral originality.

The Experience of Useless Bottles

> Nor do they put new wine into old wineskins, or else the wine-skins break, the wine is spilled, and the wineskins are ruined. But they put new wine into new wineskins, and both are preserved. Matthew 9:17

The old systems of religion were distinctly ordained of God. All the ordinances to which the Pharisees held had been given by God, but the Pharisees had become second editions of the Almighty, they had usurped the place of God. There is always a danger of Pharisaism cropping up. In our own day its form is evangelical, people become little gods over their own crowd doctrinally. The idea the Pharisees had of the kingdom of God was that it belonged to certain favorites of God and its laws were to be worked out by the select few. According to Jesus, the kingdom of God is love. "How sweet and simple," you say! But where are we going to begin? How are we going to have the love that has no lust in it, no self-interest, no sensitivity to "pokes," the love that is not provoked, that thinks no evil, is always kind? The only way is by having the love of God poured out in our hearts until there is not a bit of the old order left. The love of God in us will produce an amazing sweetness in disposition toward Jesus Christ, but if we try to put that sweetness into the "wineskin" we give to some earthly friend, the wineskin will break and the wine will be lost. We have to be careless of the expression and heed only the Source. We say, "No, I must pay attention to the outflow, I am going to try and be a blessing there." We have to pay attention to the Source, Jesus Christ, see that we love *Him* personally, passionately, and devotedly, and He will look after the outflow. Then it is not new wine in old wineskins, it is new wine creating its own wineskin. Is the love that is being exhibited by us the love of God or the love of our own natural hearts? God does not give us power to love as He loves; the love of God, the very nature of God, possesses us, and He loves through us.

How many amateur providences there are! "I must do this and that, and this one must not do this and that," and God retires and lets us go our own ways. When we say, "But it is common sense to do this and that," we make our common sense almighty God, and God has to retire right out, then after a while He comes back and asks us if we are satisfied. There must not be a bit of that order left. God totally recreates us on the inside until "all things are from God" (1 Corinthians 11:12). May God enable us to stop trying to help Him, and may we let Him do what He likes with us.

Getting There

Come to Me, all you who labor and are heavy laden, and I will give you rest. Matthew 11:28

Where the Sin and Sorrow Cease and the Song and the Saint Commence

Come *to* Me

The questions that matter in life are remarkably few, and they are all answered by these words: Come to Me. Not, "Do this," and "Don't do that," but, Come. "Come to Me, all you who labor and are heavy laden"—why "labor"? The word labor is a picture of the type of mind that realizes that longings and ideals are not being worked out, the reality is not there, and there is an encroachment of sorrow that makes these words a description of the soul. You say, "I have thought about sanctification and of the way God delivers from sin and gives the Holy Spirit and alters the shadow of death to life," but are you actually sanctified? Are you actually delivered from sin, from sorrow, from meanness—are you actually delivered from the things that make you un-Christlike? If you are not, you have no Christian experience. "Come to Me," says Jesus, and by going to Him your actual life will be brought into accordance with the reality revealed in Jesus. You will actually cease from sin and from sorrow and actually find the song of the Lord begin; you will actually find that He has transformed you, the sinner, into a saint. But if you want this actual experience, you must go to Jesus. Our Lord makes Himself the touchstone.

Have you ever gone to Jesus? Watch the stubbornness of your heart and mind, you will find you will do anything rather than the one simple, childlike thing, "Come." Be stupid enough to go, and commit yourself to what Jesus says. The attitude of going is that the will resolutely lets go of everything and deliberately commits the whole thing to Jesus. At the most unexpected moments there comes the whisper of the Lord, "Come to Me," and we are drawn to Him. Personal contact with Jesus alters everything. He meets our sins, our sorrows, and our difficulties with the one word: *Come.*

"And I will give you rest." *Rest* means the perfection of motion. "I will give you rest," that is, I will stay you, not, I will put you to bed and hold your hand and sing you to sleep, but, I will get you out of bed, out of the languor and exhaustion, out of being half dead while you are alive; I will so imbue you with the spirit of life that you will be stayed by the perfection of vital activity. It is not a picture of an invalid in a bath chair, but of life at such a pitch of health that everything is at rest, there is no exhaustion without recuperation. Physical health is a delight because it is an exact balance between our physical lives and outer circumstances. Disease means that outer circumstances are getting too much for the vital force on the inside. Morally it is the same. No one is virtuous naturally; we may be innocent naturally, but innocence is often a hindrance because it is nothing in the world but ignorance. Virtue can only be the outcome of conflict. Everything that does not partake of the nature of virtue is the enemy of virtue in us. As soon as we fight we become moral in that particular. Spiritually it is the same, everything that is not spiritual will make for our undoing. "In the world you will have tribulation," said Jesus, "but be of good cheer, I have overcome the world" (John 16:33). Spiritual grit is what we need. We become spiritual whiners and talk pathetically about "suffering the will of the Lord." Where is the majestic vitality and might of the Son of God about that! "Come to Me, and I will give you rest," that is, I will imbue you with the spirit of life so that you will be stayed by the perfection of vital activity. Jesus will produce in us the actual experience that is exactly like the reality; that means that the very life of Jesus will be manifested in our actual lives if we will face the music in His strength. Faith is not a mathematical problem, the nature of faith is that it must be tried. How many of us are laying up "gold" for a rainy day? When we go through the trial of faith we gain so much wealth in our heavenly banking accounts, and the more we go through the trial of faith the wealthier we become in the heavenly regions.

Where the Self-Interest Sleeps and the Real Interest Awakens

Come *with* Me

"They . . . remained with Him that day" (John 1:39)—that is about all some of us have ever done, and then we awoke to actualities, self-interest arose, and the abiding was over. There is no condition of life in which we cannot abide in Jesus. We have to learn to abide in Him wherever we are placed. "You are Simon. . . . You shall be called Cephas" (verse 42). Jesus writes the new name in those places in our lives where He has erased our pride and self-sufficiency and self-interest. Some of us have the new name only in spots— like sanctified measles. When we have the best spiritual mood on, you would think we were high-toned saints, but don't look at us when we are not in that mood! Disciples are ones who have nothing but the new name written all over them, self-interest and pride have been erased entirely. Pride is the deification of myself, and that nowadays is not the order of the Pharisee but of the publican—"Oh, I'm no saint." To talk like that is acceptable to human pride, but it is unconscious blasphemy against God. It literally means I defy God to make me a saint. The reason I am not a saint is either that I do not want to be a saint or I do not believe God can make me one. "I would be all right," we say, "if God saved me and took me straight to heaven." That is exactly what He will do! "We will come to him and make Our home with him" (John 14:23)—the Triune God abiding with the saint. Do we believe it? It is a question of will. Make your will let Jesus do everything, make no conditions, and He will take you home with Him not only for a day but forever, self-interest will be done with, and the only thing left will be the real interest that identifies you with Jesus.

Where the Selective Affinity Dies and the Sanctified Abandon Lives

Come *after* Me

"Then Jesus said to them, 'Follow Me'" (Mark 1:17). If you do go after Jesus, you will realize that He pays no attention whatever to your natural affinities. One of the greatest hindrances to our going to Jesus is the talk about temperament. I have never seen the Spirit of God pay any attention to a person's temperament, but over and over again I have seen people make their temperaments and their natural affinities barriers to going to Jesus. We have to learn that our Lord does not heed our selective natural affinities. The idea that He does heed them has grown from the notion that we have to consecrate our gifts to God. We cannot consecrate what is not ours. The only thing I can give to God is my right to myself (see Romans 12:1). If I will give God that, He will make a holy experiment out of me, and God's experiments always succeed. The one mark of a disciple is moral originality. The Spirit of God is a well of water in the disciple, perennially fresh. When once the saint begins to realize that God engineers circumstances, there will be no more whine, but only a reckless abandon to Jesus. Never make a principle out of your own experience; let God be as original with other people as He is with you.

"Come to Me." Have you gone? Will you go *now*? If you do go and abandon yourself to Jesus, He will continue to say "Come" through you to others. If you have gone to Jesus Christ and to the truth of God through a servant of God, you never think of the one who took you there, because that individual is so completely one with the Lord Jesus that the thought of the person is never obtruded. Other people go to Jesus not through *you*, but through His word speaking through you.

Is your life producing the echo of Christ's "come"?

Get a Move On!

Giving all diligence, add . . . ." 2 Peter 1:5

We are made partakers of the divine nature through the promises (see 2 Peter 1:4), now, says Peter, "giving all diligence, add," screw your attention down and form habits. No one is born with habits, we have to form habits, and the habits we form most easily are those that we form by imitation. When we begin to form habits we are conscious of them. There are times when we are conscious of becoming virtuous and patient and godly, but that is only a stage; if we stop there we get the strut of the spiritual prig.

In the Domain of Drudgery

Jesus . . . took a towel. . . . After that, He . . . began to wash the disciples' feet. John 13:3–5

Are we refusing to enter the domain of drudgery? Drudgery is the touchstone of character. It is a "drudging" thing to be virtuous. Necessity is not virtue, virtue can only be the outcome of conflict. The virtuous man or the virtuous woman is like one who has gone through the fight and has added virtue, added it on the basis of the divine nature, not on the basis of human determination.

The greatest hindrance of spiritual life lies in looking for big things to do—Jesus Christ "took a towel." We are not meant to be illuminated versions, we are meant to be the common stuff of ordinary human life, exhibiting the marvel of the grace of God. The snare in Christian life is in looking for the gilt-edged moments, the thrilling times; there are times when there is no illumination and no thrill, when God's angel is the routine of drudgery on the level of towels and washing feet. Are we prepared to get a move on *there*? Routine is God's way of saving us between our times of inspiration. We are not to expect Him to give us His thrilling minutes always.

In the Domain of Determination

Abide in Me. John 15:4

The secret of bringing forth fruit is to abide in Jesus. "Abide in Me," says Jesus, in spiritual matters, in intellectual matters, in money matters, in every one of the matters that make human life what it is. Beware of putting on your religious blinkers: "I can live finely in this type of meeting or with that particular set." The Christian life is not a bandbox life. We must live where we can be tested by the whole of life. Are we preventing God from doing things in our circumstances because we imagine it will hinder our communion with Him? That is impertinence. No matter what our circumstances are, we can be as sure of abiding in Him in them as in a prayer meeting. We are not to be changing and arranging our circumstances ourselves. Our Lord and Master never chose His own circumstances, He was meek toward His Father's dispensation for Him, He was at home with His Father wherever His body was placed. Think of the amazing leisure of our Lord's life! For thirty years He did nothing. If we keep God at excitement point, there is none of the serenity of the life "hidden with Christ in God" (Colossians 3:3) about us.

"Abide in Me." Think of the things that might take you out of abiding in Christ: "Yes, Lord, I will abide when once I can get this finished; I will abide, but I must do this first; when this week is over, I shall be all right." Get a move on!

Begin to abide *now!* In the initial stage abiding is a continual effort, until it becomes so much of the law of our lives that we abide in Him unconsciously. Watch it in your bodily life, in your social life—are you abiding *there?* are you bringing forth fruit *there?* That is where My Father is glorified, says Jesus.

Are our minds stayed on Jesus? Do we brood and dwell on this line of abiding in Him? It takes the breathless panic out of us. Our Lord was never in a panic, because with Him the abiding on the inside was unsullied. It is the plague of flies, mental, moral and spiritual, that annoys us and takes us out of abiding in Jesus. There is something in human pride that can stand big troubles, but we need the supernatural grace and power of God to stand by us in the little things. The tiniest detail in which we obey has all the omnipotent power of the grace of God behind it. When we do our duty not for duty's sake but because we believe that God is engineering our circumstances in that way, then at the very point of our obedience the whole, superb grace of God is ours. It is the adding that is difficult. We say we do not expect God to carry us to heaven on "flowery beds of ease," but we act as if we did!

We have to live in the domain of drudgery by the power of God and to learn to abide in Him where we are placed. Remember that God gives us the Spirit of Jesus, but He does not give us the mind of Jesus—we have to form the mind of Christ. The Spirit of Jesus is given to us by the marvel of the Atonement, then we have to construct with patience that way of thinking which is exactly in accordance with the mind of our Lord. God will not make us think as Jesus thought, we have to do that ourselves, to bring "every thought into captivity to the obedience of Christ" (2 Corinthians 10:5). Peter's counsel to "add" means to form habits on the basis of the new life that God has put in.

In the Domain of Devotion

You are My friends if you do whatever I command you. John 15:14

God created human beings to be His friends. If we are the friends of Jesus we have to deliberately and carefully lay down our lives for Him. It is difficult, and thank God it is! When once the relationship of being the friends of Jesus is understood, we shall be called upon to exhibit to everyone we meet the love He has shown to us. Watch the kind of people God brings across your path—you will find it is His way of picturing to you the kind of person you have been to Him: You are My child, the friend of My Son, now exhibit to that "hedgehoggy" person the love I exhibited to you when you were like that toward Me, exhibit to that mean, selfish individual exactly the love I showed you when you were mean and selfish. We shall find ample room to eat humble pie all the days of our lives. The thing that keeps us going is to recognize the humor of our heavenly Father in it all; you will meet the disagreeable person with a spiritual chuckle, because you know what God is doing—He is giving you a mirror that you may see what you have been like toward Him, now you have the chance to prove yourself His friend, and the other person will be amazed and say, "Why the more I poke you, the sweeter you get!" and will tumble in where you tumbled in, into the grace of God.

You Need Not Sin

How shall we who died to sin live any longer in it? . . .

Present . . . your members as instruments of righteousness to God. For sin shall not have dominion over you, for you are not under law but under grace.

What then? Shall we sin because we are not under law but under grace? Certainly not! Do you not know that to whom you present yourselves slaves to obey, you are that one's slaves whom you obey, whether of sin leading to death, or of obedience leading to righteousness? . . . Yet you obeyed from the heart that form of doctrine to which you were delivered. And having been set free from sin, you became slaves of righteousness. Romans 6:2, 13–18

We have to build in faith on the presupposition of the perfect atonement of Jesus Christ, not build on an experience. If we construct our faith on our experiences, we produce that most unscriptural type of holiness, the isolated life, with our eyes fixed on our own whiteness. If we do not base all our thinking on the presupposition of the Atonement, we shall produce a faith conscious of itself, hysterical and unholy, that cannot do the work of the world. Beware of the piety that has no presupposition of the Atonement—it is no use for anything but leading a sequestered life, it is useless to God and a nuisance to people. We have to base resolutely in unshaken faith on the complete and perfect atonement of Jesus Christ.

"Likewise you also, reckon yourselves to be dead indeed to sin, but alive to God in Christ Jesus our Lord" (Romans 6:11). How many of us reckon like that, or do our prayers,

117

our piety, come in the way? Our prayers and our piety are the evidences that we are on the right foundation. Is the Atonement the one thing that exerts a dominating influence in my life?

If You Obey in the Matter of Dedication

> Present . . . your members as instruments of righteousness to God . . .

There is something we must do, namely, dedicate our members. Have we ever, as saved souls, dedicated our bodies to God? "Present your bodies a living sacrifice, holy, acceptable to God" (Romans 12:1), not, present your all, but present your *bodies*. If you obey in this matter of dedication, you can keep your bodily life free from vice and sin. Sin dwells in human nature, but it has no light there, it does not belong to human nature as God created it. Deny the disposition of sin, says Paul, bring it to the place of crucifixion (verse 6). Do not let not sin, that is, your right to yourself, rule any longer, deny that disposition and let Jesus Christ rule. Never let any member dominate and say, You must.

If You Obey in the Matter of Deliverance

> For sin shall not have dominion over you. . . .

"Therefore do not let sin reign in your mortal body" (verse 12), that is, do not let sin command your body. Sin is a monarch ruling on the outside, demanding obedience on the inside. We can add nothing to the Atonement, we can do nothing for our deliverance, but we must manifest that we are delivered from sin. If you obey in this matter of deliverance, you will realize that there is no bondage in the Atonement. "Likewise you also, reckon yourselves to be . . . alive to God in Christ Jesus our Lord."

If You Obey in the Matter of Discernment

> What then? Shall we sin because we are not under the law but
> under grace? . . .

Do you discern that Jesus Christ means His atonement to
be recognized *there*—in my home life, in my business? The
grace of God is absolute, but your obedience must prove that
you do not receive it in vain. Continually bring yourself to
the bar of judgment and ask, Where is the discernment of the
Atonement in this matter and in that? The grace of God in a
person is proved by the discernment of the Atonement in
unobtrusive, practical ways. The amateur-providence element, the insistence of commonsense morality, is the great
enemy of the life of Jesus in a saint because it competes with
the Atonement: "Of course God does not mean that the
Atonement is to be worked out through my fingertips, in the
getting of meals, in my business!" If the Atonement does not
work out there, it will work out nowhere. Beware of the
piety that denies the natural life—it is a fraud. We can all
shine in the sun, but Jesus wants us to shine where there is
no sun, where it is dark with the press of practical things.

If You Obey in the Matter of Debate

> Do you not know that to whom you present yourselves slaves
> to obey, you are that one's slaves whom you obey? . . .

What do you debate about in your mind? When Jesus
speaks, never say, "Let us talk this matter over." Some of us
obey God only in prayer meetings or in devotional times; we
never think of obeying Him at mealtimes or in our offices or
other places. We fail whenever we forget to do in the insignificant details those things we were delighted to see when
we were looking into the law of God (see James 1:22–25).
When things come out against us, do we sit down under
them, or have we such a habit of mind that God is always

first, not piously and pathetically, but actually? Prayer does not place God first; prayer is the evidence that our minds are fixed on God. We have to get our minds used to putting God first—it is conscious to begin with. The snare is putting common sense first. Jesus says, Reverse the order, put God first. The tiniest thing that comes between you and God will blot God out. A twinge of neuralgia is sufficient to make some of us forget the Atonement.

If You Obey in the Matter of Delight

> Yet you obeyed from the heart . . .

"Obedience of the heart is the heart of obedience." Whenever we obey, the delight of the supernatural grace of God meets our obedience instantly. Absolute Deity is on our side at once every time we obey, so that natural obedience and the grace of God coincide. If we look at obedience apart from the presupposition of the Atonement, it makes it seem absurd. Obedience means that we bank everything on the Atonement, and the supernatural grace of God is a delight. We cannot do anything pleasing to God unless there is this deliberate building on the presupposition of the Atonement.

If You Obey in the Matter of Devotion

> . . . And having been set free from sin, you became slaves of righteousness.

Thank God we can do what we ought to do—when? *Now!* We are free to become the servants of righteousness. Sin is nothing but a big bully. Sin was killed at the cross of Christ, it has no power at all over those who are set free by the atonement of Jesus and are prosecuting their lives in Him, "not in any way terrified by [their] adversaries" (Philippians 1:28).

We have to grow in "the training and admonition of the Lord" (Ephesians 6:4). The more we are taught the more we can be taught, and the more we are taught the more the growth and the glorifying of God will go on in our souls. Have we ever been taught anything? Being taught of God is a delightful life, it means the discernment is exercised. God does not put us in His showroom, we are here for Him to show His marvelous works in us and to use us in His enterprises.

We have to prosecute our lives in Christ, not be dragged in His wake, or the strain will be too heavy and down we shall go. The only place to prosecute our lives in Christ is just where we are, in the din of things, and the only way in which we can prosecute our lives in Christ is to remember that it is God who engineers circumstances and that the only place where we can be of use to Him is where we are—not where we are not. God is in the obvious things.

Am I banking, in faith, on the eternal fact of the Atonement? Am I so devoted to my Lord that He is working out His purposes in me? Or am I one of those miserable individuals who is working out my own particular type of religion by myself? We have to measure every type of experience by the Lord Jesus Christ and His atonement. We must build on the great fact of the redemption that God has performed through Christ and continually presuppose that redemption. If we fail to prosecute our lives in Jesus, building our faith on our experiences only, then the further away we get from our experiences, the dimmer will Jesus Christ become.

What Next?

I say to you, love your enemies, . . . that you may be sons of your Father in heaven; for He makes His sun rise on the evil and on the good, and sends rain on the just and the unjust. For if you love those who love you, . . . do not even the tax collectors do the same? And if you greet your brethren only, what do you do more than others? . . . Therefore you shall be perfect, just as your Father in heaven is perfect. Matthew 5:44–48

Deny Yourself More than Others

That you may be the sons of your Father in heaven.

According to the Bible, self-seeking did not begin on earth, it began in heaven and was turned out of heaven because it was unworthy to live there, and it will never get back again. If we are to be Christians after the stamp our Lord requires, we must deny ourselves more than others. Our Lord never taught us to deny sin—sin must be destroyed, not denied. Nothing sinful can ever be good. "If anyone desires to come after Me, let him deny himself" (Matthew 16:24). Our Lord is referring to the natural self, which must be denied in order that it may be made spiritual. Our Lord does not teach "Deeper Death to Self," He teaches outright death to my self, outright death to self-realization and self-seeking. Sin and self are not the same thing. Sin does not belong to human nature as God created it. Adam was innocent when God created him, and God intended him to take part in his own moral development and to transform his natural life into a spiritual life by obedience, but Adam refused to do it. Our Lord continually denied the natural and turned it into the spiritual by

122

obedience. With our Lord everything was spiritual. His eating and drinking were acts of continual subordination to His Father's will (compare Matthew 4:2–4). I have a natural life to be sacrificed and thereby turned into a spiritual life. The meaning of sacrifice is giving the best we have to God, denying it to ourselves, that He may make it an eternal possession of His and ours.

Devote Yourself to Prayer More than Others

Lord, teach us to pray. Luke 11:1

Pray without ceasing. 1 Thessalonians 5:17

Never *say* you will pray about a thing—*pray about it*. Our Lord's teaching about prayer is so amazingly simple but at the same time so amazingly profound that we are apt to miss His meaning. The danger is to water down what Jesus says about prayer and make it mean something more common sense—if it were only common sense, it was not worth His while to say it. The things Jesus says about prayer are supernatural revelations.

It is not part of the life of the "natural man" to pray. We hear it said that people will suffer in their lives if they do not pray—I question it. What will suffer is the life of the Son of God in them, which is nourished not by food but by prayer. When people are born from above, the life of the Son of God is born in them, and they can either starve that life or nourish it. Prayer is the way the life of the Son of God is nourished. God has so constituted things that prayer on the basis of redemption alters the way a person looks at things. Prayer is not a question of altering things externally but of working wonders in my disposition. One great effect of prayer is that it enables the soul to command the body. By obedience I make my body submissive to my soul, but prayer puts my soul in command of my body. It is one thing to have the body in subjection, but another thing to be able to command it. When I command my body, I make it an ally, the means by which my spiritual life is furthered.

"For your Father knows the things you have need of before you ask Him" (Matthew 6:8). If God sees that my spiritual life will be furthered by giving the things for which I ask, then He will give them, but that is not the end of prayer. The end of prayer is that I come to know God Himself. If I allow my bodily needs to get out of relationship to God, then those needs will keep me morbidly interested in myself all the time, much to the devil's enjoyment. We have to leave ourselves resolutely in God's hands and launch out into the work of intercession on the basis of faith in the perfect redemption of Jesus.

Dedicate Yourself to Love More than Others

> "You shall love the LORD your God with all your heart, with all your soul, and with all your mind." This is the first and great commandment. Matthew 22:37–38

> If you love Me, keep My commandments. John 14:15

Before we can love God we must have the Lover of God in us, namely, the Holy Spirit. When the Holy Spirit has poured out the love of God in our hearts, then that love requires cultivation. No love on earth will develop without being cultivated. We have to dedicate ourselves to love, which means identifying ourselves with God's interests in other people, and God is interested in some funny people, namely, in you and in me! We must beware of letting natural affinities hinder our walking in love. One of the most cruel ways of killing love is by disdain built on natural affinities. To be guided by our affinities is a natural tendency, but spiritually this tendency must be denied, and as we deny it we find that God gives us affinity with those for whom we have no natural affinity. Is there anyone in your life who would not be there if you were not a Christian? The love of God is not mere sentimentality; it is a most practical thing for the saint to love as God loves. The springs of love are in God, not in us. The love of God is only in us when it has been poured out in our hearts by the Holy Spirit, and the evidence that it is there is the spontaneous way in which it is manifested.

Dispose Yourself to Believe More than Others

> Did I not say to you that if you would believe, you would see the glory of God? John 11:40

> He who believes in Me, . . . out of his heart will flow rivers of living water. 7:38

"I am not ashamed of the gospel of Christ," said Paul, "for it is the power of God to salvation for everyone who believes" (Romans 1:16). So as long as we live in religious compartments, make our own theology, wear doctrinal "blinkers," and live only amongst those who agree with us, we shall not see where the shame comes in, but let God shift us and bring us into contact with those who are indifferent to what we believe, and we shall realize soon the truth of what our Lord said, "Therefore the world hates you" (John 15:19). If we really believed some phases of our Lord's teaching it would make us a laughingstock in the eyes of the world. It requires the miracle of God's grace for us to believe as Jesus taught us to.

Every time our program of belief is clear to our minds we come across something that contradicts it. Faith, before it is real, must be tried. As we dispose ourselves to believe, we see God all the time, not in spasms. We see His arm behind all the facts in individual life and in history. Are we disposing ourselves to believe more than others?

Determine to Know More than Others

> If anyone wills to do His will, he shall know concerning the doc-
> trine, whether it is from God or whether I speak on My own
> authority. John 7:17

> If you know these things, blessed are you if you do them. 13:17

If you believe in Jesus, you will not spend all your time in the smooth waters just inside the harbor, full of exhilaration and delight, but always moored; you will have to go out through the harbor bar into the great deeps of God and begin to know for yourself, begin to get spiritual discernment. If you do not cut the moorings, God will have to break them with a storm and send you out. Why not unloosen and launch all on God and go out on the great, swelling tide of His purpose? "If anyone wills to do His will, he shall know."

When you know you should do a thing and you do it, immediately you will know more. If you revise where you are stodgy spiritually, you will find it goes back to the point where there was one thing you knew you should do, but you did not do it because there seemed no immediate call to, and now you have no perception, no discernment. Instead of being spiritually self-possessed at the time of crisis, you are spiritually distracted. It is a dangerous thing to refuse to go on knowing.

When the Spirit of God has opened your mind by His incoming and you are determining to know more, you will find that external circumstances and internal knowledge go together, and by obedience you begin to fulfill your spiritual destiny. The counterfeit of obedience is the state of mind in which you work up occasions to sacrifice yourself—ardor is mistaken for the discernment built on knowledge. "To obey is better than sacrifice" (1 Samuel 15:22). It is a great deal better to fulfill the purpose of God in your life by discerning His will than it is to perform great acts of self-sacrifice.

Beware of harking back to a past knowledge when God wants to bring you into a new relationship, beware of harking back to what you once were when God wants you to be something you have never been.

Pull Yourself Together

If you abide in Me, and My words abide in you, you will ask what you desire, and it shall be done for you. John 15:7

In all Christian experience there must be the presupposition of the Atonement, we have to build in faith on the great work that God has performed through Christ. We cannot save ourselves or sanctify ourselves, we cannot atone for sin, we cannot redeem the world, we cannot make right what is wrong, pure what is impure, holy what is unholy—all that is the sovereign work of God. God has made a perfect atonement—are we in the habit of realizing it? We must never put character in the place of faith—there is a great danger of doing so. My character can never be meritorious before God—I stand before God on the basis of His grace. Character is the evidence that I am built on the right foundation. What I need is the perfect realization of the atonement of Jesus Christ. The need is not to do things but to believe. "'What must I do to be saved?' . . . 'Believe on the Lord Jesus Christ, and you will be saved'" (Acts 16:30–31).

By the Habit of Constantly Realizing

If you abide in Me . . .

If we continue to act and think and work from the center of abiding in Jesus, then Jesus says that other things will happen, namely, we shall bring forth fruit. Are we abiding in Jesus? Do we take time to abide? What is the dominating factor of power in our lives? Is it work, service, sacrifice for others? The thing that ought to exert the greatest power in our lives is the Atonement. Do we give one minute out of every sixty to make ourselves realize it? We must get into the habit of constantly realizing the Atonement, of centralizing everything there. To concentrate causes consciousness of effort, to begin with. "Abide in Me," says Jesus. It is imperative on our parts that we abide in Jesus. It is a responsibility for us to continually realize the eternal fact of the Atonement.

By the Habit of Constantly Remembering

and My words abide in you . . .

We maintain our relationship to Jesus by the use of the means that He gives us, namely, His words. Some of us can only hear God in the thunder of revivals or in public worship—we have to learn to listen to God's voice in the ordinary circumstances of life. It is not the length of time we give to a thing that matters, but whether the time we give opens the door to the greatest power in our lives. The greatest factor in life is that which exerts most power, not the element that takes most time. The five minutes we give to the words of Jesus the first thing in the morning are worth more than all the rest of the day. Beware of any experience that does not wed itself to the words of Jesus. Experience is simply the doorway into the great revelation of Jesus Christ. "The words that I speak to you are spirit, and they are life" (John 6:63). *Read* the Bible, whether you understand it or not, and the Holy Spirit will bring back some word of Jesus to you in a particular set of circumstances and make it living; the point is—will you be loyal to that word? Never ask anyone else what the word means, go direct to God about it. Are we in the habit of listening to the words of Jesus? Do we realize that Jesus knows more about our business than we do ourselves? Do we take His word for our clothes, our money, our domestic work, or do we think we can manage these things for ourselves? The Spirit of God has the habit of taking the words of Jesus out of their scriptural setting and putting them into the settings of our personal lives.

By the Habit of Constantly Requesting

> You will ask what you desire . . .

This solves the mystery of what we should pray for. If we are abiding in Jesus, we shall ask what He wants us to ask whether we are conscious of doing so or not. "You will ask what you desire," that is, what your will is in. The meaning of prayer is that we recognize we are in the relationship of a child to its father. "Your Father knows the things you have need of before you ask Him" (Matthew 6:8). When once we realize that we can never think of anything our Father will forget, worry becomes impossible. Beware of getting into a panic. Panic is bad for the natural heart, and it is destructive to the spiritual life. "Let not your heart be troubled" (John 14:1)—it is a command. Are we in the habit of constantly requesting, of continually talking to Jesus about everything? Where we go in the time of trial proves what the great, underlying power of our lives is.

By the Habit of Constantly Recognizing

> . . . and it shall be done for you.

If we are abiding in Jesus and His words are abiding in us, then Jesus says God will answer our prayers. Do we recognize that? "But," you say, "suppose I ask for something not according to God's will?" I defy you to, if you are fulfilling the abiding in Jesus. The disciple who is in the condition of abiding in Jesus *is* the will of God, and his or her apparently free choices are God's foreordained decrees. Mysterious? Logically absurd? But a glorious truth to a saint!

"And whatever you ask in My name, that I will do" (John 14:13). Are we performing this ministry of the interior? Do we pray for those in prominent places, for the "Pauls"? There is no snare or danger of infatuation or pride or the "show" business in prayer. Prayer is a hidden, obscure ministry that brings forth fruit that glorifies the Father. Severed from Me you can do nothing, that is, you will not bear My fruit, you will bear something that did not come from Me at all, but, "Abide in Me," and you will bring forth fruit that testifies to the nature of the vine, fruit whereby the Father is glorified. "The effective, fervent prayer of a righteous man," one who is abiding, "avails much" (James 5:16). Are we constantly rec-ognizing that God does answer prayer if we are abiding in Jesus? Are we building in faith on the presupposition of the Atonement and bringing everything to that one center, or are we allowing our lives to be frittered away? Is Jesus Christ dominating every interest of our lives more and more? This does not mean that we are to be thinking about God always and giving all our time to so-called religious work, but it does mean that we are to concentrate on the great fact of the Atonement with the greatest amount of our time, even to the ordinary things of life as they are engineered for us by God.

Those who use the jargon of "abiding in Christ," if not really abiding, are an annoyance and an irritation. If we make the atonement of the Lord Jesus Christ the great, exerting influence of our lives, every phase of our lives will bear fruit for God. Take time and get to know whether the Atonement is the central point of all power for you, and remember that Satan's aim is to keep you away from that point of power. Jesus said that the cares of this world and the lust of other things would choke His word. We can choke God's word with a yawn, we can hinder the time that should be spent with God by remembering we have other things to do. "I haven't time!" Of course you have not time! *Take* time, strangle some other interests and make time to realize that the center of power in your life is the Lord Jesus Christ and His atonement. Paul limited his knowledge to that one thing: "I determined not to know anything among you except Jesus Christ and Him crucified" (1 Corinthians 2:2). We have to learn to concentrate our affinities, to determine to be limited.

Don't Slack Off

But you must continue in the things which you have learned and been assured of, knowing from whom you have learned them, and that from childhood you have known the Holy Scriptures, which are able to make you wise for salvation through faith which is in Christ Jesus. 2 Timothy 3:14–15

In What You Have Been Taught

But you must continue in the things which you have learned . . .

We learn very few things, because we learn that only to which we give our wits. Are we sticking to the things we have learned? We say we believe that God is love, but have we learned that He is? Have we assimilated it? We see truths, but we are not yet in the circumstances where we can learn them. Many things are taught, but we cannot learn them all at once. We say, "Oh yes, I would like to be that," then there comes the stick-to-itiveness—sixty seconds every minute, sixty minutes every hour. The only way in which we learn is by the terrific iteration of the commonplace. Experience is never the ground of our confidence, experience is the opening of the door to a new life that must be continued in. Some of us are continually having doors opened, but we will not go through them. Don't slack off, keep on with the thing that you have learned. We speak about testifying to the experience of sanctification; what we really testify to is not an experience of sanctification but to a revelation granted us by God of what sanctification is, the experience of sanctification is the rest of life from that moment.

In What You Have Tested

and been assured of . . .

Many of us believe, but we will not confess to what we believe, consequently we are assured of nothing. "I did ask God for the Holy Spirit, but I do not feel sure of anything." Confess what you believe for, and instantly the assurance of that for which you believe will be made yours. We are so terribly afraid to venture on what God says. Confession is not for the sake of other people, but for our own sake. Confession means we have trusted God for this thing and we believe on the ground of His Word that the work is done. We realize by confessing that we have no one except God to stand by us. Have we ever taken the cross of confessing? When we believe with our hearts, we have to confess with our mouths what we believe, to those whose business it is to know. The reason some of us lack assurance is because we do not continue in what we have tested, something has made us slack off.

In Loyalty to Your Teachers

knowing from whom you have learned them . . .

God brings His own particular teachers into our lives, and we have to watch that we do not slack off in our loyalty to them. Loyalty to teachers is a very rare thing. The man or the woman used by God to teach me is not necessarily the one used to teach you. We must not foist our teachers on everyone else. Are we loyal to our teachers, or are we spiritual butterflies? Does every newcomer on the highway of spiritual life switch us off on to a new line? God very rarely teaches direct from His Word until the way for that has been opened by His own order: "and He Himself gave some to be apostles, some prophets, some evangelists, and some pastors and teachers" (Ephesians 4:11). God makes His own teachers, we have to see that we do not slack off in our loyalty to them.

In the Scripture Truth

and that from childhood you have known the Holy Scriptures . . .

It is not the thing on which we spend most time that molds us, but the thing that exerts the greatest power. Five minutes with God and His Word is worth more than all the rest of the day. Do we come to the Bible to be spoken to by God, to be made "wise for salvation," or simply to hunt for texts on which to build addresses? There are people who vagabond through the Bible, taking only sufficient out of it for the making of sermons; they never let the word of God walk out of the Bible and talk to them. Beware of living from hand to mouth in spiritual matters, do not be a spiritual mendicant. Beware of the novel things. Some of us spiritually are independent, impudent travelers—"Oh, I can find my way all right." The thing to do is to keep on the steady track: "Remember the Sabbath day, to keep it holy. . . . Honor your father and your mother," and the others. (Exodus 20:8, 12). God brings back what is old in order to test our loyalty. All the novel things slip away, the essential track remains.

In the Salvation Testimony

. . . which are able to make you wise for salvation through faith which is in Christ Jesus.

The Bible is not the Word of God to us unless we come to it through what Jesus Christ says. The Scriptures, from Genesis to Revelation, are all revelations of Jesus Christ. The context of the Bible is our Lord Himself, and until we are rightly related to Him, the Bible is no more to us than an ordinary book. We cannot know the Holy Scriptures by intellectual exercises. The key to our understanding of the Bible is not our intelligence, but our personal relationship to Jesus Christ (compare John 5:39–40). The New Testament was not written in order to prove that Jesus Christ is the Son of God but written to confirm the faith of those who believe that Jesus Christ is the Son of God. There are no problems in the New Testament. We take much for granted, but nothing is ever ours until we have bought it by pain—a thing is worth just what it costs. We seem to lose everything when we go through the suffering of experience, but bit by bit we get it back. The Bible treats us as human life does—roughly.

"He awakens Me morning by morning, He awakens My ear to hear as the learned" (Isaiah 50:4). Do we allow ourselves to be arrested when we read the Holy Scriptures? The vital relationship of Christians to the Bible is not that we worship the letter but that the Holy Spirit makes the words of the Bible spirit and life to us. When we are born from above, the Bible becomes to us a universe of revelation facts whereby we feed our knowledge of Jesus Christ.

Practicing Godliness

Work out your own salvation, . . . for it is God who works in you both to will and to do for His good pleasure. Philippians 2:12–13

When our Lord is presented to the conscience, the first thing conscience does is to rouse the will, and the will agrees with God always. You say, "I do not know whether my will is in agreement with God"—look to Jesus, and you will find that your will and your conscience are in agreement with God every time. The element in you that makes you say "I won't" to God is something less profound than your will, it is perversity or obstinacy, which are never in agreement with God. Obstinacy is a remnant of the disposition of sin, and it fights against that which a person's will and conscience indicate to be right. If we persist in being perverse and obstinate, we shall ultimately get to the place where the emotions of will and conscience are stultified.

Will is the essential element in the creation of human beings, sin is a perverse disposition that has entered into them. The profound thing in us is human will, not sin. Human nature as God made it was not sinful, and it was human nature as God made it that our Lord took on Him. Obstinacy is an unintelligent "wodge" that refuses to be enlightened. It continually surprises you, "Why didn't I do that thing?" The only cure for obstinacy is to be blown up by dynamite, and the dynamite is obedience to the Holy Spirit. When the Holy Spirit comes into my human spirit, He makes me one with Jesus as He was one with His Father—it is an identification that raises the personality to its right place.

The Way of the Working of God

For it is God who works in you . . . to will . . .

Before I am rightly related to God, my conscience may be a source of torture and distress to me, but when I am born again, it becomes a source of joy and delight because I realize that not only is my will and my conscience in agreement with God, but that God's will *is* my will, and the life is as natural as breathing; it is a life of proving, or making out, what is "that good and acceptable and perfect will of God" (Romans 12:2).

Is it possible for human nature to get to such a standard that it can work out actually what God wills? God's Word says it is. God not only gives me supernatural grace, but He is in me to will and to do for His good pleasure, and that means I can do all that God's will and my conscience indicate I should do. If I am a child of God, I realize not only that God is the source of my will, but that God is *in* me to will. I do not bring an opposed will to God's will, God's will *is* my will, and my natural choices are along the line of His will. Then I begin to understand that God engineers circumstances for me to do His will in them, not for me to lie down under them and give way to self-pity. We are called to do God's will here and now—are we doing it, or are we murmuring, "Why should I be in these trying circumstances? Why should I have these disabilities?" That is murmuring. *Do* God's will. God not only expects me to do His will, but He is in me to do it.

Doing God's will is never hard. The only thing that is hard is *not* doing His will. All the forces of nature and of grace are at the back of those who do God's will, because in obedience they let God have His amazing way with them. If some of us were taken to be specimens of doing God's will, we should be sorry recommendations! We ought to be super-abounding with joy and delight because God is working in us to will and to do for His good pleasure. The "goodest" thing there is is the will of God. God's will is hard only when it comes up against our stubbornness, then it is as cruel as a plowshare and as devastating as an earthquake. God is merciless with the thing that tells against the relationship of a soul to Him. When once God does have His way, we are emancipated into the very life of God, that is, into the life that Jesus lived. The only estimate of a consistent Christian character is that the life of the Son of God is being manifested in the bodily life.

The Way of the Working of the Godly

Work out your own salvation . . .

If I am practicing godliness, that is, practicing in my life day by day and week by week, working out what God works in, then I shall find when the crisis comes that my nature will stand by me, because I have disciplined and trained my nature to work out what God works in. I make what I practice second nature, and in the crisis as well as in the details of life I find that not only does God's grace stand by me, but also my own nature—I have made it an ally. If I have not been practicing in the daily round, it is not God's grace that fails when the crisis comes, but my nature that deserts me, and I fail. God does not make our habits for us or do the practicing—God alters our dispositions and we are left to work out the new disposition He has put in, by practice and the forming of habits. If we have had a great illumination of God's grace, we have to go on to work out all that God has worked in; the danger is that we become stationary.

"Work out your own salvation." We have not to work out that which tells for our salvation, but to work out in the expression of our lives the salvation that God has worked in. What does my tongue say? What things do my ears like to listen to? What kind of bodily associates do I like to be with?

These things reveal whether we are working out the salvation God has worked in. The inward working is God's, the outward working is ours. In regeneration, God puts us into line with Himself so that by the expression of that union in our bodily lives we may prove whose we are. The first lesson to learn is that God works on the inside, and we have to work on the outside what He has wrought inside. The place for yielding and surrendering comes just there. We hinder God when we try to work on the inside. So many of us put prayer and consecration in place of God's work, we make ourselves the workers. God is the Worker, and He is after spirituality. God does nothing other than the profound, we have to do the practical. We have to see that we continually work out with concentration and care that which God has worked in, not *work* our own salvation, but *work it out*. We have to work out what God works in while we base resolutely in unshaken faith on the complete and perfect redemption of the Lord Jesus Christ.

If You Will Be Perfect

The Philosophy of Perfection

But when that which is perfect has come, then that which is in part will be done away. 1 Corinthians 13:10

"That which is perfect" is a Being, who hath comprehended and included all things in Himself and His own Substance, and with-out whom, and besides whom, there is no true Substance, and in whom all things have their Substance. *(Theologia Germanica)*

That Which Is Perfect

The Bible reveals that "that which is perfect" is a Being. God is the only perfect Being; no human being is perfect apart from God. We make the blunder of applying to human beings terms that the Bible applies to God only. Our Lord, in replying to the rich young ruler who used the term "Good Teacher," said, "No one is good but One, that is, God" (Matthew 19:16–17). There is only one Being to whom the term good can be applied, and that is the perfect Being; the term cannot be applied to good people. In the Sermon on the Mount our Lord places God as the model for Christian character; He does not say, Be good as a human is good, but: "Therefore you shall be perfect, just as your Father in heaven is perfect" (Matthew 5:48). We are to be perfect as our Father in heaven is perfect, not by struggle and effort, but by the impartation of that which is perfect. We are accustomed to the use of the word perfect in connection with our relationship to God (for example, Philippians 3:12–15), but here the word is used in a bigger sense, namely, perfect as God is perfect.

Love is another term we are apt to apply wrongly. We emphasize perfect love toward other people, the Bible emphasizes perfect love to God. *Love* is an indefinable word, and in the Bible it is always used as directly characteristic of God: "God is love" (1 John 4:8). In Romans 5:5, Paul says that "the love of God has been poured out in our hearts," not the power to love God, but the love of God. Or take truth. *The* truth is our Lord Himself, consequently any part of the truth may be a lie unless it leads to a relation to *the* truth. Salvation, sanctification, the Second Coming are all parts of the truth, but none is the truth, and they are only parts of the truth as they are absorbed by the truth, our Lord Himself. We are not told to expound the way of salvation or to teach sanctification, but to lift up Jesus, that is, to proclaim the truth.

That Which Is in Part

> If anyone thinks that he knows anything, he knows nothing yet as he ought to know. 1 Corinthians 8:2

God wants us to lose our definitions and become rightly related to Himself, the Perfect One. If we try and state before God where we are in experience, we find we cannot do it, though we know with a knowledge "which passes knowledge" (Ephesians 3:19).

The purpose of God is to get the part into the whole; if we remain in the part by sticking to our convictions, to that which we know, we shall fizzle off. An experience that is true and vivid cannot be stated in words, the lines of definition are gone. Our experience is only part of the perfect. Jesus Christ is much more than we have experienced Him to be.

> But "that which is in part," or the imperfect, is that which hath its source in, or springeth from the Perfect, just as a brightness or a visible appearance floweth out from the sun or a candle, and appeareth to be somewhat, this or that. And it is called a creature, and of all these "things which are in part," none is the Perfect. (*Theologia Germanica*)

Are we resting in our experience of the truth, or in the truth? The part has its source in the perfect. The experiences of salvation and sanctification spring from the perfect Source, and it is this that gives the devil his chance to come as an angel of light and make us seek experiences instead of Christ. Do we lift up Jesus, or are we busy carefully defining our religious experiences, having this measuring rod for the Almighty and that measuring rod for the saints, which if they do not come up to we say they are wrong? There is always a danger of doing this, so long as we walk by convictions. If our experiences come from the true Source and are untouched, they will lead to one place only—to the fullness of the life of God, but if they are tampered with they will lead away from God. Satan does not tempt saints to tell lies or to steal or drink, he does not come to them in that way; he comes along the line of their experiences, he seeks to separate Christian experience from the Lord Jesus and make us want to hug a certain type of experience for ourselves.

When we have part of the perfect nature in us and are walking in the light of the Holy Spirit, He will take us surely and certainly to the Source from which the experience sprang, namely, God—unless we prefer to stay in our experiences. Are we living in the light of our convictions, prescribed and confined, or are we living lives hidden with Christ in God? To those who have had no spiritual experience it sounds absurd to talk about being one with God in Christ, absurd to talk about being guided by the Spirit; they are impatient with it—of course they are, they must be made part of the perfect (that is, be born from above) before they can understand the language of the perfect in experience.

Jesus Christ must always be much more than any Christian experience. This throws a flood of light on experiences. That which is perfect is God, that which is part is the creature experience. The creature experience has its source in

God, but if looked at in itself it is apart altogether from God; when looked at in God it takes us straight to God Himself. When God ceases a way of guiding, when He removes the symbols of His presence, when answers to prayer do not come, it is because He is bringing us to the place where the part is merged in the perfect, and we in our degree are becoming what Jesus wants us to be.

There is only one way to understand the perfect—and the part in relation to it—and that is by receiving the Holy Spirit; God will give us the Holy Spirit if we ask Him (see Luke 11:13). We need to receive the Holy Spirit not only for Christian experience but to bring us into perfect union with God.

That Which Is Perception

> For what man knows the things of a man except the spirit of the man which is in him? Even so no one knows the things of God except the Spirit of God. 1 Corinthians 2:11; see verses 12–16

> The anointing which you have received from Him abides in you. 1 John 2:27

Perception means the power of discernment. "To whom has the arm of the LORD been revealed?" (Isaiah 53:1). We all see the common occurrences of daily life, but who amongst us can perceive the arm of the Lord behind them? Who can perceive behind the thunder the voice of God? The characteristic of those without the Spirit of God is that they have no power of perception, they cannot perceive God's working behind ordinary occurrences. The events of ordinary days and nights present facts we cannot explain, the only way to explain them is by receiving the Spirit of God, who will impart to us an interpretation that will keep the heart strong and confident in God, because it gives us an understanding of God, who is behind all things; but to the one who is not there, the explanations seem absurd. Perception in the natural world is called intuition—I know I know, although I do not know how I know. In the spiritual world this knowledge is the "anointing" the apostle John alludes to. When the Holy Spirit is in us He will never let us stop at the part experience. He will cause the part experience to keep us always one with the perfect and will reveal God to us. If ever we imagine that the Spirit of God gives us an illumination apart from the written Word, Satan is twisting the truth, and it is this kind of passage that he distorts most.

> The things which are in part cannot be appre-hended, known and expressed; but the Perfect can-not be apprehended, known and expressed by any creature as creature. (*Theologia Germanica*)

Peter tells us to "always be ready to give a defense to everyone who asks you a reason for the hope that is in you" (1 Peter 3:15). He did not say give reasonings, but a reason. We can give a reason for what we know, but we cannot rea-son it out with someone who has not the same Spirit. We can state that we are right with God because we have received His Spirit on the word of Jesus, but our reasonings are nonsense to the individual who has not accepted the Holy Spirit.

The Coming of the Perfect

> That they may be one just as We are one. John 17:22

> Now when that which is Perfect is come, then that which is in part shall be done away. But when doth it come? I say, when as much as may be, it is known, felt and tasted of the soul. . . . So also God who is the Highest Good, willeth not to hide Himself from any, wheresoever He findeth a devout soul, that is thoroughly purified from all creatures. For in what measure we put off the creature, in the same mea-sure are we able to put on the Creator, neither more nor less. (*Theologia Germanica*)

"That they may be one"—in experience? No, "that they may be one just as We are one." That is infinitely beyond experience, it is a perfect oneness not only in adjustment but in realization. In spiritual experience it means knowing that "In all the world there is none but Thee, my God, there is none but Thee." Other people have become shadows, the creature I used to rely upon has proved a broken reed, the spiritual experience I built upon has deserted me, the methods of guidance that used to bless my soul starve me now. This is illustrated in the purifying of Abraham's faith; the purification went on until Abraham was lost in God. He did not lose his identity, he reached his identity in God. The hymns that are full of absorption in God are true of deepest spiritual experience, but only true in the fundamental sense, in the surface sense they are in error.

The psalmist prayed, "Unite my heart to fear Your name" (86:11)—the whole spirit, soul, and body so united with God that the individual does not think separately of body, soul, or spirit, but only of God. There are false unities possible in human experience whereby the spirit, soul, and body are brought into harmony. Paul calls these things idolatry, because idolatry is the uniting of body, soul, and spirit to the wrong god.

If we are despising the chastening of the Lord and being discouraged when rebuked by Him (see Hebrews 12:5), it is because we do not understand what God is doing; He is weaning us from creatures to Himself, from the things we have been united to instead of being united to Him only. When God is weaning a soul from creatures, from Christian experience, from teachers and friends, then is the time that the devil begins the advocacy of self-pity. Satan tried to make Jesus realize Himself apart from God (see Matthew 16:23), but He would not: "For I have come down from heaven, not to do My own will, but the will of Him who sent Me" (John 6:38). When we are filled with the Holy Spirit, He unites us, body, soul, and spirit, with God until we are one with God even as Jesus was. This is the meaning of the Atonement—at-one-ment with God.

The one perfect personality is our Lord. When we separate ourselves from Jesus we are in part, we are not perfect, but when the life of Jesus comes into us we no more think of the separating of spirit, soul, and body, we think of Jesus only. Remember, we are not sanctified for our sakes but for God's sake. How many of us are trying to exploit God with the diplomacy that the world uses? We try to exploit God when we pray, "O Lord, give me this gift, this experience." That is the spirit which springs from the devil; we are trying to ape being devout souls, trying to be like Christians, but wanting a relationship to God on our own lines. We can only get rightly related to God through Jesus Christ. The coming of the perfect means that we are made one with God by Jesus. As soon as we are rightly related to God, perfectly adjusted to Him, the perfect life comes to us and through us.

The Conversion of the Part

> . . . it is impossible to the creature in virtue of its creature nature and qualities, that of which it saith "I" and "myself" to be perfect. For in whatsoever creature the Perfect shall be known, therein the creature-nature and qualities, I, the Self and the like, must all be lost and done away. (*Theologia Germanica*)

Our Lord told the rich young ruler to fling away all he had, to think of himself as possessing nothing. Be a mere conscious man and give that manhood to Me. Lose altogether the sense of yourself as one who wants to be blessed and be related to God in Me (see Matthew 19:21).

> So long as we think much of these things, cleave to them with love, joy, pleasure or desire, so long

remaineth the Perfect unknown to us. *(Theologia Germanica)*

If we seek the baptism of the Holy Spirit in order that God may make us great servants of His, we shall never receive anything. God baptizes us with the Holy Spirit that He may be all in all.

Numbers of people say, "I have asked God to sanctify me and He has not done it." Of course He has not! Do we find one word in the Bible that tells us to pray, "Lord, sanctify me"? What we do read is that God sanctifies what we give. An unconditional "give up" is the condition of sanctification, not claiming something for ourselves. This is where unscriptural Holiness teaching has played so much havoc with spiritual experience. We receive from God on one condition only, namely, that we yield ourselves to Him and are willing to receive nothing. As soon as we state conditions and say, I want to be filled with the Holy Spirit, I want to be delivered from sin, I want to be the means of saving souls—we may pray endlessly, but an answer will never come that way. That is all the energy of the flesh, it has no thought of the claims of Jesus on the life. Are we willing to be baptized into His death? How much struggle is there in a dead body? How much assertion of "I" and "me" and "mine"; "I have had such a wonderful experience"? The Spirit of God will never witness to testimonies along that line; they are not true to the genius of the Holy Spirit, not true to the nature of Jesus. "Whoever confesses Me before men" (Matthew 10:32), said Jesus. If there is a tightness and a dryness in my experience it is because I have begun to take the advice of someone other than God, have begun to try and make my experience like someone else said it should be. "But they, measuring themselves by themselves, and comparing themselves among themselves, are not wise" (2 Corinthians 10:12).

The Concentration of Perception

Without Me you can do nothing. John 15:5

> That which hath flowed forth from it, is no true
> Substance, and hath no Substance except in the Per-
> fect, but is an accident, or a brightness, or a visible
> appearance, which is no Substance, and hath no
> Substance except in the fire whence the brightness
> flowed forth, such as the sun or a candle. *(Theologia
> Germanica)*

"Without Me you can do nothing." If we are not spiritual we
will say that is not true, but if we are spiritual we know it is
true. Our Lord said many things that are only true in the
domain in which He spoke them. For instance, He said, "You
have no life in you" (John 6:53). We have life, but not in the
domain Jesus means. We are alive physically, alive morally
and intellectually without Jesus, but we are not alive spiritually. You have not *this* life in yourselves. "If anyone wills to do
His will, he shall know concerning the doctrine, whether it is
from God or whether I speak on My own authority" (7:17).
What is God's will? That we should receive His Spirit, and
God will give us the Holy Spirit if we ask. If we put ourselves
in the condition of paupers and waive all right to the gift and
are willing to receive, then, Jesus said, God will put into us
the Spirit that is in Him. When we have received the Holy
Spirit we begin to realize that what Jesus said is true, "without Me you can do nothing"—in the spiritual life. If some of us
are asked to give our testimonies, to speak in the open air, to
take meetings, we faint because we have not learned the lesson of drawing on the perfect life, of drawing on Jesus.
"Without Me"—nothing, but, "I can do all things through
Christ who strengthens me" (Philippians 4:13).

Have we ever come to the place of saying, "Lord, do in
me all You do want to do"? We ask God to do much less than

this and think we are asking for tremendous things; we have to come to the place of saying, "Lord, I ask that Your will may be done in me." The will of God is the gladdest, brightest, most bountiful thing possible to conceive, and yet some of us talk of the will of God with a terrific sigh; "Oh, well, I sup-pose it is the will of God," as if His will were the most calam-itous thing that could befall us.

Are we learning to think and perceive and interpret Christian experience along this line? When people come to us, are we so relying on the Holy Spirit that He can easily lead them to Jesus, or are we trying to make their square lives fit into our round experiences, trying to fit their broad expe-rience into our poor narrow, waistcoat-pocket experiences? We are off our territory on those lines; we are here for one purpose only—to be taken up with Jesus.

The Principle of Sin

I do not speak on My own authority; but the Father who dwells in Me does the works. John 14:10

The Scripture and the Faith and the Truth say, Sin is nought else, but that the creature turneth away from the unchangeable Good and betaketh itself to the changeable; that is to say, that it turneth away from the Perfect to "that which is in part" and imperfect, and most often to itself. *(Theologia Germanica)*

This is the principle of sin. Anything in spiritual life or in sensual life that makes us draw life from anything less than God is of the essence of sin. God made humankind to have dominion over the life of the sea and air and earth, but God was to have dominion over humankind. Adam sinned by tak-ing his claim to his right to himself. This claim to my right to myself works in those who are born again, and it is called "the carnal mind." It expresses itself like this: I want the baptism of the Holy Spirit, I want to be sanctified, I want to be filled with the Spirit, I want to be used of God. All that springs from the wrong source, it is not drawing its life from the right place. When we receive and recognize and rely on the Holy Spirit, all that stops forever. We have to walk in the light as God is in the light, the light that Jesus walked in (see John 6:38; 1 John 5:8–12).

The Presence of Sin

I do not seek My own will but the will of the Father who sent Me. John 5:30

Who . . . worshiped and served the creature rather than the Creator, who is blessed forever. Romans 1:25

> When the creature claimeth for its own anything good, such as Substance, Life, Knowledge, Power, and in short whatever we should call good, as if it were that, or possessed that, or that were itself or that proceeded from it—as often as this cometh to pass, the creature goeth astray. (*Theologia Germanica*)

The one characteristic of love is that it thinks of nothing for itself, it is absorbed in God. "Love suffers long and is kind; love does not envy; . . . thinks no evil" (1 Corinthians 13:4–5). We cannot live as Jesus lived by trying to imitate Him. "Jesus called a little child to Him, set him in the midst of them, and said, 'Assuredly, I say to you, unless you are converted and become as little children, you will by no means enter the kingdom of heaven'" (Matthew 18:2–3). Our Lord was not setting up a child as an ideal but as a fact. A child does not work from a conscious ambition, a child obeys the law of the life that is in him or in her, without thinking. When we are born again and rightly related to God, we will live the right kind of life without thinking. As soon as we begin to think about it, we fix our eyes on our own whiteness and go wrong. Much of the Holiness teaching of today makes people fix their eyes on their own whiteness, not on Jesus Christ; "I give up this and that, I fast here, I do this and the other, I will give up anything and everything to possess a perfect life." We will never get it in that way, but only by the passion of an absolute devotion to Jesus, and that is only possible by receiving the Holy Spirit and obeying Him.

The Propagation of Sin

> For this purpose the Son of God was manifested, that He might destroy the works of the devil. 1 John 3:8; see verses 4–8; Isaiah 14:12–13; Colossians 2:20–23; 2 Thessalonians 2:4

> What did the devil do else, or what was his going astray and his fall else, but that he claimed for himself to be also somewhat, and would have it that somewhat was his, and something was due to him? This setting up of a claim and his "I" and "me" and "mine," these were his going astray, and his fall. And thus it is to this day. (*Theologia Germanica*)

John's argument is not to do with an act of sin but with the disposition of sin. It is this that the devil propagates in human beings. Why don't we realize what God's Book says? We talk about chopping off this and doing that and having times of consecration to God. The only test of holiness is that the life of Jesus is being manifested in our mortal flesh and that we are not appealed to on the lines He was not appealed to on, nothing springs up in us and says, "Now that is mine." The perfect love is given to us freely by the grace of God, and we can hinder it when we like, no matter what our experience has been, if we cease drawing on the life of God. Anything we possess as our own, as possessions of our own personalities, is the very essence and principle of sin at work. "If anyone desires to come after Me," said Jesus, "let him deny himself" (Matthew 16:24), literally, let him give up his right to himself to Me and take up that cross daily and follow Me. Our Lord said this over and over again, but we have come to the conclusion that He did not mean what He said, and we piously and reverently pass it over.

The Philosophy of the Fall—I

Boundless Inheritance of Covetousness

> What shall we say then? Is the law sin? Certainly not! On the
> contrary, I would not have known sin except through the law.
> For I would not have known covetousness unless the law had
> said, "You shall not covet." Romans 7:7

> It is said, it was because Adam ate the apple that he
> was lost, or fell. I say, it was because of his claiming
> something for his own, and because of his I, Mine,
> Me and the like. Had he eaten seven apples, and yet
> never claimed anything for his own, he would not
> have fallen: but as soon as he called something his
> own, he fell, and would have fallen if he had never
> touched an apple. *(Theologia Germanica)*

What is true of Adam is true of every man and woman, and
"not all mankind could amend his fall, or bring him back from
going astray." This inheritance of covetousness is the very
essence of the Fall, and no praying and no human power, sin-
gly or banded together, can ever avail to touch it; the only
thing that can touch it is the great atonement of our Lord
Jesus Christ. Lust and covetousness are summed up in the
phrase, "I must have it at once and for myself." It is an absolute flood in the human nature, it overtakes the spirit, it overtakes the soul and the body. In some natures the spirit of
covetousness works through the body and is seen in sordid
ways, sometimes it is kept back and only in human reason is
it manifested, and sometimes it is held still further back and
suppressed, but it is there. The background of the whole
thing is the lust of possessing according to my affinities.

(a) Birth of Death

For in the day that you eat of it you shall surely die. Genesis 2:17

Death is the inheritance of the whole human race; since Adam, no one has ever been alive to God except by the supernatural act of rebirth. Do not get the idea that because humanity did not die suddenly physically, it is not dead. The manifestation of death in the body is simply a matter of time: "For *in the day that you eat of it* you shall surely die." The birth of death was in that moment—not the birth of death for one individual, but the birth of the death of the whole human race. God's attitude revealed in the Bible toward the race is that people are "dead in trespasses and sins" (Ephesians 2:1), no touch with God, not alive toward God at all, they are quite indifferent to God's claims.

(b) The Bylaw of Death

For if by the one man's offense death reigned through the one. Romans 5:17

A bylaw is a supplementary regulation, and the bylaw of death is a supplementary regulation on account of disobedience. "I was alive once without the law," said the apostle Paul, "but when the commandment came, sin revived, and I died. And the commandment, which was to bring life, I found to bring death" (Romans 7:9–10). We are all alive apart from God in our own consciousness, and when preachers talk about being dead in trespasses and sins, good, worldly-minded men and women are amused at our being so stupid as to tell them they are dead. They say, "I am alive, my body is alive, my mind and heart and soul and spirit are alive—what do you mean by being dead?" But as soon as a soul comes into contact with Jesus Christ's standard, instantly the realization comes of what death means.

(c) Branded by Death

For the wages of sin is death. Romans 6:23

Every natural virtue is death-branded, because the natural virtues are remnants of a ruined humanity—they are not promises of an evolving perfection. Take the life of the intellect or of the spirit—where does it end? "He who increases knowledge increases sorrow" (Ecclesiastes 1:18). Love produces such pain (apart from a knowledge of God) that it makes the sensitive soul wonder if it is worthwhile to love. Death is everywhere, on the attainments of the mind, of the heart and spirit. When you try to approach God in prayer and draw near to Him, you find the curse of this disposition of covetousness, "I must have this for myself, I want to be right with God for my own sake"—and it saps the energy out of devotion, out of communion with God and Christian service, until the soul is almost wrung to despair. It is that kind of thing that made the apostle Paul say, "sold under sin" (Romans 7:14). We have to get down to this aspect of sin, which is not familiar to us as a rule.

Talk about conviction of sin! I wonder how many of us have ever had one five minutes' conviction of sin. It is the rarest thing to know of a woman or of a man who has been convicted of sin. I am not sure but that if, in a meeting, one or two people came under the tremendous conviction of the Holy Spirit, the majority of us would not advocate they should be put in a lunatic asylum instead of referring them to the cross of Christ. We are unfamiliar nowadays with this tremendous conviction of sin, which Paul refers to as being "sold under sin," but it is not a bit too strong to say that when once the Spirit of God convicts anyone of sin, it is either suicide or the cross of Christ, no one can stand such conviction long. We have any amount of conviction about pride and wrong dealing with one another, but when the Holy Spirit convicts He does not bother us on that line; He gives us the deep conviction that we are living in independence of God, of a death away from God, and we find all our virtues and goodness and religion have been based on a ruinous thing, namely, the boundless inheritance of covetousness. That is what the Fall means. Let it soak into your thinking, and you will understand the marvel of the salvation of Jesus Christ, which means deliverance from covetousness, root and branch. Never lay the flattering unction to your soul that because you are not covetous for money or worldly possessions you are not covetous for anything. The fuss and distress of owning anything is the last remnant of the disposition of sin. Jesus Christ possessed nothing for Himself (see 2 Corinthians 8:9). Right through the warp and woof of human nature is the ruin caused by the disposition of covetousness that entered into the human race through the Fall, and it is this disposition that the Holy Spirit convicts of.

Beatific Incarnation

Therefore, having been justified by faith, we have peace with God through our Lord Jesus Christ. Romans 5:1; see verses 1–11

But how shall my fall be amended? It must be healed as Adam's fall was healed, and on the self-same wise. . . . And in this bringing back and healing, I can, or may, or shall do nothing of myself, but just simply yield to God, so that He alone may do all things in me and work, and I may suffer Him and all His work and His divine will. *(Theologia Germanica)*

The Atonement means that in the cross of Jesus Christ God redeemed the whole human race from the possibility of damnation through the heredity of sin. Jesus Christ never applied the words *children of the devil* to ordinary sinners, He applied them to religious disbelievers. Nowhere is it taught in the Bible that we are by nature children of the devil; Paul says we "were by nature children of wrath" (Ephesians 2:3). How many men and women do we know who have seen what Jesus Christ came to do, who really knew He came to save them from sin, and who have deliberately said, "No, I won't let Him"? The majority of people are sheep, as Jesus said, and the bias of the Fall leads them astray.

(a) Ruined Race

> And I will put enmity between you and the woman, and between your seed and her Seed; He shall bruise your head, and you shall bruise His heel. Genesis 3:15

The prophecy here does not refer to the destruction of sin in the individual but to the destruction of what the apostle Paul calls "the body of sin," symbolized in the first incarnation of the devil as a serpent. The body of sin stands as the counterpart of the mystical body of Christ. The fountainhead of the body of sin is the devil, the Fountainhead of the mystical body of Christ is God. The disposition of covetousness that entered in at the Fall connects me with the body of sin; in the personal experience of sanctification this disposition of covetousness is identified with the cross of Christ, "that the body of sin might be done away with" (Romans 6:6). The more people there are who enter into sanctification through Jesus Christ, the more is Satan's dominance ruined. The body of sin is maimed and paralyzed by every being who enters into the mystical body of Christ through His salvation. The carnal mind, which "is enmity against God" (Romans 8:7), is my connection with the body of sin, but the body of sin is something infinitely greater than the carnal mind—it is the mystical body of sin with the devil at its head, which Jesus Christ came to destroy (see 1 John 3:8), and in His sanctified children is manifested the bruising of Satan and the enfeebling of the body of sin, until at the final windup of everything, the body of sin and the devil are absolutely removed, not only in the individual saints but from the presence of the saints. Satan is not removed now from the presence of the saints, but the saints are still kept in the world where the Evil One rules, consequently the saints are continually being badgered by the Evil One. Jesus prayed, not that we should be taken out of the world, but that we should be kept "from the evil one" (John 17:15).

(b) Realized Right of Saved Souls

> Therefore do not let sin reign in your mortal body, that you should obey it in its lusts. Romans 6:12

Paul is strong in urging us to realize what salvation means in our bodily lives; it means that we command our bodies to obey the new disposition. That is where you find the problems on the margins of the sanctified life. Paul argues, in Romans 6:19, that you are perfectly adjusted to God on the inside by a perfect Savior, but your members have been used as servants of the wrong disposition; now begin to make those same members obey the new disposition. As we go on, we find every place God brings us into is the means of enabling us to realize, with growing joy, that the life of Christ within is more than a match not only for the Enemy on the outside but for the impaired body that comes between. Paul urges, with passionate pleading, that we present our bodies a living sacrifice and then realize, not presumptuously, but with slow, sure, overwhelming certainty, that every command of Christ can be obeyed in our bodily life through the Atonement.

(c) Restricting Remains of Sin

> What then? Shall we sin because we are not under the law but under grace? Certainly not! Do you not know that to whom you present yourselves slaves to obey, you are that one's slaves whom you obey, whether of sin leading to death, or of obedience leading to righteousness? Romans 6:15–16

A partial realization on the part of a child of God of the salvation of Jesus Christ is the very thing Satan delights in, because it leaves within that one the remains of the sinful disposition. In regeneration, a twofold experience ought to be ours: the introduction into a new kingdom by the incoming of the Holy Spirit and the realization of forgiveness of sins, and then being borne on to a moral identification with the death of Jesus whereby we know that "our old man was crucified with Him" (6:6). Impaired lives, impaired judgments and experiences—all that makes us limp and compromising—come about because we have realized only partially what Jesus Christ came to do, and the great rouser up out of that sleep of indifference is the apostle Paul. Read his epistles, rely on the Spirit of God, and let Him drive home these truths to you.

Freedom for God

I am the LORD, that is My name; and My glory I will not give to another. Isaiah 42:8

If I call any good thing my own, as if I were it, or of myself had Power or did or knew anything, or as if anything were mine or of me, or belonged to me, or were due to me or the like, I take unto myself somewhat of honour and glory, and do two evil things: First, I fall and go astray as aforesaid; Secondly, I touch God in His honour and take unto myself what belongeth to God only. For all that must be called good belongeth to none but to the true eternal Goodness which is God only, and whoso taketh it unto himself committeth unrighteousness and is against God. (Theologia Germanica)

The subtlety of Satan as an angel of light comes just here, and we hear the saints, unwittingly and without any intention of doing it, taking the glory to themselves. To say a thing is the

sure way to thinking it. That is why it is so necessary to testify to what Jesus Christ has done for us. A testimony gets
hold of the mind as it has hold of the heart, but the same
thing is true of the opposite: if we say a wrong thing often
enough we begin to think it. The only way to be kept from
taking glory to ourselves is to keep steadfastly faced by our
Savior and not by the needs of the people. Did you ever
notice how God lets you go down when you trust good people? The best of men and women are but the best of men and
women, the only good is God, and Jesus Christ always brings
the soul face-to-face with God, and that is the one great
thought we have to be soaked with. The spirit of covetousness is a flood, and when the apostle Paul talks about the
Spirit, his idea is of a flood: "Be being filled with the Spirit"
(see Ephesians 5:18), invaded by the personal, passionate
Lover of God until we realize there is only one good, and we
have no time or inclination for any other kind of goodness.
"In all the world there is none but Thee, my God, there is
none but Thee." Are we there? We will deal treacherously
with the Bible records if we are not soaked in the revelation
that only God is good. We will put the saints on the throne,
not God. There is only one unshakable goodness, and that is
God. It takes time to get there because we will cling to things
and to people. Those of us who ought to be princes and princesses with God cling to the shows of God's goodness
instead of God Himself. The only influence that is to tell in a
servant of God is God. Let people think what they like about
you, but be careful that the last thought they get is God.
When we have gone from them, there must be no beauty or
fascination in us that makes them long for us, the only
remembrance left must be, *That woman was true to God; That
man was true to God.*

The Philosophy of the Fall—II

By the Fall, the human race not only died from God, but it fell into disunion with itself; that means it became possible for someone to live in one of the three parts of his or her nature. We want to live spiritual lives, but we forget that those lives have to work out in rational expression in our souls, or, we want to live clear lives in our souls and forget altogether that we have bodies and spirits, or else we want to live like splendid animals and forget altogether the life of the soul and the spirit. When I am born again of the Spirit of God, I am introduced to life with God and union with myself. The one thing essential to the new life is obedience to the Spirit of God who has energized my spirit; that obedience must be complete in spirit, soul, and body. I must not nourish one part of my being apart from the other parts.

Margins of the Spirit

> Now the works of the flesh are evident. . . . But the fruit of the Spirit is love. . . . And those who are Christ's have crucified the flesh with its passions and desires. Galatians 5:19–24

The margins of our spirits retain the damage done by the Fall, even after sanctification, and unless we are energized by the Spirit of God and continually draw life from God, Satan will come in as an angel of light and deceive us, and the first way he does it is by habits of ecstasy.

(a) Habits of Ecstasy

That is, the tendency to live a spiritual life before God apart from the rational life of one's soul and the physical life of one's body. In many a life the idea that creeps in slowly is that one must develop a spiritual life altogether apart from the rational and the physical life. God is never in that type of teaching. There are people we call naturally spiritual people who devote all their time to developing the spirit, forgetting altogether the rational life and the physical life. When we look at them or read about them, they seem all right—spiritual and fine—but they lack the one marvelous stamp of the religion of Jesus Christ that keeps spirit, soul, and body going on together. God never develops one part of one's being at the expense of the others, spirit, soul, and body are kept in harmony. Remember, our spirits do not go further than we bring our bodies. The Spirit of God always drives us out of the visionary, out of the excitable, out of the ecstasy stages, if we are inclined that way. This blind life of the spirit, a life that delights to live in the dim regions of the spirit, refusing to bring the leadings of the Holy Spirit into the rational life, gives occasion to supernatural forces that are not of God. It is impossible to guard our spirits, the only One who can guard all the spirit's entrances is God. Never give way to spiritual ecstasy unless there is a chance of working it out rationally—check it every time. Nights and days of prayer and waiting on God may be a curse to our souls and an occasion for Satan. So always remember that the times you have in communion with God must be worked out in your soul and in your body.

(b) Habits of Election of Days

> When you did not know God, you served those which by nature are not gods. But now after you have known God, . . . how is it that you turn again to the weak and beggarly elements. . . ? Galatians 4:8–9

The habits Paul refers to here are superstitious habits in which the mind fixes on "days, and months and seasons and years" (verse 10)—on certain days God will bless us, on other days He won't; if I am careful about this and that, it will bring me into the presence of God. The days and months and seasons and years are appointed by God, but the Galatians were fixing on them altogether apart from God, and Paul says, "I am afraid for you, lest I have labored for you in vain" (verse 11). Nowadays superstition is growing again, and people are held in bondage to it. Are we in danger of fixing on means other than God for maintaining our spiritual lives? Do we put the means of grace in the place of grace itself? If we make devotional habits the source from which we draw life, God will put us through the discipline of upsetting those times. You say, "God does not upset them in other lives, why should He in mine?" Because you are putting them in the place of God. When you put God first you will easily get your times of communion, because God can entrust them to the soul who does not use them in an irrational way and give occasion to the Enemy to enter in. When our spirits are awakened by God we must bring ourselves into subordination to the Spirit of God and not fly off at a tangent, fixing on days and seasons and ritual, thus giving a chance to the mysterious background of our lives that we know nothing about, but which the Bible reveals and which Satan is on the watch for all the time. The only soul Satan cannot touch is the soul whose spiritual life and rational life and physical life is hidden with Christ in God, that soul is absolutely secure.

(c) Habits of Enervation by Dreaming

> Likewise also these dreamers defile the flesh, reject authority, and speak evil of dignitaries. Jude 8

Ecstasy of spirit leads to external ritual in the rational life and makes the bodily life spend its time in dreaming. The las-

situde that creeps over an unhealthy soul produces the physical madness of hysteria. All animal magnetism, all the power
of one person over another, and all the hysterics of self-pity
that makes some people absolutely useless unless they are in
the presence of certain other people, all spring from this
source. It begins in a wrong relationship to God first—a real
life with God was started, but instead of drawing the whole
life from God and working it out through the body, the
bodily life is spent in dreams, in fastings, in prayings, and
slowly there develops a madness of the nerves, which is
what hysteria really is. Hysteria is a physical, morbid craving
for sympathy from other people, which can go to such an
extent that people cannot live apart from certain other people. There is no power of God in such lives. Hysteria is the
actual nervous manifestation of fundamental self-pity, consequently it has been regarded for long by the medical world as
a psychophysical disease; it is more a disposition than a disease. In this domain we get the sympathy cures of Christian
Science, that is, a stronger personality, coming in contact
with a soul that has gotten out of touch with God through
disobedience, can soothe the hysteria of the nerves and inject
a cure by its sympathy, which has nothing to do with God or
with the devil but entirely to do with the influence of a
strong personality over a weak one. Animal magnetism does
not come from the devil, but remember that animal magnetism always gives occasion to the devil. In reading the
records of French physicians who used hypnotism in operat-
ing, in the past more than they do now, case after case is
recorded where a good-living physician used hypnotism but
always stated his dread and dislike of it, simply because he
found that he could never be sure what would happen to the
person after the cure had been effected. And today we find
over and over again that cures are genuine, the disease disap-
pears, but there is a derangement in the life toward God and

toward other people. In every case of healing by God it comes through a childlike trust in Jesus Christ.

Anyone who is inclined to spend time dreaming when he or she should be working out actually through the fingertips what the Spirit of God is working in, is in danger of degenerating into "these dreamers [who] defile the flesh." God never allows a Christian to carry on life in sections—so much time for study and meditation and so much for actual work; the whole life, spirit, soul and body must progress together.

Are you forming habits of ecstasy? Beware. Are you forming habits of ritual? habits of physical dreaming, wanting to get away from the active rush of things? Beware. When we get into the healthy life of God all the margins of spirit and soul and body are merged in a complete oneness with God, "that you may be filled with all the fullness of God" (Ephesians 3:19).

(d) Habits of Envy

> Wrath is cruel and anger a torrent, but who is able to stand before jealousy? Proverbs 27:4

Spiritual envy starts from having gotten something from God in the way of quickening and then trying to use it in my way, not God's. Spiritual envy is a terrible evil of the soul and will always follow the tendency to develop a spiritual life apart from the rational life and the bodily life. All kinds of sour distempers will be ours spiritually, we shall be envious of people who are growing in their lives with God in ways we are not, and we will have almost diabolical suggestions about them, suggestions we would never have gotten through our own unaided spirits. Spiritual envy is an awful possibility to any soul who does not obey the Spirit of God (compare 1 Corinthians 13:4).

(e) Habits of Emotions of Dread

> Let no one cheat you of your reward, taking delight in false humility and worship of angels, intruding into those things which he has not seen, vainly puffed up by his fleshly mind. Colossians 2:18

If we separate the life of the spirit from the rational life, we experience emotions of dread, forebodings, and spiritual nightmares in the soul, which are not imaginary but real. The cause is not always to be found in the physical condition but in the margins of the spirit life. Remember that through the Fall the human being fell into disunion, spirit, soul, and body were separated from one another—that means we are liable to influences from God or from the devil. It is only when we get full of dread about life apart from God that we leave our-selves in His hands. As soon as we try to live spiritual lives with God and forget our souls and bodies, the devil pays attention to our bodies, and when we pay attention to our bodies he begins to get at our spirits, until we learn there is only one way to keep right—to live hidden with Christ in God, then the very life and power of God garrisons all three domains, spirit, soul, and body—but it depends on us whether we allow God to do it. God cannot garrison us if we try to live spiritual lives on our own or if we go off on emotions in our rational lives. God never garrisons us in bits. Whenever marrings come to our lives it is because we have gotten twisted off somewhere, we are not living in simple, full, child-like union with God, handing the keeping of our lives over to Him and being carefully careless about everything except our relationship to Him; keep that right, and He will guard every avenue. "Kept by the power of God" (1 Peter 1:5).

(f) Habits of Exceptional "Drugging"

> They feast with you without fear, serving only themselves. They are clouds without water, . . . raging waves of the sea, foaming up their own shame. Jude 12–13

There are hidden perils in our lives with God whenever we disobey Him. If we are not obeying God physically, we experience a craving for drugs, not only physical drugs out of a bottle, but drugs in certain types of meetings and certain types of company—anything that keeps away the realization that the habits of the bodily life are not in accordance with what is God's will. If in the providence of God, obedience to God takes me into contact with people and surroundings that are wrong and bad, I may be perfectly certain that God will guard me, but if I go there out of curiosity, God does not guard me, and the tendency is to drug it over, "I went with a good idea to try and find out about these things." Well, you plainly had no business to go, and you know you had no business to go because the Spirit of God is absolutely honest. The whole thing starts from disobedience on a little point. We wanted to utilize God's grace for our own purposes, to use God's gifts for our own reasoning out of things in a particular way.

(g) Habits of Enmity

The carnal mind is enmity against God. Romans 8:7

The carnal mind is a dangerous power alongside the Spirit of God in our personalities before identification with Jesus Christ in His death and resurrection is reached. When someone has received the Holy Spirit, the watching of Satan is keen, his whole desire is to split up the personality. "For the flesh lusts against the Spirit, and the Spirit against the flesh; and these are contrary to one another" (Galatians 5:17). The carnal mind is enmity against God, and it is the carnal mind that connects us with the body of sin, of which Satan is the head and of which there is ultimately to be a new manifestation (see 2 Thessalonians 2:3). Every soul who enters into the experience of entire sanctification limits the body of sin, consequently the great, yearning eagerness of the preach-

ing of the Gospel is to get God's children to the place of sanctification where spirit, soul, and body are one, one
personality absolutely ruled by God, where the life of the
spirit is instantly manifested in the life of the soul and body
(see 1 Thessalonians 5:23). If this place of entire sanctification is not reached, there is always that in us which has a
strong affinity with the devil, and this is the remarkable
thing, we never knew it before we were introduced into the
kingdom of God by the initial experience of regeneration, but
we find after a while the strong, lustful hate of something in
us against what the Spirit God has put in, and the lust is for
one thing—I want to dominate this personality.

(h) Habits of Earnest Devotions

> If you died with Christ from the basic principles of the world,
> why, as though living in the world, do you subject yourselves to
> regulations. . . ? These things indeed have an appearance of wis-
> dom in self-imposed religion, false humility, and neglect of the
> body, but are of no value against the indulgence of the flesh.
> Colossians 2:20–23

Have we any helps to keep us living godly lives? That is
the risk. Slowly and surely God will purify our lives from
props that separate us from Him. As soon as the means of
grace are taken to be grace itself, they become a direct hindrance to our lives with God. The means are simply scaffold-
ing for the time being, and as long as they are in their right
place they are an assistance; as soon as we put them as the
source, we give occasion to the Enemy. Have we helped ourselves in work for God from any other source than God?
"You are complete in Him" (Colossians 2:10).

(1) Habits of Extraordinary Defying

> The coming of the lawless one is according to the working of
> Satan . . . and with all unrighteous deception among those who

perish, because they did not receive the love of the truth, that they might be saved. And for this reason God will send them strong delusion, that they should believe the lie, that they all may be condemned. 2 Thessalonians 2:9–12

A spiritual woman or a spiritual man going astray can use the extraordinary powers awakened by the Spirit of God against God. The only safeguard, and it is an absolute safeguard, is to live hidden with Christ in God. The life that steadily refuses to think from its right to itself, that steadily refuses to trust its own insight, is the only life that Satan cannot touch. Watch every time you get to a tight feeling spiritually, to a dry feeling rationally, to a hindered feeling physically, it is the Spirit of God's quiet warning that you should repair to the heavenly places in Christ Jesus. There is never any fear for the life that is hidden with Christ in God, but there is not only fear but terrible danger for the life unguarded by God. "He who dwells in the secret place of the Most High" (Psalm 91:1)— once there, and, although God's providence should take you into hell itself, you are as safe and secure as almighty God can keep you.

The Philosophy of Discernment

A philosopher is a lover of wisdom, and spiritual philosophy means the love of wisdom not only in our hearts, but in our heads—the last place Christians get to. Usually we leave our heads barren, we simply use our brains to explain our hearts' experiences. That is necessary, but we have to let our brains be guided by the Holy Spirit into thinking a great many things we have not experienced. That is, we are committed to Jesus Christ's view of everything, and if we only allow our brains to dwell on what we have experienced, we shut ourselves off from a great deal we ought to be exercised in. The heart experience always outstrips the head statement, and when the experience begins to be stated explicitly, the heart witnesses to it: "Why, I know that, but I never realized before how it worked." Discernment is the power to interpret what we see and hear.

The Path of Discernment

For without Me you can do nothing. John 15:5

> . . . man's knowledge should be so clear and perfect that he should acknowledge of a truth (that in himself he neither hath nor can do any good thing, and that none of his knowledge, wisdom and art, his will, love and good works do come from himself, nor are of man, nor of any creature, but) that all these are of the eternal God from whom they all proceed. (*Theologia Germanica*)

Have I learned to think what the testimony of my heart makes me state? We all say this kind of thing: "I know that in me (that is, in my flesh) nothing good dwells" (Romans 7:18), but do we *think* it? Do we really think what Jesus has taught us to know in our hearts, that apart from Him we can do nothing? We all believe it, but do we think it? Over and over again God has to take us into desert places spiritually where there is no conscious experience at all. We have probably all had this in our experiences: you have had a grand time of living communion with God, you know you are sanctified, the witness of the Spirit has proved it over and over again—then all of a sudden there falls a dearth, no life, no quickness; there is no degeneration, no backsliding, but an absolute dearth. This may be the reason—the Lord is wanting to take you to a desert place apart that you may get to this path of discernment. All the noisy things that fret our lives when we are spiritual come because we have not discerned what we know in our hearts.

(a) The Discipline of Negatives

> For who makes you differ from another? And what do you have that you did not receive? Now if you did indeed receive it, why do you boast as if you had not received it? 1 Corinthians 4:7

Paul is talking about natural gifts as well as spiritual. Have we learned to think, when we see someone endowed with a natural gift such as a fine voice or a good brain or any of the gifts of genius, that every one of those gifts has been received, therefore they cannot be consecrated? You cannot consecrate what is not yours. In thinking, we do not really go along the scriptural lines our hearts go on. Watch your heart in relationship to God, you recognize that you cannot consecrate yourself to God; you *give* yourself to God, and yet in thinking we go along the line of consecrating our gifts to God. We have to get rid altogether of the idea that our gifts are ours, they are not; gifts are gifts, and we have to be so given over to God that we never think of our gifts, then God

can let His own life flow through us. The discipline of nega-
tives is the hardest discipline in the spiritual life, and if you
are going through it you ought to shout "Hallelujah," for it is
a sign that God is getting your mind and heart where the
mind and heart of Jesus Christ was.

Spiritual gifts must be dealt with in the same way as natural gifts. Spiritual gifts are not glorified gifts, they are the
gifts of the Spirit. "There are diversities of gifts, but the same
Spirit" (1 Corinthians 12:4). None of the gifts Paul mentions
in 1 Corinthians 12:8–11 are natural gifts. The danger is to
say, "How highly favored I must be if God gives me this great
gift, what a wonderful person I must be." We never talk like
that, but the slightest thought that looks upon the gifts of the
Spirit as a favor to us is the first thing that will take us out of
the central point of Jesus Christ's teaching. Never look at the
work of God in and through you, never look at the way God
uses you in His service; as soon as you do, you put your mind
away from where Jesus Christ wants to get it. Gifts are *gifts,*
not graces.

(b) The Development of Nobility

> Our sufficiency is from God, who also made us sufficient as min-
> isters of the new covenant. 2 Corinthians 3:5–6

Paul is calling his own mind to a halt in order to explain
to the Corinthian church why what he says and does comes
with authority. If you are right with God, you will be amazed
at what other people get in the way of real spiritual help out
of what you say—but never think about it. The temptation
comes all along to say, "It is because I brooded that God gave
me that thought." The right attitude is to keep the mind absolutely concentrated on God and never get off on the line of
how you are being used by Him. Even in the choicest of
saints there is the danger. Whenever you feel inclined to say,
"Well, of course that was not me, that was God," beware!

you ought never to be in the place where you can think it. The teaching of Jesus is, Be absorbed with Me, and out of your heart will flow rivers of living water. If we are paying attention to the Source, rivers of living water will pour out of us, but as soon as we stop paying attention to the Source, the outflow begins to dry up. We have nothing to do with our usability but only with our relationship to Jesus Christ, nothing must be allowed to come in between.

Have we allowed this path of discernment to be trodden by our feet? Are we beginning to see where we are being led, namely, to the place where we are rooted and grounded in God? The one essential thing is to live hidden with Christ in God.

The Pain of Deliverance

> Jesus called a little child to Him, set him in the midst of them, and said, ". . . Unless you . . . become as little children." Matthew 18:2–3

> For when the vain imagination and ignorance are turned into an understanding and knowledge of the truth, the claiming of anything for our own will cease of itself. *(Theologia Germanica)*

Healthy people do not know what health is, sick people know what health is because they have lost it; a saint rightly related to God does not know what the will of God is because the saint *is* the will of God. A disobedient soul knows what the will of God is because that soul has disobeyed. The illustration Jesus gives to His disciples of a saintly life is a little child. Jesus did not put up a child as an ideal but to show them that ambition has no place whatever in the disposition of a Christian. The life of a child is unconscious in its fullness of life, and the source of its life is implicit love. To be made children over again causes pain because we have to reconstruct our mental ways of looking at things after God has dealt with our heart experiences. Some of us retain our old ways of looking at things, and the deliverance is painful. Paul urges that we allow the pain: "Let this mind be in you which was also in Christ Jesus" (Philippians 2:5); "bringing every thought into captivity to the obedience of Christ" (2 Corinthians 10:5). It is hard to do it. In the beginning we are so anxious, "Lord, give me a message for this meeting," until we learn that if we live in the center of God's will, He will give us messages when He likes and withhold them when He likes. We try to help God help Himself to us; we have to get out of the way and God will help Himself to our lives in every detail. Have we learned to form the mind of Christ by the pain of deliverance, till we know we are drawing on Him for everything? Are we sacrificing our holy selves to the will of Jesus, as He did to the will of His Father? Are we beginning to speak what God wants us to speak because we are submitting our intelligence to Him? "The Son can do nothing of Himself" (John 5:19). Our Lord never allowed such a thought as, *I have done that,* in His mind. Have we spiritual discernment like that? If not, remember what the apostle James says: "If any of you lacks wisdom, let him ask of God, who gives to all liberally and without reproach, and it will be given to him" (James 1:5).

(a) The Plunge into God

> But when that which is perfect has come, then that which is in part will be done away. 1 Corinthians 13:10; see verses 8–9

> Now when a man duly perceiveth these things in himself he and the creature fall behind, and he doth not call anything his own, and the less he taketh this knowledge unto himself the more perfect doth it become. So also is it with the will and love, and desire, and the like. For the less we call these things our own, the more perfect and noble and Godlike

> do they become, and the more we think them our
> own, the baser and less pure and perfect do they
> become. *(Theologia Germanica)*

The only way to learn to swim is to take the plunge, sink or swim—that is exactly the idea here. Will I cut loose from all moorings and plunge straight into God? It is what the New Testament is continually urging—Let go. Life goes on in a series of coveting the best gifts, but, Paul says, "I show you a more excellent way" (1 Corinthians 12:31)—take an absolute plunge into the love of God, and when you are there you will be amazed at your foolishness for not getting there before. It is not the question of the surrender of a soul for sanctification but the unreserved surrender of a sanctified soul to God. We are so reserved where we ought to be unreserved and so unreserved where we ought to be reserved. We ought never to be reserved toward God, but utterly open, perfectly one with Him all through. After the experience of sanctification we have to present our sanctified selves to God, and one of the greatest difficulties in doing this is considering the conditions other people say we have to observe. "But they, . . . comparing themselves among themselves, are not wise" (2 Corinthians 10:12). Watch how tied up we are with other people's notions of what we should be. The only way to get rid of it all is to take this plunge into the love of God. We have to form the mind of Christ until we are absorbed in Him and take no account of the evil done to us. No love on earth can do this but the love of God.

(b) The Participation in Godliness

> Christ Jesus my Lord, for whom I have suffered the loss of all
> things. Philippians 3:8

> We must cast all things from us, and strip ourselves
> of them; we must refrain from claiming anything for
> our own. *(Theologia Germanica)*

To experience the loss of all things for anyone but Jesus Christ is mental suicide. Read what our Lord said to the rich young ruler: "Sell what you have, . . . and come, follow Me" (Matthew 19:21), reduce yourself until you are a mere conscious man, and then give that manhood to Me, and we read that "he was sad at this word, and went away sorrowful, for he had great possessions" (Mark 10:22). Do you possess a reputation as a Christian worker? That will be in the way when the Lord speaks to you. Are you rich in the consciousness that you are somebody spiritually? That will be in the way. You must first estimate and then experience the loss of all things and cast yourself on Jesus, then participation in godliness will be yours as it never has been.

> When we do this, we shall have the best, fullest, clearest and noblest knowledge that a man can have, and also the noblest and purest love, will and desire; for then these will be all of God alone. It is much better that they should be God's than the creature's.
> (*Theologia Germanica*)

The oneness Jesus Christ prayed for in John 17 is the oneness of identity, not of union. "I and My Father are one" (John 10:30), and by the Atonement our Lord brings us into identity with Himself: "that they may be one just as We are one" (17:22).

The Plane of Delight

> While we . . . look . . . at the things which are not seen. 2 Corinthians 4:18

> But if our inward man were to make a leap and spring into the Perfect, we should find and taste how that the Perfect is without measure, number or end, better and nobler than all which is imperfect and in part, and the Eternal above the temporal or perishable, and the foundation and source above all

that floweth or can ever flow from it. *(Theologia Germanica)*

When we think of being delivered from sin, of being filled with the Spirit, we say, "Oh, I shall never get there, it is only for exceptional people like the apostle Paul," but when by God's grace we get there we find it is the easiest place to live; it is not a mountain peak but a flat tableland of delight, with plenty of room for everyone. "May your whole spirit, soul, and body be preserved blameless" (1 Thessalonians 5:23)—that is not the life I am to live hereafter but the life God would have me live now—most of us are far too diffident about getting there.

(a) The Altitude of Love

> The greatest of these is love. 1 Corinthians 13:13

> A Master called Bœtius said, "It is of sin that we do not love that which is Best." He hath spoken the truth. That which is best should be the dearest of all things to us. *(Theologia Germanica)*

Is it? Sometimes we crave for something less than the best—beware! We ought to love the most what is best. The Spirit of God in us can teach us how to love the best through faith, through knowledge, through everything, till we are altogether in love with God, in absolute harmony with Him, absorbed in the one great purpose of God.

> And in our love of it, neither helpfulness nor unhelpfulness, advantage nor injury, gain nor loss, honour nor dishonour, praise nor blame, nor anything of the kind should be regarded. *(Theologia Germanica)*

1 Corinthians 13 is not an ideal, it is an identification that makes the ideal possible. Never put the ideal where the Spirit

of God does not put it. The ideal comes after the identification.

(b) The Atmosphere of Life

But the fruit of the Spirit is love. Galatians 5:22

Now that creature in which the Eternal Good, most manifesteth itself, shineth forth, worketh, is most known and loved, is the best, and that wherein the Eternal Good is least manifested is the least good of all creatures. (Theologia Germanica)

In days gone by we all used to love the creatures that exhibit reflections of the Eternal Good—honor and courage and strength—but when we are made one with Jesus Christ we find we love the creatures that exhibit the fruit of the Spirit. A great alteration has come over my outlook, God is altering the thing that matters.

Therefore when we have to do with the creatures and hold converse with them, and take note of their diverse qualities, the best creatures must always be the dearest to us, and we must cleave to them, and unite ourselves to them. (Theologia Germanica)

"What communion has light with darkness?" (2 Corinthians 6:14). The education God puts His children through in life is, first, that which is natural, then, that which is spiritual, until we are rooted and grounded in Him, then there is no danger evermore to that life. It is always better further on—through the natural to the spiritual. No wonder the counsel of the Spirit through the writer to the Hebrews is, "You have need of endurance" (10:36).

The Philosophy of Following Our Lord

> First, man must consider the teaching and the life of
> Jesus Christ, for He hath taught poverty and lived
> it. And a man should follow the teaching and the
> life, if he wisheth to be perfect, for He saith,
> "Whoso loveth Me keepeth My commandments
> and My counsels, and heareth My word." (John
> Tauler, in *The Following of Christ*)

In every profession under heaven the great ambition of the natural heart is to be perfect. When Jesus Christ was faced with a splendid specimen of a young man, He said, "If you want to be perfect," I will tell you what to do. (Matthew 19:21).

"If anyone loves Me, he will keep My word; and My Father will love him, and We will come to him and make Our home with him" (John 14:23). The whole outcome of following Jesus is expressed for us in these words, namely, that the triune God, Father, Son, and Holy Spirit, will come and make His home with the person who loves Jesus and keeps His word. As long as the devil can keep us terrified of thinking, he will always limit the work of God in our souls.

The Way of the Follower—Negative

> If anyone desires to come after Me, let him deny himself, and
> take up his cross daily, and follow Me. Luke 9:23

The word "deny" embraces what the apostle Paul meant when he said "put to death your members which are on the earth" (Colossians 3:5).

(a) Infirmity-Sins

> For if you live according to the flesh you will die; but if by the
> Spirit you put to death the deeds of the body, you will live.
> Romans 8:13

> It might now be said, What is man in his selfhood,
> that he must deny, if he wisheth to follow after
> Christ? Man's selfhood consisteth in four things.
> First, his frailty, and that he falleth into sins; and
> this he must needs set aside; he must die to his
> defects and sins, and mortify himself. (Tauler)

The disposition in us is either implanted naturally
through the First Adam or implanted supernaturally through
the Last Adam by regeneration and sanctification. We breed
our temperaments out of the dispositions that are in us. If we
are going to follow Jesus, we must do to death infirmity-sins.
God cannot do it—we have to do it ourselves. Satan takes
occasion of the frailty of the bodily temple and says, "Now
you know you cannot do that, you are so infirm, you cannot
concentrate your mind," and the like. Never allow bodily
infirmities to hinder you obeying the commands of Jesus.
Paul says, "I discipline my body and bring it into subjection"
(1 Corinthians 9:27); I buffet (or bruise) my body, and bring
it into bondage. Through the Atonement, God deals with the
wrong disposition in us, then He gives us the glorious privilege of making our bodies "instruments of righteousness to
God" (Romans 6:13).

(b) Inordinate Affection

> Put to death your members which are on the earth: . . . passion.
> Colossians 3:5

> Secondly, he is inclined to creatures. For man is
> inclined by nature to his like, and he must kill
> nature, and must withdraw from creatures, for God

and creatures are opposites. And therefore he who wisheth to have God must leave creatures. For the soul is so narrow that God and the creature cannot dwell together in her; and therefore if God is to dwell in thy soul, the creature must remain without. (Tauler)

In Colossians 3:5, Paul is describing an unsanctified individual, but the same person, sanctified, is inclined to creatures rather than to the Creator. Watch the hard things Jesus says about father, mother, wife, children, your own life (see Luke 14:26); He says if we are going to follow Him, these must be on the outside of the central citadel. The central citadel must be God and God alone. When once we are willing to do to death our clinging to creatures, which in certain supreme calls comes between us and God, Jesus says we will receive an hundredfold, because as soon as we are rightly related to God He can trust us with creature-relationships without fear of inordinateness. With the majority of us, these relationships are cut off not by our own doing—God has to do it for us—He has to come with strange providences and cut them off, because we have professed that we are going to follow Jesus. We forget that sanctification is only the beginning, the one purpose of sanctification is that Jesus might be "admired among all those who believe" (2 Thessalonians 1:10).

(c) Inveterate Luxury

But I discipline my body and bring it into subjection, lest, when I have preached to others, I myself should become disqualified. 1 Corinthians 9:27

The third point is, that man to part from selfhood should drop all sensual delight, for he must die to this and kill it in himself if he wisheth to have God's comfort. As St. Bernard saith, "The comfort of God is so noble that no one receiveth it who seeketh comfort elsewhere." (Tauler)

The natural life in a sanctified man or in a sanctified woman is neither moral nor immoral, it is the gift God has given the saint to sacrifice on the altar of love to God. Jesus Christ had a natural body, it was not a sin for Him to be hungry, but it would have been a sin for Him to satisfy that hunger when God had told Him not to, and Satan came to Him, when He had fasted forty days and forty nights and was hungry, and said, Satisfy that hunger *now.* The bodies we have are not sinful in themselves; if they were, it would be untrue to say that Jesus Christ was sinless. Paul's words have reference to the fact that my body has been ruled by a sinful disposition, a disposition that simply means I am going to find my sustaining in creature comforts. After I am sanctified I have the same body, but it is ruled by a new disposition, and I have to sacrifice my natural life to God even as Jesus did, so that I make the natural life spiritual by a series of direct moral choices.

(d) Intellectual Intemperance

And lest I should be exalted above measure by the abundance of the revelations. 2 Corinthians 12:7

The fourth thing a man must let go if he wisheth to follow Christ, is spiritual natural comforts, which are generated in man, by detecting the distinction between spiritual and natural knowledge. . . . Whoever tarries by this natural rational delight, hinders himself from the supernatural delight which God in His grace imparteth to the soul. (Tauler)

Intellectual intemperance is a great snare to a saint. Bodily fasting is child's play compared to the determined fasting from the intellectual apprehension of the teachings of Jesus that goes beyond what we are living out. The characteristic of many spiritual people today is intellectual intemperance, fanatical intoxication with the things of God, wild exuberance, an unlikeness to the sanity of Jesus in the very ways of God. There is a danger in the enjoyment of the delights and the power that come to us through Jesus Christ's salvation without lifting our lives into keeping with His teaching, especially in spiritual people whose minds have never been disciplined, and they wander off into all kinds of vagaries. That accounts for the distinction we find between spiritual sincerity and spiritual reality.

All this is the negative side of following our Lord. Have we told Jesus we will follow Him? Are we prepared to do our parts in bringing our bodies into subjection, for one purpose only, that we may learn the fellowship of following (see 1 Corinthians 9:27)? Are we beginning to realize that until we are born again the teachings of Jesus are simple, after we are born again they become growingly difficult, and we find clouds and darkness are round about the things we thought we knew perfectly well once, and following our Lord is one of these things?

The Way of the Fellowship—Positive

> And he who does not take his cross and follow after Me is not worthy of Me. He who finds his life will lose it, and he who loses his life for My sake shall find it. Matthew 10:38–39

It is possible to be grossly selfish in absorbing the salvation of Jesus, to enjoy all its benedictions, and never follow Him one step. So Jesus says, "If anyone desires to come after Me," this is the way, "let him deny himself, and take up his cross daily, and follow Me" (Luke 9:23).

(a) Working Virtue from God

> For just as you presented your members as slaves of uncleanness, and of lawlessness leading to more lawlessness, so now

present your members as slaves of righteousness for holiness. Romans 6:19

> First, man should kill sin in himself through virtue; for just as man is removed from God by sin must he be brought nigh again unto God by virtue . . . but let no one believe that he is free from sins, unless he hath taken unto himself all the virtues. (Tauler)

The positive side is this—that we work all the virtues of Jesus in and through our members, but this can only be done when all self-reliance has come to an end (compare 2 Corinthians 1:9). Our natural virtues are remnants of what God created humanity to be, not promises of what humanity is going to be. The natural virtues cannot be patched up to come anywhere near God's demands, and the sign that God is at work in us is that He corrupts our confidence in the natural virtues. It is simply an amplification of the old Gospel hymn—

> Nothing in my hand I bring,
> Simply to Thy Cross I cling!

(b) Willing Poverty for God

> For you know the grace of our Lord Jesus Christ, that though He was rich, yet for your sakes He became poor, that you through His poverty might become rich. 2 Corinthians 8:9

> The second thing that man must shun is the love for creatures. Poverty of spirit is a going out of yourself and out of everything earthly. Thereby he despiseth creatures, is despised by them, and is thus set free. A truly poor man taketh nothing from creatures, but all from God, be it bodily or spiritual. God alone will be the Giver. (Tauler)

To be willingly poor for God is to strip myself of all things for the sake of Jesus Christ. One of the greatest snares is built on what is really a great truth, namely, that all have

Christ in themselves. The pernicious use that is made of that statement is that therefore people draw power from themselves. Never! Jesus Christ never drew power from Himself, He drew it always from without Himself, namely, from His Father. "The Son can do nothing of Himself" (John 5:19, 30). Beware of being rich spiritually on earth—only be rich spiritually in heaven. Jesus said to the rich young ruler, If you will strip yourself and have no riches here, you will lay up for yourself treasure in heaven. Treasure in heaven is faith that has been tried (compare Revelation 3:18). As soon as we begin to have fellowship with Jesus we have to live the life of faith at all costs; it may be bitter to begin with, but afterwards it is ineffably and indescribably sweet—willing poverty for God, a determined going outside myself and every earthly thing.

(c) Watchful Purity for God

> Whoever has been born of God does not sin, for His seed remains in him; and he cannot sin, because he has been born of God. 1 John 3:9

> But who knoweth, wilt thou ask, if he have all virtues? I answer to this like John, who saith, "Whosoever is born of God cannot sin." For in the same moment in which God the Father begetteth His Son in the soul, sins and all unlikeness disappear, and all virtues are born in her in a likeness to God. (Tauler)

According to that statement of the apostle John, none are free from sin unless they are possessed of all the virtues. The apostle is not teaching sinless perfection, he is teaching perfect sinlessness, which is a different matter. If as sanctified souls we walk in the light as God is in the light, the revelation is that through the Atonement, "the blood of Jesus Christ His Son cleanses us from all sin" (1 John 1:7). That does not mean cleansing from all sin in my consciousness—if it did, it would produce hypocrisy. Any number of people are not conscious of sin, but it does not follow that they are cleansed from all sin. It is not my consciousness that is referred to, but the consciousness God has of me; what I am conscious of is walking in the light with nothing to hide. The outcome of following our Lord is a holiness of character so that God sees nothing to censure because the life of His Son is working out in every particular. Our main idea is to keep steadfastly in the blazing light of God so that He can exhibit the virtues of Jesus through us unhindered. "If you love Me, keep My commandments" (John 14:15). How many of them? All of them. Then, says Jesus, "We will come to him and make Our home with him" (verse 23)—in heaven? No, here.

(d) Wonderful Passion for God

> Therefore, since Christ suffered for us in the flesh, arm your-selves also with the same mind, for he who has suffered in the flesh has ceased from sin, that he no longer should live the rest of his time in the flesh for the lusts of men, but for the will of God. 1 Peter 4:1–2

>> And whoso would eat its fruit (the fruit of the holy cross) with profit must break it off from the cross by steadfast internal contemplation of the Passion of Our Lord.

>> All on the cross is full of fruit, and more than all tongues could in truth proclaim. Nay, angels' tongues could not describe the overflowing grace that is there hidden in the Passion of our Lord. Blessed are those who have found this treasure. (Tauler)

Steady contemplation of the passion of our Lord will do to death everything that is not of God. It is only after a long while of going on with God and steady contemplation of the Cross that we begin to understand its meaning. "Today you will be with Me in Paradise" is said at only one place, namely, at the cross (Luke 23:43).

This is not a message about our salvation and sanctification but about the outcome of salvation and sanctification in our implicit lives, that is, where we live it and cannot speak it. Jesus said, "If anyone desires to come after Me" (Matthew 16:24), not, If anyone would be saved and sanctified. "If anyone desires to come after Me"—those are the conditions. Jesus Christ always talked about discipleship with an *If*. We are at perfect liberty to toss our spiritual heads and say, "No, thank you, that is a bit too stern for me," and the Lord will never say a word, we can do exactly what we like. He will never plead, but the opportunity is there: "If."

After all, it is the great, stern call of Jesus that fascinates men and women quicker than anything. It is not the gospel of being saved from hell and enjoying heaven that attracts people, except in a very shallow mood, it is Christ crucified that attracts people; Jesus said so: "I, if I am lifted up from the earth, will draw all peoples to Myself" (John 12:32). Jesus Christ never attracts us by the unspeakable bliss of paradise, He attracts us by an ugly beam. We talk about getting down to the depths of someone's soul—Jesus Christ is the only One who ever did. If once someone has heard the appeal of Jesus from the cross, that individual begins to find there is something there that answers the cry of the human heart and the problem of the whole world. What we have to do as God's servants is to lift up Christ crucified. We can either do it as gramophones or as those who are in fellowship with Him.

Many of us have heard Jesus Christ's first "Follow Me"—to a life of liberty and joy and gladness; how many of us have heard the second "Follow Me"—deny your right to yourself and do to death in yourself everything that never was in Me?

The Philosophy of Godliness

Most assuredly, I say to you, He who believes in Me, the works that I do he will do also; and greater works than these he will do, because I go to My Father. John 14:12

The Way of the Working of God

> Then they said to Him, "What shall we do, that we may work the works of God?"
>
> Jesus answered and said to them, "This is the work of God, that you believe in Him whom He sent." John 6:28–29

> There are two kinds of work in God—a working within and a working outwardly. The working inward is God's being and nature, the outward working is the creature. . . . God worketh in souls that He may bring them to the first origin from which they have flowed, for by their works they cannot go in again. (John Tauler, in *The Following of Christ*)

These words of Jesus in John 6 sum up the whole mystery of the work of grace, namely, that to "work the works of God" we must stop working and let God work. "This is the work of God, that you believe." Unbelief is the most active thing on earth; it is negative on God's side, not on ours. Unbelief is a fretful, worrying, questioning, annoying, self-centered spirit. To believe is to stop all this and let God work.

(a) The Working Master

> Work out your own salvation with fear and trembling; for it is God who works in you both to will and to do for His good pleasure. Philippians 2:12–13

> If man is to come to God, he must be empty of all work and let God work alone. . . . Now, all that God willeth to have from us is that we be inactive, and let Him be the working Master. (Tauler)

Paul does not say, Work out something that will tell for your salvation, he says, Work out in the expression of your life the salvation God has worked in. If we think for a moment we shall soon know how much we are saved—What do our tongues say? What kind of things do our ears like to listen to? What kind of bodily associates do we like to be with? These things will always tell not only other people, but us ourselves, what kind of salvation God has worked in. In regeneration God works us into relation with Himself, that by our bodily expressions we may prove whose we are. If you are trying to be a Christian, it is a sure sign you are not one. Fancy trying to be the daughter or the son of your parents! You cannot help being their child. But try and be the child of someone else's parents! Unless God has worked in us, we shall hinder Him all the time by trying to be His children; we cannot, we have to be born from above by the will of God first, be regenerated, then our working is not working to help God, it is working to let God express through us what He has done in us so that we may prove we are the children of our Father in heaven (see Matthew 5:43–48).

So many of us put prayer and work and consecration in place of the working of God—we make ourselves the workers. God is the Worker, we work out what He works in. Spirituality is what God is after, not religiosity. The great snare in religion without genuine spirituality is that people ape being good when they are absolutely mean. There is no value whatever in religious externals, the only thing that is of value is spiritual reality, and this is spiritual reality—that I allow God to work in me to will and to do for His good pleasure, and then work out what He has worked in, being carefully careless about everything except my relationship to God.

(b) The Workable Medium

> If anyone does not abide in Me, he is cast out as a branch and is withered. John 15:6

> If we were altogether inactive we should be perfect men. For all that is good is the work of God, and if God does not work it, it is not good. (Tauler)

I wonder how many of us are living on the virtues of our grandparents! The natural virtues are remnants of what the original creation of humankind once was, they are not promises of what humankind is going to be—what humankind is going to be is seen in the life of Jesus Christ. The workable medium is humanity. God takes as the medium of working the stuff we are made of, and all He requires is for us to be inactive and let Him work. When once we are rightly related to God through the Atonement we will be inactive and not in the way of His working in us as He worked in Jesus, consequently we shall be able to work out in our natural lives all that God wills. It is the old twist: we will try to do what God alone can do, and then we mourn before God because He won't do what we alone can do. We put up sighing petitions: "I have tried to be good, I have tried to sanctify myself." All that is the work of God, and the best thing to do is to stop trying and let God do it. What we have to do—and what God cannot do—is to work out what He has worked in. We try to do God's work for Him, and God has to wait until we are passive enough to let Him work in us. To believe in Jesus means retiring and letting God take the mastership inside. That is all God asks of us. Have we ever gotten into the way of letting God work, or are we so amazingly important that we really wonder in our nerves and ways what the Almighty does before we are up in the morning! We are so certain we know what is right, and if we don't always keep at it God cannot get on. Compare that view with the grand, marvelous working of God in the life of the Lord Jesus. Our Lord did not work for God; He said, "The Father that dwells in Me, He does the works." Have we any faith in God at all? Do we really expect God to work in us the good pleasure of His will, or do we expect He will only do it as we pray and plead and sacrifice? All these things shut the door to God working. What we have to ask away from, to knock at, to seek through, are these pressing strivings of our own—

> When we stay our feeble efforts,
>   And from struggling cease,
> Unconditional surrender
>   Brings us God's own peace.

—a doctrine easily travestied, but a doctrine God never safeguards. The whole basis of modern Christian work is the great, impulsive desire to evade concentration on God. We will work for Him any day, rather than let Him work in us. When people realize what God does work in them through Jesus Christ, they become almost lunatic with joy in the eyes of the world. It is this truth we are trying to state, namely, the realization of the wonderful salvation of God.

(c) The Worker's Manner

> And now abide faith, hope, love, these three; but the greatest of these is love. 1 Corinthians 13:13

> How is a man to know if his work is of himself or from God? Shortly be it said; there are three super-natural divine virtues, Faith, Hope, and Love or Charity; whatever increaseth virtues is from God, but what diminisheth them is a sign that it is the work of man.... For what man worketh of himself, he applieth

to himself and to time. . . but what God worketh, draweth a man away from himself to eternity, and this increaseth Faith, Hope, and Charity. (Tauler)

How much of faith, hope, and love is worked in us when we try to convince somebody else? It is not our business to convince other people, that is the insistence of a merely intel- lectual, unspiritual life. The Spirit of God will do the convict- ing when we are in the relationship where we simply convey God's Word. We exploit the Word of God in order to fit it into some view of our own that we have generated, but when it comes to the great, calm peace and rest of the Lord Jesus, we can easily test where we are. To "rest in the Lord" is the per- fection of inward activity. In the ordinary human reasoning it means sitting with folded arms and letting God do everything, in reality it is being so absolutely stayed on God that we are free to do the active human work without fuss. The times God works most wonderfully are the times we never think about it. When we work of ourselves we always connect things with time. "What is the good of faith, hope, and love when I have to earn my living?" Compare that outlook with what Jesus says in the Sermon on the Mount: "Seek first the kingdom of God and His righteousness, and all these things shall be added to you" (Matthew 6:33). It means on our parts a continual carelessness about everything but that one thing. The great curse of modern Christianity is that people will not be careless about things they have no right to be careful about, and they will not let God make them careful about their relationship to Him. Sum it up for yourself—what do you think about most, not on the surface, but in the deep center of your center? What is the real, basal thought of your life: "'What shall we eat?' or 'What shall we drink?' or 'What shall we wear?'" (verse 31). None of us are so stupid or lacking in cunning as to say we do think of these things, but if we think of what will happen to "all these things" (verse 32) if we put God first, we know where we are—God is not first. If He is first you know you can never think of anything He will forget.

The Way of the Working of the Godly

> Therefore, if anyone is in Christ, he is a new creation; . . . Now all things are of God. 2 Corinthians 5:17–18

> What is the divine work? It is twofold, what God worketh in the soul, one the work of grace, the other essential and divine. By the work of grace man is prepared for the essential . . . by grace God maketh man well-pleasing, it driveth him away from all defective things on to virtue, so that with it he obtaineth all virtues. (Tauler)

The only sign that we are new creations in Christ Jesus is that we know all things are of God. When we are in difficult circumstances, when we are hard up, when friends slander us, to whom do we go? If we know that "all things are of God," then we certainly are new creations in Christ Jesus. The things that upset the external life reveal where we live. If we are in Christ the whole basis of our goings is God, not conceptions of God, not ideas of God, but God Himself. We do not need any more ideas about God—the world is full of ideas about God, they are all worthless, because the ideas of God in anyone's head are of no more use than our own ideas. What we need is a real God, not more ideas about Him. As soon as we get a real God we find that "old things have passed away; behold, all things have become new"; we are so absolutely one with God that we never think of saying we are, the whole life is hidden with Christ in God.

(a) The Experimental Virtue

> For by grace you have been saved through faith, and that not of yourselves; it is the gift of God. Ephesians 2:8

> God worketh through His grace in man, when He
> draweth him away from sin and leadeth him on to
> virtue, if man leaveth sin and exerciseth virtue, this
> is a grace of God. (Tauler)

When we are first born again of the Spirit and become rightly related to God, the whole set of our lives is along God's line, other people looking at us know how marvelously God has transformed us, we do things and wonder why we do them. That is experimental virtue, but it is accidental, that is, the expression in our lives is that of spiritual innocence not of spiritual holiness yet, then slowly and surely the Holy Spirit leads on to the next thing, the essence of virtue.

(b) The Essence of Virtue

> My little children, for whom I labor in birth again until Christ is
> formed in you. Galatians 4:19

> > The second work that God worketh in the soul is
> > essential; when man cometh to this that he hath
> > obtained all accidental virtue, and so now arriveth at
> > the essence of virtue, then God worketh all virtue in
> > him in an essential way, namely, the Heavenly Father
> > begetteth His Son in the soul, and this birth raiseth
> > the spirit above all created things into God. (Tauler)

"Until Christ"—not Jesus Christ, but Christ, the Son of God, who was incarnate once as a Man called Jesus Christ: "until Christ is formed in you." No wonder Paul talks about "the riches of the glory of this mystery among the Gentiles: which is Christ in you, the hope of glory" (Colossians 1:27). This is not an innocent state, it is a holy state, the very essence of the life is holy, and as we draw on His resurrection life, the life of Jesus is manifested in our mortal flesh.

(c) The Essential Vision

> God . . . raised us up together, and made us sit together in heavenly places in Christ Jesus. Ephesians 2:4–6

> Nevertheless grace leaveth not the man, but it directeth and ordereth the forces of man and cherisheth the divine birth in the essence of the soul . . . the spirit of man hath now passed over to the Godhead. (Tauler)

Being seated together in heavenly places in Christ Jesus does not mean lolling about on the Mount of Transfiguration, singing ecstatic hymns, and letting demon-possessed children go to the devil in the valley; it means being in the accursed places of this earth as far as the walk of the feet is concerned, but in undisturbed communion with God. In the historic Jesus Christ the human spirit passed over to the Godhead and Jesus saw essentially, not experimentally, and the same thing happens when Christ is formed in us. God's grace does not leave us after an experience of grace. The common idea of how to live the right life seems to be that it is by getting continual bouts of God's grace, that an insight into God's grace will last us several days. As a matter of fact it won't last us any time. That is not what God's grace means. "While we do not look at the things which are seen" (2 Corinthians 4:18)—that battle never stops. The things that are seen are not the devil, but the pressing things, the things that distract; when Christ is formed in us and the essential vision comes through, looking at the things that are not seen, we find that God makes other people shadows. If my saintly friends are images of God to me, I have much further to go yet. God alone must be my stay and source and everything. That is the way the godly life is lived. What is a godly life? A life like God in my bodily edition. Imitation is the great stumbling block to sanctification. Be yourself first, then go to your own funeral, and let God forever after be all in all.

The Philosophy of Reason

Essence of Reason in the Saint

> Always be ready to give a defense to everyone who asks you a reason for the hope that is in you. 1 Peter 3:15

To give an answer concerning the hope that is in us is not the same thing as convincing by reasonable argument why that hope is in us. A line we are continually apt to be caught by is that of argumentatively reasoning out why we are what we are; we cannot argue that out. There is not a saint amongst us who can give explicit reasonings concerning the hope that is in us, but we can always give this reason: we have received the Holy Spirit, and He has witnessed that the truths of Jesus are the truths for us. When we give that answer, anyone who hears it and refuses to try the same way of getting at the truth is condemned. If people refuse one way of getting at the truth because they do not like that way, they cease to be honest people.

(a) The Reach of Reason

> It is no longer I who live, but Christ lives in me. Galatians 2:20

> The reason . . . is always striving after this essential working. . . . By this act of hastening after the divine work, she empties herself of all created images, and with a supernatural light she presseth into the mystery of the hidden Godhead. (John Tauler, in *The Following of Christ*)

Reason always strives for a true expression. Soul is spirit expressing itself rationally, and whenever the work of God in

199

a person's soul (as in the apostle Paul's) is stated, it does not contradict the rational element, it transcends it. When anyone is born again the personality becomes dead to earth as the source of its inspiration and is only alive to God. The great snare is to make reason work in the circle of experience and not in the circle of God. As long as we use the image of experience, of feelings, of answers to prayer, we shall never begin to understand what the apostle Paul means when he says, "it is no longer I who live, but Christ lives in me." The whole exercise of essential human reason is drawing on God as the source of life. The hindrance comes when we begin to keep sensuous images spiritually in our minds. Those of us who have never had visions or ecstasies ought to be very thankful. Visions, and any emotions at all, are the greatest snare to a spiritual life, because as soon as we get them we are apt to build them round our reasoning, and our reasoning round them, and go no further. Over and over again sanctified people stagnate, they do not go back and they do not go on, they stagnate, they become stiller and stiller and muddier and muddier, spiritually—not morally—until ultimately there comes a sort of scum over their spiritual lives, and you wonder what is the matter with them. They are still true to God, still true to their testimonies of what God has done for them, but they have never exercised the great, God-given reason that is in them and gotten beyond the images of their experiences into the knowledge that God alone is life—transcending all we call experience. It is because people will not take the labor to think that the snare gets hold of them, and remember, thinking is a tremendous labor (see 2 Corinthians 10:5).

(b) The Reaction against Reason

> Do not be like the horse or like the mule, which have no understanding. Psalm 32:9

> For what the creature chooseth instead of God is
> done by sensuality and not by the reason . . . and
> whoso chooseth the creature instead of God, is not
> a rational man, but is as an irrational beast. (Tauler)

We use the term *rational* when we should say *sensual*.
Sensuality is a word that has lost its meaning in the higher
realm to us, we only talk of sensuality on the groveling line,
but sensuality reaches higher; it means that bodily satisfaction is taken as the source of life—what I possess, what I
feel—that is not rationalism but sensuality, and when it is
allowed to dominate it works out as Paul says, they "became
futile in their thoughts, and their foolish hearts were dark-
ened" (Romans 1:21; see verses 18–23). If we will let reason
act it will make itself so felt that we have to say, "There is
more than this"; the visible things we see and know awaken
in us a sense that there is something more than these. Reason
must not be prevented from reaching to God.

In the religious domain sensuality takes another guise; it
becomes either pietistic or ritualistic—both are irrational. The
pietistic tendency in this country is a much bigger curse than
the ritualistic tendency—that is a mere excrescence that will
be always, as long as human beings are. The real peril is the
sensual piety that is not based on a rational life with God but
on certain kinds of devotion, certain needs of consecration,
certain demands of my personal life. When you come to the
New Testament, particularly the writings of the apostle Paul,
you find that kind of piety is torn to shreds (for example,
Colossians 2:20–23). All fanaticism and the things that are
foreign to the teachings of Jesus Christ start from spiritual
sensuality, which means I have images in my mind of what I
want to be and what I am and what I have experienced. These
images hinder reason from working. Beware of any image at all
in your mind but Jesus Christ—an image of sanctification or
devotion or any other thing on earth will be the peril of your

rational spiritual life. Have we any idea that it is our devotion, our consecration, the times we give to prayer, the service rendered, what we have given up, because we have been through this and that experience we are where we are?—every one of them is a hidden, irrational snare. No wonder the apostle Paul was so anxious we should get on this rational line. The essence of reason in the saint—what is it? The Holy Spirit in me being obeyed, revealing the things of Jesus.

(c) The Right Rational Man

> The water that I shall give him will become in him a fountain of water. . . . I am the bread of life. John 4:14; 6:35

> For the right reason seeketh God, and removes from creatures whether they be bodily or spiritual, and whoso cometh to this reason is a right, rational man, whose reason is shone through with divine light, in which you know the Godhead and forget the earthy. (Tauler)

The idea left in our minds by these two symbols is water measureless and bread inexhaustible. You can never be caught up by the externals of the symbols Jesus uses, He never leaves any room for sensuality, He only leaves room for the Spirit of God, consequently the symbols are uninterpretable except to reason inspired by the Spirit of God. The Holy Spirit never swamps our personal spirits, He invades them and energizes them so that the light of God in our reason gives us the power and delight of forgetting earthly things. As we take these subjects, if you are alive, your mind will say every now and again, "Oh, stop and let us think longer of this," but the Spirit of God won't stop. The reason for it is that God's Book is packed full of overwhelming riches, they are unsearchable, the more we have the more there is to have. It is a great boon to know there are deep things to know. The curse of the majority of spiritual Christians is that they are too cocksure and certain there is nothing more to know than they know. That is spiritual insanity. The more we go on with God the more amazed we are at what there is to find out, until we begin to use the power God gives us to forget earthly things, to be carefully careless about them, but never careless about our relationship to God.

Exercise of Reason in the Saint

> But earnestly desire the greater gifts. And yet I show you a more excellent way. 1 Corinthians 12:31

Good things will always be the bane of the spiritual life until they are wedded to and lost in the best. When God begins with us He gives us good things, He showers them down (see Matthew 5:45); God does not withhold the best, He cannot give it until we are ready to receive it. Receive the Holy Spirit and let your reason be lifted out of images and out of the good, and instantly you will be lifted into the best.

Have you ever noticed the vague indefiniteness of the Bible? Unless we are spiritual we shall say, "I do wish the Bible would talk clearly, why does it not talk as clearly as some little books I have?" If it did, the Bible would be interpretable without any knowledge of God at all. The only way we can understand whether Jesus Christ's teaching [is] of God is by the Spirit that is in Jesus (see John 7:17).

(a) The More Excellent Way

> Giving all diligence. 2 Peter 1:5; see verses 4–7

> For virtue is never filled up in full measure, nor followed in the highest, except man strip himself of the love of all temporal possessions till he exerciseth himself in all virtue, and lose the image of all virtue, and cometh to the faculty of no longer being able to

work any virtue outwardly, but only essentially and
not accidentally. (Tauler)

Until you have stopped trying to be good and being
pleased with the evidences of holiness in yourself, you will
never open the wicket gate that leads to the more excellent
way. The "life . . . hidden with Christ in God" (Colossians
3:3)—that is the more excellent way. You can never talk of
Jesus Christ in the light of any one virtue—if you do, you feel
you have not described Him—you can only talk of Him as the
Bible does: God-Man. When we describe people we have to
mention some particular virtue. People who deal with Bible
characters are inclined to fix on some virtue that becomes
rotten before the end of the life. When the Spirit of God has
His way with us, we go on till there is only one thing left:
"And they realized that they had been with Jesus" (Acts
4:13). In evangelical work it is not preaching holiness or
sanctification or bodily healing, it is preaching Christ Jesus:
"I, if I am lifted up from the earth, will draw all peoples to
Myself" (John 12:32).

Watch the corruption of the natural virtues in yourself.
We have to learn that most insufferably difficult lesson that
God never patches up our natural virtues, because our natural virtues can never come anywhere near what Jesus Christ
wants. Over and over again men and women are so troubled
at finding their natural virtues break down that they dare not
say a word about it to themselves, let alone to anyone else.
The reason for it is that God wants to get us out of the love
of virtue and in love with the God of virtue—stripped of all
possessions but our knowledge of Him.

(b) The Most Extraordinary Wonder

God is able to make all grace abound toward you. 2 Corinthians
9:8; see verses 6–15

> So long as a man hath he must give, and when he
> hath nothing more he is free. Freedom is much
> nobler than giving was before, for he giveth no
> more in accident but in essence. (Tauler)

Our Lord emptied Himself and had nothing all the days of His earthly life, consequently He was free for God to lavish His gifts through Him to others. Think of the rushes with which we come in front of our heavenly Father; whenever we see an occasion we rush in and say, "I can do this, you need not trouble God." I wonder if we are learning determinedly to possess nothing? It is possessing things that makes us so conceited—"Oh, yes, I can give prayer for you, I can give this and that for you." We have to get to the place about which Jesus talked to the rich young ruler, where we are so absolutely empty and poor that we have nothing, and God knows we have nothing, then He can do through us what He likes. Would that we would quickly get rid of all we have, give it away till there is nothing left, then there is a chance for God to pour through in rivers for other people.

(c) The More Exceeding Worship

> I beseech you therefore, . . . that you present your bodies a living
> sacrifice, holy, acceptable to God, which is your reasonable ser-
> vice. Romans 12:1

> Therefore also a teacher saith, "It is good when a
> man imparts his property and cometh to the help of
> his fellow men; but it is far better to give all and to
> follow Christ in a poor life." (Tauler)

Worship is giving the best we have unreservedly to God. Jesus Christ was entirely merciful because He kept nothing at all. We are merciful in spots, in a fragmentary way, because we will stick to our opinionettes. Whatever makes us spiritually satisfied will twist our mercy at once, because

an opinionette is attached to every spot where we are satisfied, and when anyone comes in contact with that spot of satisfaction we are merciless to them. Jesus Christ was never
merciless, and it is only as we draw on His life that we are
like our Father in heaven. The only safety is to live the life
hidden with Christ in God. As long as we are consciously
there, we are not there. It is only when we are there that it
never occurs to us that we are, but the evidence is strong
because others are getting the blessings of God through us
and are helping themselves to us, even as Jesus Christ was
made broken bread and poured-out wine for us. God cannot
make some of us into broken bread because there are bits of
unbaked dough in us that would produce indigestion. We
have to go into the furnace again to be baked properly, until
we are no more like Ephraim, "a cake unturned" (Hosea 7:8).

Expression of Resurrection Reason in the Saint

> Blessed are the dead who die in the Lord. Revelation 14:13

(a) The Matter of Death

> Unless a grain of wheat falls into the ground and dies, it remains
> alone; but if it dies, it produces much grain. John 12:24

> > Therefore we should make ourselves poor, that we
> > may fundamentally die, and in this dying be made
> > alive again. (Tauler)

Death is God's delightful way of giving us life. The
monks in the early ages shut themselves away from everything to prove they were dead to it all, and when they got
away they found themselves more alive than ever. Jesus
never shut Himself away from things—the first place He took
His disciples to was a marriage feast. He did not cut Himself
off from society, He was not aloof—so much was He not
aloof that they called Him "a glutton and a winebibber!"

(Matthew 11:19). But there was one characteristic of Jesus—
He was fundamentally dead to the whole thing, it had no
appeal to Him. The "hundredfold" that Jesus promised (Matthew 19:29) means that God can trust you anywhere and
with anything when you are fundamentally dead to things.

(b) The Manner of Devotion

> If you want to be perfect, go, sell what you have, . . . and come,
> follow Me. Matthew 19:21

> > This selling means the self-denial of man; the giving
> > away is virtue, the following of Jesus is fundamen-
> > tally to die, so that dying completely to himself God
> > may live perfectly in him. (Tauler)

As soon as that is experienced we are alive with the
effulgent life of God. We use the phrase "drawing on the resurrection life of Jesus," but try it—you cannot draw on it
when you like. You will never get one breath of that life until
you are dead, that is, dead to any desire that you want a
blessing for body or soul or spirit. As soon as you die to that,
the life of God is in you, and you don't know where you are
with the exuberance of it. To put it in the negative way—the
bits in us that won't yield to God are the bits we cling to. We
are always going back to the grave and saying, "I was always
respectable here, I don't need Christ there, I always had a
good view of what was right and pure." Instantly the life of
God in us wilts, but when the dying is gone through with
and maintained (I am not talking about dying to sin, but about
dying outright to my right to myself in any shape or form),
then the life of Jesus can be manifested in my mortal flesh
(see 2 Corinthians 4:10–12).

(c) The Method of the Discipline of Death

> For you died, and your life is hidden with Christ in God. Colos-
> sians 3:3

Blessed is the man who can die all manner of deaths, but this dying is of such a nature that no man can rightly understand it, and he is the most rational who understandeth this dying the best. For no one understandeth it save he to whom God hath revealed it. (Tauler)

This secret is revealed to the humblest child of God who receives, recognizes and relies on the Holy Spirit, and it leads to only one place, the effulgent life of God, while we walk in the light as He is in the light. The trouble with most of us is that we will walk only in the light of our convictions of what the light is. If you are live to God He will never take from you the amazing mercy of having something put to death. Jesus sacrificed His natural life and made it spiritual by obeying His Father's voice, and we have any number of glorious opportunities of proving how much we love God by the delighted way we go to sacrifice for Him.

The Philosophy of Love

> Jesus answered him, "The first of all the command-
> ments is: 'Hear, O Israel, the LORD our God, the
> LORD is one. And you shall love the LORD your
> God with all your heart, with all your soul, with all
> your mind, and with all your strength.'. . . And the
> second, like it, is this: 'You shall love your neighbor
> as yourself.'" Mark 12:29–31

The Way of the Sovereign Preference of the Heart

Do you love Me? John 21:15; see verses 15–17

> And these are the right lovers of God, who love
> God with their whole heart. And they who love
> God with their whole heart give up all bodily things
> for the sake of God. (John Tauler, in *The Following of
> Christ*)

Faith, hope, love, the three supernatural virtues, have a twofold aspect in the saint's life. The first is seen in the early
experiences of grace when these virtues are accidental; the
second, when grace is worked into us and these virtues are
essential and abiding. When the work of God's grace begins,
"the love of God has been poured out in our hearts by the
Holy Spirit" (Romans 5:5), not the power to love God, but
the essential nature of God. When we experience what technically we call being born again of the Spirit of God, we have
spurts of faith, hope, love—they come but we cannot grip
them, and they go; when we experience what technically we
call sanctification those virtues abide, they are not accidental
any more. The test of the life "hidden with Christ in God"

(Colossians 3:3) is not the experience of salvation or sanctification, but the relationship into which those experiences have led us. It is only by realizing the love of God in us by His grace that we are led by His entrancing power in us where we would not go. Love is the sovereign preference of my person for another person, and Jesus says that other person must be Him. Ask yourself what sort of conception you have of loving God. The majority of us have a bloodless idea, an impersonal, ethereal, vague abstraction called "love to God." Read Jesus Christ's conception, He mentions relationships of the closest, most personal, most passionate order and says that our love for Him must be closer and more personal than any of those (see Luke 14:26). How is it to be? Only by the work of the sovereign grace of God. If we have not realized the pouring out of the essential nature of God in our hearts, the words of Jesus ought to make us realize the necessity of it: "You shall love the LORD your God with all your heart." To love God with all my heart means to be weaned from the dominance of earthly things as a guide, there is only one dominant passion in the deepest center of the personality, and that is the love of God.

The Way of the Soul's Passion for God

Whoever loses his life for My sake shall find it. Matthew 16:25

> They also love with their whole soul; that is, when they give up their life for the sake of God; for the soul giveth life to the body, and this same life they give entirely to God. (Tauler)

The only way to love God with all the soul is to give up the life for His sake, not give our lives to God—that is an elemental point—but when that has been done, after our lives have been given to God, we ought to lay them down for God (see 1 John 3:16). Jesus Christ laid down His holy life for His

Father's purposes, then if we are God's children we have to lay down our lives for His sake, not for the sake of a truth, not for the sake of devotion to a doctrine, but for Jesus Christ's sake—the personal relationship all through (compare Luke 6:22–23). Have I ever realized the glorious opportunity I have of laying down my life for Jesus? It does not mean that we lay down our lives in the crisis of death; what God wants is the sacrifice *through* death, which enables us to do what Jesus did—He sacrificed His life, His death comes in as a totally new revelation. Every morning we wake and every moment of the day, we have this glorious privilege of sacrificing our holy selves to and for Jesus Christ (see Romans 12:1). Beware of the subtle danger that gets hold of our spiritual lives when we trust in our experiences. Experience is absolutely nothing if it is not the gateway only to a relationship. The experience of sanctification is not the slightest atom of use unless it has enabled me to realize that that experience means a totally new relationship. Sanctification may take a few moments of realized transaction, but all the rest of the life goes to prove what that transaction means.

The Way of the Mind's Penetration into God

When He is revealed, we shall be like Him. 1 John 3:2

> They also love God with all their mind; that is, when their mind soareth above all created things, and penetrates into the uncreated good, which is God, and then loseth itself in the secret darkness of the unknown God. Therein it loseth itself and escapeth, so that it can no more come out. (Tauler)

To love God with all the mind, we have to soar above created things, and penetrate "into the uncreated good," namely, God. When the Spirit of God begins to deal on this side of things we shall feel at sea, if we are not spiritual, as to what is meant; when we are spiritual we feel with our hearts, not with our heads, "Yes, I begin to see what it means." When anything begins to get vague, bring yourself up against the revelation of Jesus Christ, He is a fact, and He is the pattern of what we ought to be as Christians (compare Matthew 5:48). How much of our time are we giving for God to graduate us in the essential life? We know all about the accidental life, about the sudden spurts that come to us, the sudden times of illumination and sweet inspiration from God's Book; what our Lord is getting at is not a life of that description at all, but a life that has lost all sense of its own isolation and smallness and is taken up with God. Not only is the life hidden with Christ in God, but the heart is blazing with love to God, and the mind is able to begin slowly, bit by bit, to bring every thought into captivity to the obedience of Christ, till we never trouble about ourselves or our conscious lives, we are taken up only with thoughts that are worthy of God.

The Way of the Strength of Stillness for God

That He would grant you . . . to be strengthened with might . . . , that Christ may dwell in your hearts through faith. Ephesians 3:16–17

They further love God with all their strength; that is, they ordain all their powers according to the highest discretion, and they direct all of them to one end, and with this effort they penetrate into God. (Tauler)

The whole strength of the personal life, the personal spirit, is to be so gripped by the Spirit of God that we begin to comprehend His meaning. It is always risky to use a phrase with a fringe, a phrase that has a definite kernel of meaning but a fringe of something that is not definite. The way we get off on to the fringe is by ecstasy, and ecstasies may mean anything from the devil to God. An ecstasy is something that takes us clean beyond our own control, and we do not know what we are doing, whether we are being inspired by God or the devil, whether we are jabbering with angels' tongues or demons'. When you come to the words of our Lord or of the apostle Paul, the one great safeguard is the absolute sanity of the whole thing. "That you may be able to comprehend . . . , to know" (Ephesians 3:18–19)—there is no ecstasy there, no being carried out of yourself into a swoon, no danger of what the mystics of the Middle Ages called Quietism, no danger of losing the conditions of morality, but slowly and surely we begin to comprehend the love of Christ, that is, the essential nature of God that the Holy Spirit has imparted to us, that enables us to live the same kind of life that Jesus lived down here through His marvelous atonement. Anything that partakes of the nature of swamping our personalities out of our control is never of God. Do we ever find a time in the life of the Lord Jesus Christ when He was carried beyond His own control? Never once. Do we ever find Him in a spiritual panic, crediting God with it? Never once, and the one great marvel of the work of the Holy Spirit is that the sanity of Jesus Christ is stamped on every bit of it. Jesus said we should know the work of the Holy Spirit by these signs: "He will glorify Me" (John 16:14); "He will teach you all things, and bring to your remembrance all things that I said to you" (14:26); and, "He will guide you into all truth" (16:13) The Spirit of God does not dazzle and startle and amaze us into worshipping God, that is why He takes such a long while—it is bit by bit, process by process, with every power slowly realizing and comprehending "with all the saints." We cannot comprehend it alone, the "together" aspect of the New Testament is wonderful. Beware of all those things that run off on a tangent spiritually. They begin by saying, "God gave me an impulse to do this"—God never gave anyone any impulse. Watch Jesus Christ; the first thing He checked in the training of the Twelve was impulse. Impulse may be all right morally and physically, but it is never right spiritually. Wherever spiritual impulse has been allowed to have its way, it has led the soul astray. We must check all impulses by this test—Does this glorify Jesus, or does it only glorify us? Does it bring to our remembrance something Jesus said, that is, does it connect itself with the Word of God, or is it beginning to turn us aside and make us seek great things for ourselves? That is where the snare comes. Nowadays, people seem to have an idea that these ecstatic, visionary, excitable, lunatic moments glorify God—they do not, they give an opportunity to the devil. The one thing Jesus Christ did when He came in contact with lunacy was to heal it, and the greatest work of the devil is that he is producing lunacy in the name of God all over the world in the spiritual realm, making people who did know God go off on tangents. What did Jesus say? "to deceive, if possible, even the elect" (Mark 13:22). Beware of being carried off into any kind of spiritual ecstasy either in private or in public. There is nothing about ecstasy in these verses: "You shall love the LORD your God with all your heart"—the sovereign preference of your personality for God. Can I say before God, "For in all the world there is none but Thee, my God, there is none but Thee"? Is it true? Is there a woman there? Is there a man there? Is there a child there? Is there a friend there? "You shall love the LORD your God with all your heart." Do you say, "But that is so stern"? The reason it is stern is that when once God's mighty grace gets my heart wholly absorbed in Him, every other love of my life is safe, but if my love to God is not dominant, my love may prove to be lust. Nearly all the cruelty in the world springs from not understanding this. Lust in its highest and lowest forms simply means I seek for a creature to give me what God alone can give, and I become cruel and vindictive and jealous and spiteful to the one from whom I demand what God alone can give.

"With all your soul." What are we laying down our lives for? Why do so many Christians go a-slumming? Why do so many go to the foreign field? Why do so many seek for the salvation of souls? Let us haul ourselves up short and measure ourselves by the standard of Jesus Christ. He said, "The Son of Man has come to seek and to save that which was lost" (Luke 19:10). The mainspring of His love for human souls was His love to the Father; then, if I go a-slumming for the same reason, I can never do too much of it, but if my desire for the salvation of souls is the evangelical, commercial craze, may God blast it out of me by the fire of the Holy Spirit. There is such a thing as commercialism in souls as there is in business. When we testify and speak, why do we? Is it out of the accident of a poor little paltry experience that we have had, or is it because the whole life is blazing with an amazing desire, planted there by the Holy Spirit, for God to glorify Himself?

> Arrived here, all the powers keep silence and rest;
> this also is the highest work that the powers can
> perform, when they are inactive and let God only
> work. (Tauler)

It is only when our lives are hidden with Christ in God that we learn how to be silent to God—not silent about Him, but silent with the strong, restful certainty that all is well, behind everything stands God, and the strength of the soul is that it knows it. There are no panics intellectual or moral. What a lot of panicky sparrows we are, the majority of us. We chatter and tweet under God's eaves until we cannot hear His voice at all—until we learn the wonderful life and music of the Lord Jesus telling us that our heavenly Father is the God of the sparrows, and by the marvelous transforma- tion of grace He can turn the sparrows into His nightingales that can sing through every night of sorrow. A sparrow cannot sing through a night of sorrow, and no soul can sing through a night of sorrow unless it has learned to be silent to God—one look, one thought about my Father in heaven, and it is all right.

The Way of the Freedom of the Will

But now having been set free from sin. Romans 6:22

> Thus is the mind bound by God. To this it might be said, If this is so, the freedom of the will is taken away. I answer, the freedom of the will is not taken away but given to it, for then is the will quite free when it cannot bear anything save what God willeth. (Tauler)

"Thus is the mind bound by God." The complaint of someone who is not spiritual when you talk like that is that human free will is destroyed. It is not, it is given to us. The only thing that gives a personality freedom of will is the salvation of Jesus Christ. The will is not a faculty, will is the whole person active—body, soul, and spirit. Let me get right with God through the Atonement and my activity becomes in that manner and measure akin to Jesus Christ—the whole of my will free to do God's will—that means a holy scorn of putting my neck under any yoke but the yoke of the Lord Jesus Christ. Where are Christians putting their necks nowadays? Why, nine out of every nine and a half of us are absolute cowards, we will only put our necks under the yoke of the set we belong to. It means, "outside the camp, bearing His reproach" (Hebrews 13:13; see John 14:15; 15:9–10).

The Way of Hearing the Eternal Word

If anyone loves Me, he will keep My word. John 14:23

> Now man . . . cometh to the third degree of perfection, in which he heareth, in a silent, secret speak

ing, the everlasting Word which God the Father speaketh in the ground of souls. (Tauler)

We all know how certain verses jump out of a page of the Bible and grip us, full of infinite sweetness and inspiration; at other times they do not. That is what people mean when they say God gave them a message—by the way, do not say that unless God does, we use phrases much too glibly. God may give you the kind of message He gave Isaiah, a blistering, burning message of the altar of God. To be able to hear the "silent, secret speaking" of the Father's voice in the words of the Bible is the essential groundwork of the soul of every saint. "The words that I speak to you are spirit, and they are life" (John 6:63). God makes His own Word respeak in us by His Spirit. He safeguarded that, He uses the words His Son used, and the words those used He determined should write them (see 2 Peter 1:21). The great insubordination of today is, "Who are the apostles? God spoke through them, why can't He speak through me?" He will not, unless we let the Spirit of God interpret to us what those people said, then He will talk through us, but in no other way. When once we have learned to hear with the inner ear the Word of God, we discard our selfhood, and the natural delight in God's Word is lost in the realization that it is God who is speaking. Do you want to know how selfhood works out? "I have such a fine message, it will do for such and such an audience, I have got a wonderful exposition of this text." Well, burn it and never think any more about it. Give the best you have every time and everywhere. Learn to get into the quiet place where you can hear God's voice speak through the words of the Bible, and never be afraid that you will run dry, He will simply pour the Word until you have no room to contain it. It won't be a question of hunting for messages or texts but of opening the mouth wide and He fills it.

The outcome of Mark 12:29–31 is God four times over—God the King of my heart, God the King of my soul, God the King of my mind, God the King of my strength—nothing other than God, and the working out of it is that we show the same love to others as God has shown us. That is the external aspect of this internal relationship, the sovereign preference of my person for God. The love of the heart for Jesus, the life laid down for Jesus, the mind thinking only for Jesus, the strength given over to Jesus, the will working only the will of God, and the ear of the personality hearing only what God has to say.

The Philosophy of Sacrificing

Then Jesus said to His disciples, "If anyone desires to come after Me, let him deny himself, and take up his cross, and follow Me. For whoever desires to save his life will lose it, but whoever loses his life for My sake will find it. For what profit is it to a man if he gains the whole world, and loses his own soul? Or what will a man give in exchange for his soul?" Matthew 16:24–26

I wonder if I will or if I won't

God does not take the willful "won't" out of us by salvation, at any stage we may say, "No, thank you, I am delighted to be saved and sanctified, but I am not going any further." Our Lord always prefaced His talks about discipleship with an if; it has no reference whatever to a soul's salvation or condemnation, but to the discipleship of the personality.

We must bear in mind that our Lord in His teaching reveals unalterable and eternal principles. In Matthew 16:25: "For whoever desires to save his life will lose it, but whoever loses his life for My sake shall find it"—Jesus says that the eternal principle of human life is that something must be sacrificed; if we won't sacrifice the natural life, we do the spiritual. Our Lord is not speaking of a punishment to be meted out, He is revealing what is God's eternal principle at the back of human life. We may rage and fret, as people have done, against God's just principles, or we may submit and accept and go on, but Jesus reveals that these principles are as unalterable as God Himself.

"I wonder if I will or if I won't." In sanctification the free-dom of the will is brought to its highest critical point. A good many people, in order to express the marvelous emancipation that comes by God's salvation, make the statement, "I cannot now do the things that are wrong." It is only then we have the choice; when Jesus Christ emancipates us from the power of sin, that second we have the power to disobey; before we had not the power, we were almost obliged to dis-obey because of the tendency in that direction. So this princi-ple in its full meaning, "I wonder if I will or if I won't," works on the threshold of sanctification: "I wonder if I will devote myself to Jesus Christ or to a doctrine or a point of view of my own." Jesus says if we are to be His disciples we must sacrifice everything to that one thing.

Innocent Light under Identification

Take My yoke upon you and learn from Me . . . and you will find rest for your souls. Matthew 11:29

> But what use doth it bring if a man alway dieth? It bringeth a fivefold use. First, man draweth nigh thereby to his first innocence. . . . They are best in this who have most died to themselves for in that death and denial of self a new delight springeth up, for the death that man suffereth thereby openeth up the hidden joy. Christ also said, "Take My yoke upon you—that is, My Passion—and ye will find rest unto your souls." (John Tauler, in *The Following of Christ*)

The only place we shall find rest is in the direct education by Jesus in His cross. A new delight springs up in any saint who suffers the yoke of Christ. Beware of dissipating that yoke and making it mean the yoke of a martyr. It is the yoke of someone who owes all she or he has to the cross of Christ. Paul wore the yoke when he said, "I determined not to know anything among you except Jesus Christ and Him crucified" (1 Corinthians 2:2). "Take My yoke upon you" —it is the one yoke people will not wear.

Have I taken the yoke of Christ upon me, and am I walking in the innocent light that comes only from the Spirit of God through the Atonement? When we are born again of the Spirit of God we are made totally new creatures on the inside; that means we have to live according to the new life of innocence that God has given us and not be dictated to by the clamoring defects of the temple into which that life has been put. The danger is to become wise and prudent, cumbered with much serving, and these things choke the life God has put in (compare Mark 4:19).

Implicit Love under Identification

Who shall separate us from the love of Christ? Romans 8:35

> The second use is, that in each such dying a new life ariseth to man, and with this life every time a new love, so that man is overflooded with grace, and his reason is enlightened with divine light, his will is glowing with the fire of divine love . . . so that no one can any more separate him from God. (Tauler)

The natural life of a saint is neither pure nor impure; it is not pure necessarily because the heart is pure, it has to be made pure by the will of the saint. To delight in sacrificing the natural to the spiritual means to be overflowing with the grace and love of God, and the manner and measure of the sacrificing depends on "I wonder if I will or if I won't." Never say, if you are a thoughtful saint, "Since I have been sanctified I have done what I liked." If you have, you are immoral in that degree. If it were true, it would be true of the holiest Being who ever lived, but it is said of Him that "even Christ did not please Himself" (Romans 15:3; compare John 8:28; Hebrews

5:8). There must be something to sacrifice. Jesus says, "If any-one desires to come after Me," you must sacrifice the natural life, that is, the life that is moral and right and good from the ordinary human standpoint. We cannot use the terms of nat-ural virtue in describing Jesus Christ. If you say that Jesus was a holy Man you feel at once it is not sufficient, or take the terms of intense saintliness—you can never fit them on to Jesus Christ, because there is an element of fanaticism in every saint that there never was in the Lord. There is an amazing sanity in Jesus Christ that shakes the foundations of death and hell; no panic, absolute dominant mastery over everything—such a stupendous mastery that He let people take His strength from Him: "He was crucified in weakness" (2 Corinthians 13:4)—that was the acme of Godlike strength.

Identity of Liberty under Identification

> Most assuredly, I say to you, unless one is born again, he cannot see the kingdom of God. John 3:3

> Thirdly, if a man is quite pure he is emptied of all defective accident, and receptive of God alone. God is present in all things; if you accomplish all things so, then God only remaineth to us; but this purity must be sought by dying, and if the soul is freed from everything else, she is in a condition to bring forth the Son of God within her. (Tauler)

Bear in mind the audience of Jesus when He said these words; Jesus said them to a mature, upright, godly man, there is no mention of sin—that will come in due course, it comes in the order Jesus said it would, by the Holy Spirit (see John 16:8–9). When the Son of God is born in us He brings us into the liberty of God. "Whoever has been born of God does not sin" (1 John 3:9). The only way we can be born again is by renouncing all other good. The "old man," or the man of old, means all the things that have nothing to do with the new life. It does not mean *sins*—any coward among us will give up wrong things, but will we give up right things? Will we give up the virtues, the principles, the recognition of things that are dearer to the "Adam" life than the God life? The nature of the Adam disposition in us rebels against sacrificing natural good. Jesus says, If you don't sacrifice natural good, you will barter the life I represent. This is the thing people resent with what Paul calls "enmity" (Romans 8:7). The preachers and teachers who have not taken on them the yoke of Christ are always inclined to exalt natural good, natural virtues, natural nobility and heroism; the consequence is Jesus Christ pales more and more into the background until He becomes "as a root out of dry ground" (Isaiah 53:2). Imagine a pagan who worshipped natural virtues being told that the Nazarene carpenter was God's idea expressed in His last syllable to this order of things—it would be, as Paul said, "foolishness to him" (1 Corinthians 2:14). The same thing persists today.

Infusion of Likeness under Identification

If we walk in the light as He is in the light. 1 John 1:7

> The fourth use ariseth if God is born in the soul, when God ravisheth the spirit from the soul and casteth her into the darkness of His Godhead, so that she becometh quite like unto God . . . so that the man becometh a son of grace, as he is a son of nature. (Tauler)

To be a son or a daughter of God is to be free from the tyranny of the show of things. Adam preferred to take the show of things for the substance; that is, he preferred not to see that the "garment" was not the person, he refused to listen to the voice of the Creator behind the garment, and when the Creator moved quickly, all Adam could do was to hang on to the skirts of the garment, clutch at the show of things, and the human race has been doing it ever since. Exactly what Jesus said, the spiritual has been bartered because we preferred the natural. The natural is only a manifestation of what is behind. If we walk in the light, not as holy people are in the light, but as God is in the light, we see behind the show of things—God. We become the offspring of God by a regenerating internal birth, and when that regenerating principle inside takes its marvelous sway over the natural on the outside, the two are transformed into exactly what God intended them to be. That is the full meaning of the redemption, but in order to get there the natural must be sacrificed. If I prefer to hug my Father's skirt, I must not be surprised at finding myself in darkness when He gives it a sudden pull, but if I let my Father take me up in His arms, then He can move His skirts as He likes: "Therefore we will not fear, even though the earth be removed, and though the mountains be carried into the midst of the sea" (Psalm 46:2). I am no longer caught up in the show of things. The saints who are alive when Jesus comes will be "changed—in a moment, in the twinkling of an eye" (1 Corinthians 15:51–52), all the show of things will be changed instantly, by the touch of God, into reality.

Incorporation of Life under Identification

> For as many as are led by the Spirit of God, these are sons of God. Romans 8:14; compare Philippians 2:15

> Fifthly, if the soul be raised into God, it reigneth also with God. . . . Thus the spirit can do all things with God; he commandeth all with God, he ordereth and leadeth all with God; what God omits, he omitteth; what God doeth, he doeth with God; he worketh all things with God. This unspeakable perfection we obtain through dying. (Tauler)

Being born again of the Spirit is not contrary to God's original plan; for a time it has to be apparently contrary to it because Adam refused to sacrifice the life of nature to the will of God and transform it into a spiritual life by obeying the voice of God. The natural has to be sacrificed for a time, but we shall find the redemption of Jesus works out via the natural in the end: "Now I saw a new heaven and a new earth" (Revelation 21:1). In the meantime, to be a disciple of Jesus means to be taboo in this order of things.

Remember, it was not the offscouring that crucified Jesus, it was the highest reach of natural morality crucified Him. It is the refined, cultured, religious, moral people who refuse to sacrifice the natural for the spiritual. When once you get that thought, you understand the inveterate detestation of the cross of Christ. Where are we with regard to this barter? Are we disciples of Jesus? Who is first, or what is first, in my life? Who is the dominating personality that is dearer to me than life—myself or someone else? If it is someone else, who is it? It is only on such lines as these that we come to understand what Jesus meant when He said, "If anyone desires to come after Me, let him deny himself" (Matthew 16:24). What He means is that He and what He stands for must be first. The enemies of the cross of Christ, whom Paul characterizes so strongly, and does it weeping, are those who represent the type of things that attract far more than Jesus Christ. Never put a false issue before others or before yourself. We begin to compare ourselves with ourselves: "Oh, well, I have always had refined susceptibilities, I have always had an admiration for what is noble and true and good"; Jesus says, Die to it all. Read Philippians 3: "What things were gain to me, these I have counted loss for Christ" (verse 7).

"Then Jesus said to His disciples, 'If anyone desires to come after Me, let him deny himself.'" The first "Follow Me" was a fascination for natural ideals.

"Are you able to drink the cup that I drink? . . ."

"We are able." Mark 10:38–39

There is no arrogance there, only hopeless misunderstanding. We all say, "Yes, Lord, I will do anything," but will you go to the death of that—the death of being willing to go to the death for the noble and true and right? Will you let Jesus take the sense of the heroic right out of you? Will you let Him make you see yourself as He sees you, until for one moment you stand before the Cross and say, "Nothing in my hands I bring"? How many of us are there today? Talk about getting people to hear that, they won't have it! Jesus says they won't. No crowd on earth will ever listen to that, and if under some pretense you get them and preach the cross of Christ they will turn with a snubbing offense from the whole thing, as they did in our Lord's day (John 6:60, 66). The abominable "show" business is creeping into the very ranks of the saved and sanctified; "We must get the crowds." We must not—we must keep true to the Cross; let folks come and go as they will, let movements come and go, let us be swept along or not, the one main thing is—true to the yoke of Christ, His cross. The one thing we have to stand against is what is stated in Hebrews 12:1: "Therefore . . . let us lay aside every weight, and the sin which so easily ensnares us," the sin that is admired in many—the sin that gathers round your feet and stops you running—get stripped of the whole thing and run, with your eye on your File Leader, making "straight paths for your feet, so that what is lame may not be dislocated" (verse 13).

The Philosophy of Discipleship

Let no man think that sudden in a minute
All is accomplished and the work is done:
Though with thine earliest dawn thou
    shouldst begin it
Scarce were it ended in thy setting sun.

Discipleship must always be a personal matter, we can never become disciples in crowds or even in twos. It is so easy to talk about what "we" mean to do—"we" are going to do marvelous things, and it ends in none of us doing anything. The great element of discipleship is the personal one.

    The disciples, in the days of His flesh, were in a relationship to our Lord that we cannot imagine, they had a unique relationship that no other people have had or will have. We may use the relationship of these people to Jesus as illustrative of those who are devoted to Him but not yet born from above, or we may take them as pointing out lines of discipleship after the work of grace has been begun. Discipleship may be looked at from many aspects, because it is not a dogma but a declaration. We are using discipleship in this study as an illustration of what happens after salvation. Salvation and discipleship are not one and the same thing. Whenever our Lord speaks of discipleship, He prefaces what He says with an *If*. "If anyone desires to come after Me" (Matthew 16:24). Discipleship is based on devotion to Jesus Christ, not on adherence to a doctrine.

Potential Position by Grace

> Then Peter answered and said to Him, "See, we have left all and followed You. Therefore what shall we have?" Matthew 19:27; compare 15:24

Potential means existing in possibility, not in reality. By regeneration, in its twofold phase of salvation and sanctification, we are potentially able to perform all the will of God. That does not mean we are doing it, it means that we can do it if we will, because God has empowered us (see Philippians 2:12–13). Anyone in whom the grace of God has begun its work—the grace of God does not respect persons, so I mean any kind of person you can think of—is potentially in the sight of God as Christ, the possibility of being as Christ is there. Whenever the grace of God strikes the human consciousness and we begin to realize what we are in God's sight, we become fanatical if we are healthy. We have to make allowance in ourselves and others for the swing of the pendulum that makes us go to the opposite extreme of what we were before. When once the grace of God has touched our hearts we see nothing but God, we do not see Him in relation to anything else but only in relation to ourselves on the inside, and we forget to open the gate for gladness. Fanaticism is the insane sign of a sane relationship to God in its initial working. The joy of the incoming grace of God always makes us fanatical. It is the potential position by grace, and God leaves us in that nursery of bliss just as long as He thinks fit, then He begins to take us on another step—we have to make that possible relationship actual. We have not only to be right with God inside, we have to be manifestly rightly related to God on the outside, and this brings us to the painful matter of discipline.

Practical Path in Grace

> So Jesus said to them, "Assuredly I say to you, that in the regeneration, when the Son of Man sits on the throne of His glory,

you who have followed Me will also sit on twelve thrones." Matthew 19:28; compare 10:38

> To abandon all, to strip one's self of all, in order to seek and follow Jesus Christ naked to Bethlehem, where He was born, naked to the hall where He was scourged, and naked to Calvary where He died on the cross, is so great a mystery that neither the thing, nor the knowledge of it, is given to any but through faith in the Son of God. (John Wesley)

The practical path in grace is to make what is possible actual. That is where many of us hang back; we say, "No, I prefer the bliss and the delight of the simple, ignorant babyhood of 'Bethlehem,' I like to be carried in the arms of God, I do not want to transform that innocence into holy character." The following in the steps of Jesus in discipleship is so great a mystery that few enter into it. When once the face of the Lord Jesus Christ has broken through, all ecstasies and experiences dwindle in His presence, and the one, dominant leadership becomes more and more clear. We have seen Jesus as we never saw Him before, and the impulsion in us, by the grace of God, is that we must follow in His steps. As in the life of Mary, the mother of our Lord, a sword pierced through her own soul because of the Son of God, so the sword pierces our natural lives as we sacrifice them to the will of God and thus make them spiritual. That is the first lesson in the practical path of grace. We go through bit by bit and realize that there are things Jesus says and the Holy Spirit applies to us at which the natural cries out, "That is too hard!"

Practice of Pain in Grace

> "And everyone who has left houses . . . , for My name's sake, shall receive a hundredfold." Matthew 19:29

"If anyone comes to Me and does not hate . . . , he cannot be My disciple" (Luke 14:26). The word "hate" sounds harsh, and yet it is uttered by the most human of human beings; because Jesus was divine, there was never a human breast that beat with more tenderness than Jesus Christ's. The word "hate" is used as a vehement protest against the pleas to which human nature is only too ready to give a hearing. If we judge our Lord by a standard of humanity that does not rec' ognize God, we have to put a black mark against certain things He said. One such mark would come in connection with His words to His mother at Cana: "Woman, what does your concern have to do with Me?" (John 2:4). Another would come in connection with John the Baptist; instead of Jesus going and taking His forerunner out of prison, He sim' ply sends a message to him through his disciples: "Go and tell John. . . . And blessed is he who is not offended because of Me" (Luke 7:22–23). But if we could picture the look of our Lord when He spoke the words, it would make a great differ' ence to the interpretation. There was no being on earth with more tenderness than the Lord Jesus, no one who under' stood the love of a mother as He did, and if we read this into His attitude toward His mother and toward John we shall find the element of pain to which He continually alludes; that is, we have to do things that hurt the best relationships in life, without any explanation. If we make our Lord's words the reply of a callous nature, we credit Him with the spirit of the devil, but interpret them in the light of what Jesus says about discipleship, and we shall see that we must sacrifice the natural in order to transform it into the spiritual. All through our Lord's teaching that comes: If you are going to be My disciple, you must barter the natural. Our Lord is not talking about sin but about the natural life that is neither moral nor immoral, we make it moral or immoral. Over and over again we come to the practice of pain in grace, and it is the only explanation of the many difficult things Jesus said that make people rebel or else say that He did not say them.

Have we begun to walk the practical path in grace? Do we know anything about the practice of pain? Watch what the Bible has to say about suffering, and you will find the great characteristic of the life of a child of God is the power to suffer, and through that suffering the natural is transformed into the spiritual. The thing we kick against most is the question of pain and suffering. We have naturally the idea that if we are happy and peaceful we are all right. "I did not come to bring peace but a sword," said our Lord (Matthew 10:34)—a striking utterance from the Prince of Peace. Happiness is not a sign that we are right with God, happiness is a sign of satisfaction, that is all, and the majority of us can be satisfied on too low a level. Jesus Christ disturbs every kind of satisfaction that is less than delight in God. Every strand of sentimental satisfaction is an indication of how much farther we have to go before we understand the life of God, it is the satisfaction of a smug self-interest that God, by circumstances and pain, shocks out of us as we go in the discipline of life.

Protest of Power through Grace

> You who have followed Me will also sit on twelve thrones.
> Matthew 19:28; compare Luke 14:53

Physical power is nothing before moral power. A frail, simple young woman can overcome a brute who has the strength of an ox—by moral superiority. Think of our Lord's life. The New Testament does not refer to the scene in the Garden as a miracle: "Now when He said to them, 'I am He,' they drew back and fell to the ground" (John 18:6)—it was the inevitable protest of power of a pure, holy Being, facing unholy people, from whom all power went. The wonder is not that Jesus showed His marvelous power, but that He did not show it. He continually covered it up.

Oh! wonderful the wonders left undone!
And scarce less wonderful than those He wrought!
Oh, self-restraint, passing all human thought,
To have all power and be—as having none!

The great marvel of Jesus was that He was voluntarily weak. "He was crucified in weakness," and, says Paul, "we also are weak in Him" (2 Corinthians 13:4). Any coward amongst us can hit back when hit, but it takes an exceedingly strong nature not to hit back. Jesus Christ never did. "Who, when He was reviled, did not revile in return; when He suffered, He did not threaten" (1 Peter 2:23), and if we are going to follow His example we shall find that all His teaching leads along that line. But ultimately, at the final windup of His great purpose, those who have followed His steps reign with Him. Those who reign with Him are not the sanctified in possibility, in ecstasy, but those who have gone through actually. Equal duties, not equal rights, is the keynote of the spiritual world—equal rights is the clamor of the natural world. The protest of power through grace, if we are following Jesus, is that we no longer insist on our rights, we see that we fulfill our duty.

That is the philosophy of a poor, perfect, pure discipleship. Remember, these are not conditions of salvation but of discipleship. Those of us who have entered into a conscious experience of the salvation of Jesus by the grace of God, whose whole inner lives are drawn toward God, have the privilege of being disciples, if we will. The Bible never refers to degrees of salvation, but there are degrees of it in actual experience. The spiritual privileges and opportunities of all disciples are equal, they have nothing to do with education or natural ability. "One is your Teacher, the Christ" (Matthew 23:8, 10). We have no business to bring in that abomination of the lower regions that makes us think too little of ourselves; to think too little of ourselves is simply the obverse side of conceit. If I am a disciple of Jesus, He is my Master, I am looking to Him, and the thought of self never enters. So crush on the threshold of your mind any lame, limping "Oh, I can't; you see, I am not gifted." The great stumbling block in the way of some people being simple disciples is that they are gifted, so gifted that they won't trust God. So clear away all those things from the thought of discipleship, we all have absolutely equal privileges, and there is no limit to what God can do in and through us.

Jesus Christ never allows anywhere any room for the disciple to say, "Now, Lord, I am going to serve You." It never once comes into His outlook on discipleship that the disciple works for Him. He said, "As the Father has sent Me, I also send you" (John 20:21). How did the Father send Jesus? To do His will. How does Jesus send His disciples? To do His will. "You shall be witnesses to Me" (Acts 1:8)—a satisfaction to Me wherever you are placed. Our Lord's conception of discipleship is not that we work for God but that God works through us, He uses us as He likes, He allots our work where He chooses, and we learn obedience as our Master did (see Hebrews 5:8).

The one test of a teacher sent from God is that those who listen see and know Jesus Christ better than ever they did. If you are a teacher sent from God your worth in God's sight is estimated by the way you enable people to see Jesus. How are you going to tell whether I am a teacher sent from God or not? You can tell it in no other way than this—that you know Jesus Christ better than ever you did. If a teacher fascinates with a doctrine, the teaching never came from God. The teacher sent from God is the one who clears the way to Jesus and keeps it clear, souls forget altogether about the teacher because the vision of Jesus is the only abiding result. When people are attracted to Jesus Christ through you, see always that you stay on God all the time, and their hearts and affections will never stop at you. The enervation that has crippled many churches, many Sunday school classes and Bible classes, is that the pastors or teachers have won people to themselves, and the result when they leave is enervating sentimentality. The true man or true woman of God never leaves that behind, every remembrance of him or of her makes you want to serve God all the more. So beware of stealing the hearts of the people of God in your mind. If once you get the thought, "It is my winsome way of putting it, my presentation of the truth that attracts"—the only name for that is the ugly name of thief, stealing the hearts of the sheep of God who do not know why they stop at you. Keep the mind stayed on God, and I defy anyone's heart to stop at you, it will always go on to God. The peril comes when we forget that the duty is to present Jesus Christ and never get in the way in thought. The practical certainty that we are not in the way is that we can talk about ourselves; if we are in the way, self-consciousness keeps us from referring to ourselves. The apostle Paul looked upon himself as an exhibition of what Jesus Christ could do, consequently he continually refers to himself: "Christ Jesus came into the world to save sinners, of whom I am chief. However, for this reason I obtained mercy, that in me first Jesus Christ might show all longsuffering, as a pattern to those who are going to believe on Him for everlasting life" (1 Timothy 1:15–16).

The Philosophy of the Perfect Life

> One came and said to Him, "Good Teacher, what good thing shall I do that I may have eternal life?"
>
> So He said to him, "Why do you call Me good? No one is good but One, that is, God. But if you want to enter into life, keep the commandments. . . ."
>
> The young man said to Him, "All these things I have kept from my youth. What do I still lack?"
>
> Jesus said to him, "If you want to be perfect, go, sell what you have and give to the poor, and you will have treasure in heaven; and come, follow Me."
>
> But when the young man heard that saying, he went away sorrowful, for he had great possessions. Matthew 19:16–22

The occasion of a conversation is in many respects as important to consider as its subject. The occasion of this conversation was the coming to Jesus of a splendid, upright, young aristocrat who was consumed with a master passion to possess the life he saw Jesus possessed. He comes with a feeling that there is something he has not yet, in spite of his morality and integrity and his riches, something deeper, more far-reaching he can attain to, and he feels instinctively that this Jesus of Nazareth is the One who can tell him how to possess it. It is to this type of individual that Jesus presents a most powerful attraction.

The Occasion of the Conversation of Perfection

The "what" and "may" of Matthew 19:16

> Good Teacher, what good thing shall I do that I may have eternal life?

Never confound eternal life with immortality. *Eternal* has reference to the quality of life, not to its duration. Eternal life is the life Jesus exhibited when He was here on earth, with neither time nor eternity in it, because it is the life of God Himself (see John 17:3). Jesus said, You do not have this life in yourselves (see John 6:53). What life? The life He had. People have moral life, physical life, and intellectual life apart from Jesus Christ. This rich young ruler felt the fascination of the marvelous life Jesus lived and asked how he might become possessed of the same life. His question was not asked in a captious spirit. Watch the atmosphere of your mood when you ask certain questions. "Good Teacher, what good thing shall I *do* that I may have eternal life?" The great lesson our Lord taught him was that it is not anything he must do, but a relationship he must be willing to get into that is necessary. Other teachers tell us we have to do something, "Consecrate here; do this, leave off that." Jesus Christ always brings us back to one thing: Stand in right relationship to Me first, then the marvelous doing will be performed in you. It is a question of abandoning all the time, not of doing.

The Obedience to the Conditions of Perfection

The "why" and "if" of Matthew 19:17

> Why do you call Me good? . . . But if you want to enter into life keep the commandments.

It looks at first as if Jesus was captious, as if the young man's question had put Him in a corner, but our Lord wishes him to understand what calling Him "good" and asking Him about "good things" meant, If I am only a good man, there is no use coming to Me more than to anyone else, but if you mean that you are discerning who I am—then comes the condition—"If you want to enter into life, keep the commandments." The commonplace of the condition must have staggered this clean-living noble; "All these things I have kept from my youth" (Matthew 19:20).

"Then Jesus, looking at him, loved him" (Mark 10:21). The nobility of moral integrity and sterling natural virtue was lovely in the sight of Jesus, because He saw in it a remnant of His Father's former handiwork.

In listening to some evangelical addresses, the practical conclusion we are driven to is that we have to be great sinners before we can be saved, and the majority of people are not great sinners. This man was an upright, sterling, religious man, it would be absurd to talk to him about sin, he was not in the place where he could understand what it meant. There are hundreds of clean-living, upright people who are not convicted of sin, I mean sin in the light of the commandments Jesus mentioned. We need to revise the place we put conviction of sin in and the place the Spirit of God puts it in. There is no mention of sin in the apprehension of Saul of Tarsus, yet no one understood sin more fundamentally than the apostle Paul. If we reverse God's order and refuse to put the recognition of who Jesus is first, we present a lame type of Christianity that excludes forever the kind of people represented by this rich young ruler. The most staggering thing about Jesus Christ is that He makes human destiny depend not on goodness or badness, not on things done or not done, but on who we say He is.

"What do I still lack?" Jesus then instantly presses another "if": "If you want to be perfect." The second "if" is much more penetrating than the first. Entrance into life is through the recognition of who Jesus is, that is, all we mean by being born again of the Spirit—If you want to enter into life, that is the way. The second "if" is much more searching: "If you want to be perfect," perfect as I am, perfect as your Father in heaven is—then come the conditions. Do we really want to be perfect? Beware of mental quibbling over the word "perfect." Perfection does not mean the full maturity and consummation of a person's powers, but perfect fitness for doing the will of God (compare Philippians 3:12–15). Supposing Jesus Christ can perfectly adjust me to God, put me so perfectly right that I shall be on the footing where I can do the will of God—do I really want Him to do it? Do I want God, at all costs, to make me perfect? A great deal depends on what is the real, deep desire of our hearts. Can we say with Robert Murray McCheyne, "Lord, make me as holy as You can make a saved sinner"? Is that really the desire of our hearts? Our desires come to light always when we press this "if" of Jesus: "If you want to be perfect."

The Obliterating Concessions to Perfection

The "go" and "come" of Matthew 19:21

Go, sell what you have, . . . and come, follow Me.

After you have entered into life, come and fulfill the conditions of that life. We are so desperately wise, we continually make out that Jesus did not mean what He said, and we spiritualize His meaning into thin air. In this case there is no getting out of what He meant: "If you want to be perfect, go, sell what you have and give to the poor." The words mean a voluntary abandoning of property and riches, and a deliberate devoted attachment to Jesus Christ. To you or me Jesus might not say that, but He would say something equivalent over anything we are depending upon. Never push an experience into a principle by which to guide other lives. To the rich young ruler Jesus said, Loosen yourself from your property because that is the thing that is holding you. The principle is one of fundamental death to possessions while being obliged to use them. "Sell what you have"—reduce yourself till nothing remains but your consciousness of yourself, and then cast that consciousness at the feet of Christ. That is the bedrock of intense, spiritual Christianity. The moral integrity of this man made him see clearly what Jesus meant. Anyone who had been morally twisted would not have seen, but this man's mind was unwarped by moral damage, and when Jesus brought him straight to the point, he saw it clearly.

"Go, sell what you have." Do you mean to say that it is necessary for a soul's salvation to do that? Our Lord is not talking about salvation, He is saying, "If you want to be perfect." Do mark the *ifs* of Jesus. "If anyone desires to come after Me" (Luke 9:23). Remember, the conditions of discipleship are not the conditions for salvation. We are perfectly at liberty to say, "No, thank you, I am much obliged for being delivered from hell, very thankful to escape the abominations of sin, but when it comes to these conditions it is rather too much, I have my own interests in life, my own possessions."

The Obstructing Counterpoise to Perfection

The "when" and "went" of Matthew 19:22

> But when the young man heard that saying, he went away sorrowful, for he had great possessions.

Counterpoise means an equally heavy weight in the other scale. We hear a thing not when it is spoken but when we are in a state to listen. Most of us have only ears to hear what we intend to agree with, but when the surgical operation of the Spirit of God has been performed on the inside and our perceiving powers are awakened to understand what we hear, then we get to the condition of this young man. When he heard what Jesus said he did not dispute it, he did not argue, he did not say, I fail to perceive the subtlety of Your meaning; he heard it, and he found he had too big an interest in the other scale and he drooped away from Jesus in sadness, not in rebellion.

Our Lord's statements seem so simple and gentle that we swallow them and say, "Yes, I accept Jesus as a Teacher," then

His words seem to slip out of our minds; they have not, they have gone into our subconscious minds, and when we come across something in our circumstances, up comes one of those words and we hear it for the first time, and it makes us reel with amazement. "He who has ears to hear, let him hear" (Matthew 11:15). What have we ears for?

"Go, sell what you have and give to the poor." Remember, Jesus did not claim any of the rich young ruler's possessions; He did not say, Consecrate them to Me, He did not say, Sell what you have and give it to My service; He said, "Sell what you have and give to the poor," and for you, "come, follow Me," and you will have treasure in heaven. One of the most subtle errors is that God wants our possessions—they are not any use to Him. God does not want our possessions, He wants us.

In this incident, our Lord reveals His profound antipathy to emotional excitement. The rich young man's powers were in unbewitched working order when Jesus called him to decide. Beware of the "seeking great things for yourself" idea—cold shivers down the back, visions of angels, and visitations from God. "I can't decide in this plain, commonplace, ordinary evening as to whether I will serve Jesus or not." That is the only way Jesus Christ ever comes to us. He will never take us at a disadvantage, never terrify us out of our wits by some amazing manifestation of His power, and then say, "Follow Me." He wants us to decide when all our powers are in full working order, and He chooses the moment when the world, not He, is in the ascendant. If we chose Him when He was in the ascendant, in the time of religious emotion and excitement, we would leave Him when the moment of excitement passed, but if we choose Him with all our powers about us, the choice will abide.

"And come, follow Me." It is not only a question of binding the sacrifice with cords to the horns of the altar, it is a rising in the might of the Holy Spirit, with your feet on the earth but your heart swelling with the love of heaven, conscious that at last you have reached the position to which you were aspiring. How long are some of us, who ought to be princes and princesses for God, going to be bound up in the show of things? We have asked in tears, "What do I still lack?" This is the road and no other: "Come, follow Me."

"And you will have treasure in heaven"—and on earth, what? A hundredfold of all you left *for My sake.*

The devotion to Jesus Christ of our persons is the effectual working of the evangelical doctrine of Christian perfection.

The Disciple and the Lord of Destiny

Revelation 3

His Divine Integrity

> These things says He who is holy, He who is true. Revelation 3:7

(a) Harmony with God's Character

These words suggest that our Lord's unlimited sovereignty over human souls rests upon moral fitness. In Revelation 5, this aspect is again alluded to: "Who is worthy to open the scroll?" (verse 2). The appeal made to us by Jesus Christ is that He is worthy not only in the domain of God but in the human domain, consequently He "has prevailed to open the scroll" (verse 5). The disciple's Lord is in absolute harmony with the highest humanity knows and with the highest God has revealed. The Bible is not the authority, the church is not the authority, the Lord Jesus Christ alone is the authority. The tendency is strong to make the statements of the Bible simpler than God makes them, the reason being that we will not recognize Jesus Christ as the authority. It is only when we rely on the Holy Spirit and obey His leadership that the authority of Jesus Christ is recognized. The Holy Spirit will glorify Jesus only, consequently the interpretation of the Bible and of human life depends entirely on how we understand the character of Jesus Christ. If there is anything hidden from us as disciples today it is because we are not in the fit state to understand it. As soon as we become fit in spiritual character, the thing is revealed; it is concealed at God's discretion until the life is developed sufficiently.

(b) Holiness Supreme with Man

The disciple's Lord is the supreme authority in every relationship of life the disciple is in or can be in. That is a very obvious point, but think what it means—it means recognizing it as impertinent to say, "Oh, well, Jesus Christ does not know my circumstances, the principles involved in His teachings are altogether impracticable for me where I am." That thought never came from the Spirit of God, and it has to be gripped in a vice on the threshold of the mind and allowed no way. If, as we obey God, such a circumstance is possible where Jesus Christ's precepts and principles are impracticable, then He has misled us. The idea insinuates itself, "Oh, well, I can be justified from my present conduct because of—such and such." We are never justified as disciples in taking any line of action other than that indicated by the teaching of our Lord and made possible for us by His Spirit. The providence of God fits us into various settings of life to see if we will be disciples in those relationships.

(c) Highest Authority Conceivable

The highest authority conceivable for a human being is that of a holy character. The holiest character is the Lord Jesus Christ, therefore His statements are never dogmas, they are declarations. In the Epistles we find the dogmas of belief stated and formulated, but our Lord never taught dogma—He declared. There is no argument or discussion in what He says, it is not a question of the insight of a marvelous individual but a question of speaking with authority. "He taught them as one having authority" (Matthew 7:29). The disciple realizes that our Lord's statements never spring from a personal point of view, they reveal the eternal character of God as applied to the practical details of life.

His Divine Imperialism

He who has the key of David. Revelation 3:7

(a) Abiding Sacredness of His Inheritance

The disciple's Lord has the key to every situation in heaven above or on earth beneath. Other powers that are not of Jesus Christ claim they can open the book, but the unmeasured blight of God rests on an intellectual curiosity that divorces itself from moral and spiritual worth. It is necessary to bear that in mind, for this is a day of intolerant inquisitiveness, people will not wait for the slow, steady, majestic way of the Son of God, they enter in by this door and that, and the consequence is moral, spiritual, and physical insanity. All kinds of terrible and awful evils come through people having pressed open domains for themselves. They have refused to have the only authority there is, the authority of a moral, holy character. "I fear," Paul says, "lest somehow . . . your minds may be corrupted from the simplicity that is in Christ" (2 Corinthians 11:3).

(b) Antagonists Scared by His Servants

The easy supremacy of the Lord Jesus Christ in and through the life of a disciple brings the blatant terror of the synagogue of Satan to bow at the disciple's feet. "Indeed, I will make those of the synagogue of Satan . . . come and worship before your feet, and to know that I have loved you" (Revelation 3:9). This is the age of humiliation for the saints, just as it was the age of humiliation for our Lord when He was on earth—we cannot stand the humiliation unless we are His disciples, we want to get into the show business, we want to be successful, to be recognized and known, we want to compromise and put things right and get to an understanding. Never! Stand true to Jesus Christ, "not in any way terrified by your adversaries" (Philippians 1:28). We find the features of the synagogue of Satan everywhere, but if the disciple will obey, all that power will crumble down as bluff by the marvelous authority of Jesus Christ. "Do not fear, little flock, for it is your Father's good pleasure to give you the kingdom" (Luke 12:32). When once fear is taken out, the world is humiliated at the feet of the humblest of saints, it can do nothing, it cannot touch the amazing supremacy that comes through the divine imperialism of the saint's Lord and Master.

(c) Alpha and Omega

"I am the Alpha and the Omega, the First and the Last" Revelation 1:11

Jesus Christ is the last word on God, on sin and death, on heaven and hell, the last word on every problem that human life has to face. If you are a disciple, be loyal to Him; that means you will have to choke off any number of things that might fritter you away from the one center. Beware of prejudices being put in place of the sovereignty of Jesus Christ, prejudices of doctrine, of conviction, or experience. When we go on Jesus Christ's way, slowly and steadily we find He builds up spiritual and moral character along with intellectual discernment—these develop together; if we push one at the expense of the other, we shall get out of touch with God. If intellectual curiosity pushes the barriers further than God has seen fit to open, the moral character will get out of hand, and we shall have pain that God cannot bless, suffering from which He cannot protect us. "The way of the unfaithful is hard" (Proverbs 13:15).

"I am . . . the First and the Last." Is Jesus Christ the first and the last of my personal creed, the first and last of all I look to and hope for? Frequently the discipline of discipleship has to be delayed until we learn that God's barriers are put there not by sovereign deity only, they are put there by a God whose will is absolutely holy and who has told us plainly, Not that way (compare Deuteronomy 29:29).

His Divine Invincibility

> He who opens and no one shuts, and shuts and no one opens.
> Revelation 3:7

(a) Defied but Never Frustrated

The word *door* is used elsewhere in the New Testament for privileges and opportunities ("For a great and effective door has opened to me" [1 Corinthians 16:9]), but here it means that Jesus Christ's sovereignty is effective everywhere, it is He who opens the door and He who shuts. "See, I have set before you an open door, and no one can shut it" (Revelation 3:8). Behind the devil is God. God is never in a panic, nothing can be done that He is not absolute master of, and no one in earth or heaven can shut a door He has opened nor open a door He has shut. God alters the inevitable when we get in touch with Him. We discover the doors our Lord opens by watching the things unsaved human nature reacts against. Everything Jesus Christ has done awakens a tremendous reaction against Him in those who are not His disciples: "I won't go that way." Insubordination is the characteristic of today. People defy, but they cannot frustrate, and in the end they come to see that Jesus Christ's is the only way. The Gospel gives access into privileges that no one can reach by any other way than the way Jesus Christ has appointed. Unsaved human nature resents this and tries to make out that Jesus Christ will bow in submissive weakness to the way it wants to go. The preaching of the Gospel awakens an intense craving and an equally intense resentment. The door is opened wide by a God of holiness and love, and any and every one can enter in through that door who will. "I am the way" (John 14:6). Jesus Christ is the exclusive way to the Father.

(b) Divine and Forever "Never"

Some doors have been shut by God and they will never again be opened. God opens other doors, but we find these closed doors all through human history. Some people believe in an omnipotence with no character—they are shut up in a destiny of hopelessness; Jesus Christ can open the door of release and let them right out. There is no door that human or devil has closed but Jesus Christ can open, but remember, there is the other side, the door He closes no one can open.

(c) Desired Communion

In Revelation 3:20, the metaphor is changed: "Behold, I stand at the door and knock." If it is true that no one can open the doors Jesus Christ has closed, it is also true that He never opens the door for His own incoming into the heart and life of a church or an individual. "If anyone . . . opens the door, I will come in to him." The experience into which Jesus Christ by His sovereignty can bring us is at-one-ment with God, a full-orbed, unworrying oneness with God.

Disciples Indeed

"If you abide in My word, you are My disciples indeed."

John 8:31

Belief

The only noble sense in which we can claim to believe a thing is when we ourselves are living in the inner spirit of that thing.

I have no right to say I believe in God unless I order my life as under His all-seeing eye.

I have no right to say I believe that Jesus is the Son of God unless in my personal life I yield myself to that eternal Spirit, free from all self-seeking, which became incarnate in Jesus.

I have no right to say that I believe in forgiveness as an attribute of God if in my own heart I cherish an unforgiving temper. The forgiveness of God is the test by which I myself am judged.

Belief is a wholesale committal; it means making things inevitable, cutting off every possible retreat. Belief is as irrevocable as bereavement (compare 2 Samuel 12:21–23).

Belief is the abandonment of all claim to merit. That is why it is so difficult to believe.

A believer is one whose whole being is based on the finished work of redemption.

It is easier to be true to our convictions than to Jesus Christ, because if we are going to be true to Him our convictions will need to be altered.

Where we blunder is in trying to expound the Cross doctrinally while refusing to do what Jesus told us to do, namely, lift Him up. "And I, if I am lifted up from the earth, will draw all peoples to Myself" (John 12:32).

We are not sent to specialize in doctrine but to lift up Jesus, and He will do the work of saving and sanctifying souls. When we become doctrine mongers God's power is not known, only the passion of an individual appeal.

God has a way of bringing in facts that upset people's doctrines, if these stand in the way of God getting at their souls.

Doctrine is never the guide into Christian experience; doctrine is the exposition of Christian experience.

The further we get away from Jesus the more dogmatic we become over what we call our religious beliefs, while the nearer we live to Jesus the less we have of certitude and the more of confidence in Him.

You cannot understand Jesus Christ unless you accept the New Testament revelation of Him; you must be biased for Him before you can understand Him.

Beware of going to Jesus with preconceived notions of your own, go relying on the Holy Spirit, "He will glorify Me," said Jesus (John 16:14).

Once allow that Jesus Christ is all the New Testament proclaims Him to be, and you are borne on irresistibly to believe that what He says about Himself is true.

The most conspicuous thing in the New Testament is the supremacy given to our Lord; today the supremacy is apt to be given to phases of the truth, to doctrines, and not to Jesus Christ.

Truth is a person, not a proposition; if I pin my faith to a logical creed I will be disloyal to the Lord Jesus.

The most fundamental heresies that split the Christian church are those built on what Jesus Christ can do instead of on Jesus Himself. Wreckage in spiritual experience always follows.

Many people spurn Jesus Christ in any phase other than that of their particular religious ideas.

Every partial truth has so much error in it that you can dispute it, but you can't dispute truth as it is in Jesus.

Watch the things you say you can't believe, and then recall the things you accept without thinking, for example, your own existence.

It is impossible to prove a fact, facts have to be swallowed, and the person who swallows revelation facts is no more of a fool than the one who swallows commonsense facts on the evidence of his or her senses. Face facts, and play the skeptic with explanations.

The "always learning and never able to come to the knowledge of the truth" stage (2 Timothy 3:7) is the cause of all spiritual epidemics; we won't realize what God has revealed.

You can't unveil truth when you like; when the unveiling comes, beware. That moment marks your going back or your going on.

Truth is of the implicit order; you can't define truth, and yet everyone is so constituted that at times the longing for truth is insatiable. It is not sufficient to remain with a longing for truth, because there is something at the basis of things that drives us to the truth if we are honest.

When people say they can't believe, don't argue with them on what they don't believe, but ask them what they do believe, and proceed from that point; disbelief as often arises from temperament as from sin. Everyone believes in a good character—then refer to Jesus Christ as the best character in history, and ask people to believe that what He says is likely to be true (for example, Luke 11:13; John 3:16), and get them to transact business on that.

When once you come in contact with Jesus you are not conscious of any effort to believe in Him.

If I believe the character of Jesus, am I living up to what I believe?

The danger of pietistic movements is that we are told what we must feel, and we can't get near God because we are so hopelessly dependent on pious attitudes; consequently what is seen is not the New Testament stamp of saint but the mixture of an insubordinate intellect along with an affected clinging to Jesus with devotion.

Whenever a Holiness movement raises its head and begins to be conscious of its own holiness, it is liable to become an emissary of the devil, although it started with an emphasis on a neglected truth.

We must continually take stock of what is ours in Christ Jesus because only in that way will we understand what God intends us to be.

If you preach holiness or sanctification or divine healing or the Second Coming, you are off the track because you decentralize the truth. We have to fix our eyes on Jesus Christ, not on what He does. "I am . . . the truth" (John 14:6).

If I am going to know who Jesus is, I must obey Him. The majority of us don't know Jesus because we have not the remotest intention of obeying Him.

Our deadliest temptations are not so much those that destroy Christian belief as those that corrupt and destroy the Christian temper.

The great paralysis of our hearts is unbelief. As soon as I view anything as inevitable about any human being, I am an unbeliever.

There is a difference between believing God and believing about Him; you are always conscious of the latter, it makes you a prig. If by letting your beliefs go you get hold of God Himself, let them go.

Beware of worshipping Jesus as the Son of God and professing your faith in Him as the Savior of the world, while you blaspheme Him by the complete evidence in your daily life that He is powerless to do anything in and through you.

The greatest challenge to a Christian is to believe. Matthew 28:18: "All authority has been given to Me in heaven and on earth." How many of us get into a panic when we are faced by physical desolation, by death or war, injustice, poverty, disease? All these in all their force will never turn to panic the ones who believe in the absolute sovereignty of their Lord.

The Bible

"The Word" is Jesus Himself (John 1:1), therefore we must have an experimental knowledge of Him before we understand the literal words of the Bible

The danger today is that people are being nourished not with the Bible so much as with conceptions that ignore Jesus Christ.

Bible facts are either revelation facts or nonsense. It depends on me which they are to me.

God does not thunder His truth into our ears; the attitude of our minds must be submissive to revelation facts. All of us bring certain prejudices, civilized prejudgments, that greatly hinder our understanding of revelation facts.

Our attitude to the Bible is a stupid one; we come to the Bible for proof of God's existence, but the Bible has no meaning for us until we know God does exist. The Bible states and affirms facts for the benefit of those who believe in God; those who don't believe in God can tear it to bits if they choose.

People can dispute the words of the Bible as they like, but get a soul in whom the craving for God has come, and the words of the Bible create the new life in that soul: "having been born again . . . through the word of God" (1 Peter 1:23).

If we understood what happens when we use the Word of God, we would use it more often. The disablement of the devil's power by means of the Word of God conveyed through the lips of a servant of God is inconceivable.

The main characteristic that is the proof of the indwelling Spirit is an amazing tenderness in personal dealing and a blazing truthfulness with regard to God's Word.

There is no true illumination apart from the written Word. Spiritual impressions generated from my own experience are of no importance, and if I pay attention to them I will pay no attention to the words of Jesus.

The test of God's truth is that it fits you exactly; if it does not, question whether it is His truth.

Beware of bartering the Word of God for a more suitable conception of your own.

All impulses must wed themselves to the express statements of the Bible, otherwise they will lead astray.

The thing to ask yourself is, "Does the Bible say it?" not, "I don't think that is a good view of God."

Profoundly speaking, it is not sufficient to say, "Because God says it," or, "Because the Bible says it," unless you are talking to people who know God and know the Bible to be His Word. If you appeal from the authority of God or of the Bible to people not born again, they will pay no attention to you because they do not stand on the same platform. You have to find a provisional platform on which they can stand with you, and in the majority of cases you will find that the platform is that of moral worth. If Jesus Christ is proved worthy on the plane people are on, they will be ready to put Him as the Most Worthy One, and all the rest will follow.

Whenever human nature gets driven to the end of things, the Bible is the only Book, and God the only Being, in the world.

The reason some of us are not healthy spiritually is because we don't use the Bible as the Word of God but only as a textbook.

Beware of making a fetish of a word God once spoke to you; if you stick to the word God spoke, you will leave Him, and the result is harshness and stagnation, a refusal to budge from the precedent you have established.

Watch every time the Word of God is made a sacrament to you through someone else—it will make you retune your ears to His Word.

There are saints who are being rattled out of holiness by fussy work for God, whereas one five minutes of brooding on God's truth would do more good than all their work of fuss.

It is what the Bible imparts to us that is of value.

The Bible does not thrill, the Bible nourishes. Give time to the reading of the Bible and the re-creating effect is as real as that of fresh air physically.

If I have disobeyed, the Word of God is dried up, there is no "open vision." As soon as I obey, the Word is poured in.

To read the Bible according to God's providential order in your circumstances is the only way to read it, namely, in the blood and passion of personal life.

The statements of Scripture apart from the Holy Spirit's illumination are dull; it needs no spiritual insight to regard Jesus Christ as a Man who lived beyond His time, but when I am born again I have insight into the person of Jesus, an insight that comes through communion with God by means of the Bible.

Beware of interpreting Scripture in order to make it suit a prearranged doctrine of your own.

Exegesis is not torturing a text to agree with a theory of my own, but leading out its meaning.

Beware of reasoning about God's Word—obey it.

An absurd thing to say is, "Give me a text to prove it." You cannot give a text to prove any one of God's revelations, you can only give a text to prove your simplification of those revelations. A proof text is generally used to bolster up a personal spiritual affinity of my own.

We are to be servants of the Gospel, not devotees of the Bible, then God can make us living mediums whereby His Word becomes a sacrament to others.

The Call of God

If you only know what God can do, your talk is altogether of that—a logical exposition of doctrine, but if you have heard God's call you will always keep to the one center, the person of the Lord Jesus Christ.

Discard any emotion or call to work that cannot find itself at home in the absolute mastery of Jesus Christ.

If I hear the call of God and refuse to obey, I become the dullest, most commonplace of Christians, because I have seen and heard and refused to obey.

No experience on earth is sufficient to be taken as a call of God; you must know that the call is from God, for whom you care more than for all your experiences, then nothing can daunt you.

You can never toil the life out of the one whose service springs from listening to the voice of God, its inspiration is drawn not from human sympathy but from God Himself.

The call is the inner motive of having been gripped by God—spoiled for every aim in life except that of disciplining people to Jesus.

One man or one woman called of God is worth a hundred who have elected to work for God.

It is an erroneous notion that you have to wait for the call of God; see that you are in such a condition that you can realize it (see Isaiah 6:8).

If God has called some of you in this College into His service, as He undoubtedly has, never allow anyone to interfere with your obedience to His call. Let God do what He likes,

He knows exactly where you are and when the time is fit to make you broken bread in His hands.

We need no call of God to help other people—that is the natural call of humanity—but we do need the supernatural work of God's grace before we are fit for God to help Himself through us.

If you are called to preach the Gospel, God will crush you till the light of the eye, the power of the life, the ambition of the heart, is all riveted on Him. That is not done easily. It is not a question of saintliness, it has to do with the call of God.

The Character of God

"No one has seen God at any time. The only begotten Son, who is in the bosom of the Father, He has declared Him" (John 1:18). Christians accept all they know about God on the authority of Jesus Christ, they can find out nothing about God by their own unaided intellects.

The God I infer by my common sense has no power over me at all.

The vindication of God to the intelligence is the most difficult process. Only when we see righteousness and justice exhibited in the person of Jesus Christ can we vindicate God.

In the face of problems as they are, we see in Jesus Christ an exhibition of where our faith is to be placed, namely, in a God whose ways we do not understand.

Jesus Christ reveals not an embarrassed God, not a confused God, not a God who stands apart from the problems, but One who stands in the thick of the whole thing with us.

When a so-called rationalist points out sin and iniquity and disease and death and says, "How does God answer that?" you have always a fathomless answer—the cross of Christ.

God's ways are past finding out! We often state the character of God in terms of brutal harshness while our motive is to glorify Him.

Never accept an explanation that travesties God's character.

There are some questions God cannot answer until you have been brought by obedience to be able to stand the answer. Be prepared to suspend your judgment until you have heard God's answer for yourself.

There *is* a dark line in God's face, but what we do know about Him is so full of peace and joy that we can wait for His interpretation.

God's order is clearly marked out in the first and the last; His permissive will is seen in the process in between, where everything is disorganized because of sin. The Christian is one who, by the power of the indwelling Spirit, sees the final issue.

The psalmist was perplexed when he saw the prosperity of the wicked (see Psalm 73:1–12); God's final purpose is holiness, holy men and holy women, and He restrains none of the forces that go against that purpose.

Beware lest your attitude to God's truth reminds Him that He is very unwise. Everything worthwhile in life is dangerous, and yet we would have God such a tepid Being that He runs no risks!

Believe what you do believe and stick to it, but don't profess to believe more than you intend to stick to. If you say you believe God is love, stick to it, though all Providence becomes a pandemonium shouting that God is cruel to allow what He does.

Never attempt to explain God to an exasperated soul, because you cannot. Don't take the part of Job's friends and say you can explain the whole thing; if you think you can, you are very shallow. You have to take on the attitude of vicarious waiting till God brings the light.

Remember, each life has a solitary way, alone with God. Be reverent with His ways in dealing with other souls because you have no notion, any more than Job had, why things are as they are. Most of us are much too desirous of getting hold of a line that will vindicate us in our views of God.

It is perilously possible to make our conceptions of God like molten lead poured into specially designed molds, and when they are cold and hard we fling them at the heads of the religious people who don't agree with us.

God is true to the laws of His own nature, not to my way of expounding how He works.

We have to get out of the old pagan way of guiding ourselves by our heads and get into the Christian way of being guided by faith in a personal God, whose methods are a perpetual contradiction to our every preconceived notion.

We only see others in the light of what we think they are—it takes an amount of surgery on the inside to make us see other people as they really are, and it is the same with what we think about God, we take the facts revealed in the Bible and try to fit them into our own ideas of what God is like.

Am I becoming more and more in love with God as a holy God, or with the conception of an amiable Being who says, "Oh, well, sin doesn't matter much"?

God never coerces, neither does He ever accommodate His demands to human compromise, and we are disloyal to Him if we do.

Watch the margins of your mind when you begin to take the view that it doesn't matter whether God is holy or not, it is the beginning of being a traitor to Jesus Christ.

Spiritual insight does not so much enable us to understand God as to understand that He is at work in the ordinary things of life, in the ordinary stuff human nature is made of.

Learn to give honor to God when good works are done, but also learn to discern whether or not they are done by God's servants. The most outrageous moment for the devil will be when he finds that in spite of himself he has done God's will, and the same with people who have been serving their own ends.

Everything the devil does, God overreaches to serve His own purpose.

Have I ever had a glimpse of this—that God would not be altered if all our civilized life went to pieces?

Overrefinement in civilization turns God's order upside down.

God has no respect for our civilizations because He did not found them. While civilization is not God's, it is His providential protection for people, generally restraining the bad and affording His children the means of developing their lives in Him.

When the present phase is over, God won't have elbow-room; it will be all insurance and combine, and God won't be able to get in anywhere. What is true of civilization will be true of us individually unless we remember to put God first.

In a time of calamity God appears to pay scant courtesy to all our art and culture, He sweeps the whole thing aside till civilization rages at Him. It is "the babe" and "the fool" who get through in the day of God's visitation.

God cannot come to me in any way but His own way, and His way is often insignificant and unobtrusive.

Never accept an explanation of any of God's ways that involves what you would scorn as false and unfair in a human being.

God does not act according to His own precedents, therefore logic or a vivid past experience can never take the place of a personal faith in a personal God.

God never crushes people beneath the fear of judgment without revealing the possibility of victorious virtue.

We say that God foresaw sin and made provision for it; the Bible revelation is that "the Lamb slain from the foundation of the world" (Revelation 13:8) is the exact expression of the nature of God.

Experience

Experiences are apt to be exalted out of all due measure, whereas they are but the outward manifestation of the one-ness with God made possible for us in Christ Jesus.

Get into the habit of chasing yourself out of the sickly morbid experiences that are not based on having been with Jesus (see Acts 4:13), they are not only valueless but excessively dangerous.

The great bedrock of Christian experience is the outside fact of the resurrection made inwardly real by the incoming of the Holy Spirit. "That I may know Him and the power of His resurrection" (Philippians 3:10).

If your experience is not worthy of the risen, ascended Christ, then fling it overboard.

Whenever ecstasies or visions of God unfit us for practical life, they are danger signals that the life is on the wrong track.

Our identity with Jesus Christ is immediately practical or not at all; that is, the new identity must manifest itself in our mortal flesh, otherwise we can easily hoax ourselves into delusions. Becoming "the righteousness of God in Him" (2 Corinthians 5:21) is the most powerfully practical experience in a human life.

Insubordination characterizes much of what is called the Higher Christian Life; it is spiritual anarchy based on *my* intuitions, *my* private interpretations, *my* experiences, while refusing to submit to the words of the Lord Jesus.

My experience of salvation never constitutes me an expounder of the Atonement. I am always apt to take my experience for an inclusive interpretation instead of its being merely a gateway for *me* into salvation.

We continually want to present our understanding of how God has worked in our own experiences, consequently we confuse people. Present Jesus Christ, lift Him up, and the Holy Spirit will do in them what He has done in you.

A great deal of what we have to proclaim can never be experienced, but whenever God's standard is presented we are either exonerated or condemned by the way we ourselves carry out the dictates of the Holy Spirit.

Experience as an end in itself is a disease, experience as a result of the life being based on God is health.

Spiritual famine and dearth, if it does not start from sin, starts from dwelling entirely on the experience God gave me instead of on God who gave me the experience.

When I plant my faith on the Lord Jesus, my experiences don't make me conscious of them, they produce in me the life of a child.

If my experience makes anyone wish to emulate me, I am decoying that one away from God.

"Because I have had more experience of life than you have, therefore I can discern God's will better than you can." Not at all. Whenever I put my experience of life or my intelligence or anything other than dependence on God as the ground of understanding the will of God, I rob Him of glory.

It is on the line of impulse that Satan leads the saints astray, in spite of Jesus Christ's warning, "to deceive, if possible, even the elect" (Mark 13:22). It is spiritual impulse that leads off at a tangent. Satan does not come as an angel of light to anybody but a saint.

Whenever we get light from God on a particular phase we incline to limit God's working to that phase, forgetting that we cannot tie up almighty God to anything built up out of our own experiences.

One person's experience is as valuable as another's, but experience has nothing to do with facts. Facts pay no attention to us, facts have to be accepted; they are the real autocrats in life.

You cannot deal with facts as you like; you may object to them, but a fact is a fact, whether a commonsense fact or a revelation fact.

In spiritual experience, it is not your intellect that guides you; intellect illuminates what is yours, and you get a thrill of delight because you recognize what you have been going through but could not state.

Whenever the Bible refers to facts of human experience, look to your experience for the answer; when the Bible refers to standards of revelation, look to God, not to your experience.

Beware of making your religious experiences a cloak for a lack of reality.

If you have been going on with God, you find He has knocked the bottom board out of your fanaticism; where you used to be narrow and bigoted, you now exhibit His Spirit.

Would to God we got finished once for all with the experience of being adjusted to God and let Him send us forth into vicarious service for Him!

The Holy Spirit

It is not what we feel or what we know, but ever what we receive from God—and a fool can receive a gift. "If you then, being evil, know how to give good gifts to your children, how much more will your heavenly Father give the Holy Spirit to those who ask Him?" (Luke 11:13). It is so simple that everyone who is not simple misses it.

Beware of telling people they must be worthy to receive the Holy Spirit; you can't be worthy, you must know you are unworthy, then you will ask for the gift: "If you then, being evil."

The biggest blessing in your life was when you came to the end of trying to be a Christian, the end of reliance on natural devotion, and were willing to come as a pauper and receive the Holy Spirit. The humiliation is that we have to be quite sure we need Him, so many of us are quite sure we don't need Him.

It is extraordinary how things fall off from people like autumn leaves once they come to the place where there is no rule but that of the personal domination of the Holy Spirit.

We continually want to substitute our transactions with God for the great, mystic, powerful work of the Holy Spirit. "The wind blows where it wishes, and you hear the sound of it, but cannot tell where it comes from and where it goes. So is everyone who is born of the Spirit" (John 3:8).

By regeneration we are put into right relationship with God, then we have the same human nature, working on the same lines, but with a different driving power expressing itself, so that the "members" that were used for the wrong are now used for the good (see Romans 6:17–21).

The strenuous effort of the saints is not to produce holiness but to express in actual circumstances the disposition of the Son of God that is imparted to us by the Holy Spirit.

Beware of seeking power, rather than the personal relationship to Jesus Christ that is the grand avenue through which the Holy Spirit comes in His working power. "But you shall receive power when the Holy Spirit has come upon you; and you shall be witnesses to Me" (Acts 1:8).

The message of Pentecost is an emphasis not on the Holy Spirit but on the risen and ascended Christ (see John 16:13–15).

The Holy Spirit takes care that we fix our attention on Jesus Christ, then He will look after the presentation given of our Lord through us.

Devotion to Jesus is the expression of the Holy Spirit's work in me.

The Holy Spirit is concerned only with glorifying Jesus, not with glorifying our human generosities.

The deep and engrossing need of those of us who name the name of Christ is reliance on the Holy Spirit.

Jesus Christ reinstates us to the position lost through sin (see Romans 5:12); we come at this knowledge experimentally, but it is never our understanding of salvation that leads to salvation. Salvation is *experienced* first, then to understand it needs the work of the Holy Spirit, which is surprising and incalculable.

We "may be partakers of the divine nature" (2 Peter 1:4) by receiving the Holy Spirit, who has poured out "the love of God . . . in our hearts" (Romans 5:5), and the oneness is manifested in lives of abandon and obedience—both unconscious.

If you are being checked by the Holy Spirit over a wrong thing you are allowing in yourself, beware of only captiously seeing the limitations in other people; you will diverge further away from God if you don't recognize that it is the still, small voice of God to you.

There is nothing so still and gentle as the checks of the Holy Spirit if they are yielded to; emancipation is the result, but let them be trifled with, and there will come a hardening of the life away from God. Don't quench the Spirit.

There is no room for harsh judgment on the part of a child of God. Harsh judgment is based not on the sternness of the Holy Spirit but on my refusal to bear someone else's burden.

Beware of everything in which you have to justify yourself to yourself, because the underlying fact is that you have cajoled yourself into taking a decision born of temperamental convictions instead of in entire reliance on the Holy Spirit.

The inspiration of the Holy Spirit is not an impulse to make me act but to enable me to interpret God's meaning; if I do act on the impulse of the inspiration, it is a mere physical reaction in myself. Impulse is God's knock at my door that He might come in—not for me to open the door and go out.

The salvation of Jesus Christ makes a personality intense—very few of us are real until the Holy Spirit gets hold of us.

The Holy Spirit does not obliterate personality, He lifts it to its highest use, namely, for the portrayal of the mind of God.

Beware of the "show" business—"I want to be baptized with the Holy Spirit so that I may do wonderful works." God never allows anyone to do wonderful works; *He* does them, and the baptism of the Holy Spirit prevents my seeing them in order to glory in them.

"When He ascended on high, He . . . gave gifts to men" (Ephesians 4:8; compare Acts 2:33). The only sign that a particular gift is from the ascended Christ is that it edifies the church. Much of our Christian work today is built on what the apostle pleads it should not be built on, namely, the excellencies of the natural virtues.

Be careful to notice the difference between an offended personal prejudice, which makes you feel ruffled and huffy, and the intuitive sense of bondage produced by the Holy Spirit when you are listening to something that is not God's truth.

We must distinguish between the bewilderment arising from conviction of sin and the bewilderment arising from confusion in thinking; the latter is the inevitable result in a traditionally Christian mind on first receiving the Holy Spirit, but a curious thing to note is that a heathen mind experiences no such bewilderment on receiving the Holy Spirit, because there are no preconceived notions to be gotten rid of.

The mind that is not produced by obedience to the Holy Spirit in the final issue hates God.

If you are in danger of building on the natural virtues, which are a remnant of the former creation, the Holy Spirit will throw a searchlight and show you things that cause you to shudder. He will reveal a vindictiveness, a maliciousness you never knew before.

Let God bring you through some midnight, when the Holy Spirit reminds you of what you once were, of your religious hypocrisies—the things the devil whispers you should forget, let God bring you to the dust before Him. This experience will always come in the path of those God is going to take up into His purposes.

The baptism of the Holy Spirit means the extinction of life fires that are not of God, and everything becomes instinct with the life of God.

The Holy Spirit is the One who regenerates us into the family to which Jesus Christ belongs, until by the eternal efficacy of the Cross we are made partakers of the divine nature.

The Holy Spirit is not a substitute for Jesus. The Holy Spirit is all that Jesus was, made real in personal experience *now.*

There is one thing we cannot imitate: we cannot imitate being full of the Holy Spirit.

The mark of the Holy Spirit in people's lives is that they have gone to their own funerals, and the thought of themselves never enters.

The sign that the Holy Spirit is being obeyed by me is that I am not dominated by my sensualities. "And those who are Christ's have crucified the flesh with its passions and desires" (Galatians 5:24). Sensualities are not gross only, they can be very refined.

"Do you not know that your body is the temple of the Holy Spirit who is in you?" (1 Corinthians 6:19). The indwelling of the Holy Spirit is the climax of redemption.

The great, impelling power of the Holy Spirit is seen in its most fundamental working whenever an issue of will is pushed. It is pleasanter to listen to poetical discourses, more agreeable to have your affinities appealed to, but it is not good enough, it leaves you exactly as you were. The Gospel appeal comes with a stinging grip: "Will you?" or "Won't you?"; "I will accept," or "I'll put it off"—both are decisions, remember.

We have to distinguish between acquiring and receiving. We *acquire* habits of prayer and Bible reading and we *receive* our salvation, we *receive* the Holy Spirit, we *receive* the grace of God. We give more attention to the things we acquire, all God pays attention to is what we receive. Those things we receive can never be taken from us because God holds those who receive His gifts.

The fruit of pseudoevangelism is different from the fruit of the Spirit (see Galatians 5:22–23).

Guard as your greatest gift the anointing of the Holy Spirit, namely, the right of access to God for yourself. "The anointing which you have received from Him abides in you" (1 John 2:27).

It is the fine art of the Holy Spirit to be alone with God.

The Moral Law

It has been a favorite belief in all ages that if only people were taught what good is, everyone would choose it, but history and human experience prove that that is not so. To know what is good is not to be good.

My conscience makes me know what I ought to do, but it does not empower me to do it. "For what I will to do, that I do not practice; but what I hate, that I do" (Romans 7:15).

To say that if I am persuaded a thing is wrong I won't do it is not true. The mutiny of human nature is that it will do it whether it is wrong or not.

The problem in practical experience is not to know what is right but to do it. My natural spirit may know a great many things, but I never can be what I know I ought to be until I receive the life that has life in itself, namely, the Holy Spirit. That is the practical working of the redemption.

"Morality is altogether based on utilitarian standards"; it is not—your conscience will come in every time when you don't want it to.

Conscience resides in one's essential spirit, not in one's reasoning faculty; it is the one thing that assists people in their unregenerate days.

Why are people not worse than they are? The reason is the existence of the moral law of God that restrains people in spite of the impulse toward wrong, consequently you find remnants of the strivings of the moral law where you least expect it, because the moral law is independent entirely of the opposition to it on the part of individuals.

When God's law is presented, beware of the proud self-confidence that says, "This is good enough for me, I don't intend to soar any higher."

In dealing with the question of disease, both moral and physical, we must deal with it in the light of the redemption. If you want to know how far wrong the world has gotten, you learn it not in a hospital but at the Cross. We learn by what it cost God to redeem the world how criminally out of moral order the universe has gotten.

The guilt abroad today can never be dealt with by pressing a social ethic or a moral order or by an enfolding sympathy for humanity, while pooh-poohing the demands of a holy God.

Very few of us know what *love of God* is; we know what *love of moral good* is, and the curious thing is that that leads us away from God more quickly than does a terror of moral evil—"the good is ever the enemy of the best."

Our lawlessness can be detected in relation to the words, "Come to Me" (Matthew 11:28).

Liberty means ability not to violate the law, *license* means personal insistence on doing what I like.

If one is not holy, one is immoral; it does not matter how good a person seems, immorality is at the basis of the whole thing. It may not show itself as immoral physically, but it will show itself as immoral in the sight of God (see Luke 16:15).

Intellectual skepticism is good, but we are to blame for moral skepticism. We all believe in goodness and uprightness and integrity, until we pervert the taste by going wrong ourselves.

Beware of giving way to spiritual ecstasies, it disconnects you from the great ordinances of God and shakes the very basis of sane morality God has made.

There is no such thing as a *wrong* wrong, only a *right* that has gone wrong. Every error had its start in a truth, else it would have no power.

In the moral realm, if you don't do things quickly you will never do them. Never postpone a moral decision.

Second thoughts on moral matters are always deflections.

It is only when a moral act is performed and light thrown on realities that we understand the relationship between our human lives and the cross of Christ.

Personality

Nothing in connection with the personality is so disastrously enervating as disillusionment about ourselves. We much prefer our own ideas of ourselves to the stern realization of what we really are. Paul warns, Let no one "think of himself more highly than he ought to think" (Romans 12:3). Watch how God has disillusioned you over yourself and see the value of it for the future.

There is a difference between the reality of personality and its actuality—the latter is continually changing—you are sensitive now where you were indifferent before, and vice versa.

Individuality can never become a sacrament, it is only personality that can become a sacrament through oneness with Jesus Christ.

You often find people in the world are more desirable, easier to get on with, than people in the kingdom. There is frequently a stubbornness, a self-opinionatedness in Christians not exhibited by people in the world.

If there is to be another revival, it will be through the readjustment of those of us on the inside who call ourselves Christians.

It is obvious that as we have grown physically we have developed into more useful human beings, but have we grown finer morally and spiritually? grown more pure and holy? We may have become broader minded and yet not be so fine in perception as we used to be. It takes a lot of self-scrutiny to know whether we are evolving all the time in every domain of our beings. "Therefore by their fruits you will know them" (Matthew 7:20).

The greatest test of Christianity is the wear and tear of daily life; it is like the shining of silver—the more it is rubbed the brighter it grows.

It is well to remember that our examinations of ourselves can never be unbiased or unprejudiced, so that we are only safe in taking the estimate of ourselves from our Creator instead of from our own introspection, whether conceited or depressed.

The modern Pharisee is the one who pretends to be the publican: "Oh, I would never call myself a saint!" Exaggerated self-depreciation and exaggerated conceit are both diseased.

God has an alchemy of providence by means of which the inner spirit precipitates itself—obliged to be holy if you are holy, obliged to be impure if you are impure. It is impossible to repress the ruling spirit when in the presence of the Spirit of God in another.

Crisis reveals character. When we are put to the test, the hidden resources of our characters are revealed exactly.

We have to do more than we are built to do naturally, we have to do all the Almighty builds us to do.

The phrase "Self-mastery" is profoundly wrong, although practically correct. Profoundly, one can never be master of what one does not understand, therefore one's only master is not oneself or another human being, but God. "Self-mastery" is correct if it means carrying out the edicts of God in myself.

Leave no subject connected with your own soul until you have landed at the door of the supernatural. Natural resources are liable to break down in a crisis, but if your life is based on the supernatural God, His power will manifest itself and turn the moment that might have been tragic into triumph.

Unity of self is difficult to describe; it is the state in which there is no consciousness of myself, only of unity in myself. A false unity is fictitious because at any moment it may fall to pieces in an agony of remorse.

How long it takes for all the powers in a Christian to be at one depends on one thing only, namely, obedience.

The reason self-interest is detected in me is because there are whole tracts of my nature that have never been fused by the Spirit of God into one central purpose.

If all Jesus Christ came to do is to produce disunity in me, He had better never have come, because I am created to have such harmony in myself that I am unconscious of it.

Self-complacency and spiritual pride are always the beginning of degeneration. When I begin to be satisfied with where I am spiritually, instantly I begin to degenerate.

There is no pride equal to spiritual pride, and no obstinacy equal to spiritual obstinacy, because they are nearest to the throne of God and are most like the devil.

It is never our wicked hearts that are the difficulty, but our obstinate wills.

"Show me what to do and I'll do it"—you won't. It is easy to knock down one type of pride and erect another.

The only reason I can't get to God is pride, no matter how humble I seem.

When any personal position is credited by me to myself, God's decree is that it hardens my heart in pride.

The only sacrifice acceptable to God is "a broken and a contrite heart" (Psalm 51:17), not a moral, upright life built on pride. When I stand on the basis of penitence, God's salvation is manifested immediately.

Note the thing that makes you say, "I don't believe it"; it will prove where you are spiritually. What I resent reveals who governs me.

If excellence of character is made the test, the grace of God is made void, because a person can develop an amazing perfection of character without a spark of the grace of God.

If we put a saint or a good woman or a good man as the standard, we blind ourselves to ourselves—personal vanity makes us do it; there is no room for personal vanity when the standard is seen to be God Himself.

To cling to my natural virtues is quite sufficient to obscure the work of God in me.

There is a domain of the nature that we as Christians do not cultivate much, namely, the domain of the imagination. Almost the only way we use our imaginations is in crossing bridges before we come to them. The religion of Jesus embraces every part of human makeup—the intellectual part, the emotional part—no part must be allowed to atrophy, all must be welded into one by the Holy Spirit.

Learn to distinguish between what isolates you and what insulates you. God insulates, sin isolates—a gloomy, sardonic standing off from everything, the disdain of superiority—only when you are closest to God do you understand that that is its nature.

The natural virtues in some people are charming and delightful, but let a presentation of truth be given they have not seen before, and there is an exhibition of the most extraordinary resentment, proving that all their piety was purely temperamental, an unexplored inheritance from ancestors.

It is an appalling fact that our features tell our moral characters unmistakably to those who can read them—and we may be very thankful there are few who can—our safety is in other people's ignorance. In spite of the disguise of refinement, sensuality, selfishness, and self-indulgence speak in our features as loud as a thunderclap. The inner spirit tells with an indelible mark on every feature, no matter how beautiful or how ugly the features may be. Let us remember that that is how God sees us.

Nothing can hinder God's purpose in personal lives but the persons themselves.

In this life we must forgo much in order that we might develop spiritual characters that can be a glory to God for time and eternity.

In His teaching about discipleship, Jesus Christ bases everything on the complete annihilation of individuality and the emancipation of personality. Until this is understood, all our talk about discipleship passes into thin air.

When I am baptized with the Holy Spirit, my personality is lifted up to its right place, namely, into perfect union with God, so that I love Him without hindrance.

Anything that partakes of the nature of swamping my personality out of control is never of God.

Personal Relationship

The essence of Christianity is a personal relationship to Jesus Christ with any amount of room for its outworking.

The appeal of the Gospel is not that it should be preached in order that people might be saved and put right for heaven but that they might enter into a personal relationship with Jesus Christ here and now.

Discipleship and salvation are two different things: disciples are ones who, realizing the meaning of the Atonement, deliberately give themselves up to Jesus Christ in unspeakable gratitude.

The one mark of discipleship is the mastership of Jesus— His right to me from the crown of my head to the sole of my foot.

"If anyone desires to come after Me, let him deny himself" (Matthew 16:24), that is, deny his right to himself. Jesus never swept people off their feet in ecstasy, He always talked on the line that left people's wills in the ascendant until they saw where they were going. It is impossible for me to give up my right to myself without knowing I am doing it.

Naturally, we regard our right to ourselves as the finest thing we have, yet it is the last bridge that prevents Jesus Christ having His way in our lives.

The approaches to Jesus are innumerable, the result of coming to Him can be only one—the dethroning of my right to myself, or I stop short somewhere.

Jesus Christ is always unyielding to my claim to my right to myself.

The one essential element in all our Lord's teaching about discipleship is abandon—no calculation, no trace of self-interest.

Is Jesus Christ absolutely necessary to me? Have I ever shifted the basis of my reasoning on to incarnate reason? ever shifted my will on to His will? my right to myself on to His right to me?

What is the personal history between Jesus Christ and me? Is there anything of the nature of the new creation in me? Or is what I call my "experience" sentimental rubbish placed on top of "me" as I am?

Disciples are those who not only proclaim God's truth, but who manifest that they are no longer their own—they have been bought with a price.

My service is to be a living sacrifice of devotion to Jesus, the secret of which is identity with Him in suffering, in death, and in resurrection (see Philippians 3:10).

It is possible to be first in suffering for the truth and in reputation for saintliness and last in the judgment of the great searcher of hearts. The whole question is one of heart-relationship to Jesus.

If you remain true to your relationship to Jesus Christ, the things that are either right or wrong are never the problem—it is the things that are right but that would impair what He wants you to be that are the problem.

The mark of the saint is the good right things he or she has the privilege of not doing. There are a hundred and one right and good things which, if you are a disciple of Jesus, you must avoid as you would the devil, although there is no devil in them. If our Lord's words in Matthew 5:29–30 were read more often we would have a healthier young manhood and womanhood: "If your right eye causes you to sin, pluck it out and cast it from you; . . . And if your right hand causes you to sin, cut it off and cast it from you; for it is more profitable for you that one of your members perish, than for your whole body to be cast into hell."

Beware of the people who tell you life is simple. Life is such a mass of complications that no one is safe apart from God. Coming to Jesus does not simplify life, it simplifies my relationship to God.

The implicit relationship tells more than the explicit; if you put the explicit first you are apt to produce skeptics.

When Jesus Christ is bringing daughters and sons to glory, He ignores the work they have done, the work has been allowed as a discipline to perfect their relationships to the Father.

The work we do for God is made by Him a means till He has gotten us to the place where we are willing to be purified and made of worth to Him.

Too much organization in Christian work is always in danger of killing God-born originality; it keeps us conservative, makes our hands feeble. A false, artificial flow of progress swamps true devotion to Jesus.

Whenever a spiritual movement has been true to Jesus Christ it has brought forth fruit in a hundred and one ways the originator of the movement never dreamed of.

Neither usefulness nor duty is God's ultimate purpose, His aim is to bring out the message of the Gospel, and if that can only be done by His "bruising" me, why shouldn't He? We put our intelligent fingers on God's plan.

God's idea is that individual Christians should become identified with His purpose for the world. When Christianity becomes overorganized and denominational, it is incapable of fulfilling our Lord's commission; it doesn't feed His sheep—it can't.

"I have had visions on the mount, wonderful times of communion with God"—but is it turning you into an individual infinitely superior to your Lord and Master? one who won't wash feet but will only give yourself up to certain types of meeting?

"If I then, your Lord and Teacher, have washed your feet, you also ought to wash one another's feet" (John 13:14); the highest motive is the only motive for the lowliest service. Where do we stand in God's sight under that scrutiny?

A false religion makes me hyperconscientious: "I must not do this or that"; the one lodestar in the religion of Jesus is personal, passionate devotion to Him and oneness with His interests in other lives. Identify yourself with Jesus Christ's interests in others, and life takes on a romantic risk.

Christianity is not service for Jesus Christ, not winning souls, it is nothing less than the life of Jesus being manifested more and more in my mortal flesh.

Beware of allowing the historic Jesus Christ to be taken from you in any shape or form, make it the most intense concern of your spiritual life to accompany the disciples as He went in and out among them in the days of His flesh.

"What has my religion done for me I could not do for myself?" That is a question every individual is forced to ask. Religion, ostensibly, is faith in someone or a form of belief in some power I would be the poorer if I did not have, and I should be able to state in what way I would be poorer.

If my religion is not based on a personal history with Jesus, it becomes something I suffer from, not a joyous thing, but something that keeps me from doing what I want to do.

Occasionally we have to revise our ways of looking at God's providence. The usual way of looking at it is that God presents us with a cup to drink, which is strangely mixed. But there is another aspect that is just as true, perhaps more vitally true, namely, that we present God with a cup to drink, full of a very strange mixture indeed. God will never reverse the cup. He will drink it. Beware of the ingredient of

self-will, which ought to have been dissolved by identification with the death of Jesus, being there when you hand the
cup of your life back to God.

Prayer

God is never impressed with our earnestness; He promises to answer us when we pray on one ground only, namely, the ground of the redemption. The redemption of the Lord Jesus provides me with a place for intercession.

The only way to get into the relationship of asking is to get into the relationship of absolute reliance on the Lord Jesus. "Now this is the confidence that we have in Him" (1 John 5:14; see verses 14–16).

Remember, you have to ask things that are in keeping with the God whom Jesus Christ reveals. When you pray, what conception have you in your mind—your need, or Jesus Christ's omnipotence? (see John 14:12–13).

Asking in prayer is at once the test of three things: simplicity, stupidity, and certainty of God. Prayer means that I come in contact with an almighty Christ, and almighty results happen along the lines He laid down.

It is not that our prayers are so important, that is not the point; God has so made it that by means of intercession certain types of blessing come upon people. In Christian work that is where the "filling up" comes in; we are apt to bank much more on talking to people.

If I am a Christian, I am not set on saving my own skin but on seeing that the salvation of God comes through me to others, and the great way is by intercession.

The Bible knows nothing about a gift of prayer—the only prayer the Bible talks about is the prayer that is able to bring down something from God to people.

How impatient we are in dealing with other people! Our actions imply that we think God is asleep, until God brings us to the place where we come on them from above.

The illustrations of prayer our Lord uses are on the line of importunity, a steady, persistent, uninterrupted habit of prayer.

God puts us in circumstances where He can answer the prayer of His Son (see John 17) and the prayer of the Holy Spirit (see Romans 8:26).

The reason for intercession is not that God *answers* prayer but that God tells us to pray.

God never answers prayer to prove His own might.

The answers to prayer never come by introspection but always as a surprise. We don't hear God because we are so full of noisy, introspective requests.

Spiritual certainty in prayer is God's certainty, not a side eddy of sanctimony.

Prayer is the vital breath of the Christian—not the thing that makes you alive, but the evidence that you *are* alive.

The very powers of darkness are paralyzed by prayer. No wonder Satan tries to keep our minds fussy in active work till we cannot think to pray.

God is not meant to answer *our* prayers, He is answering the prayer of Jesus Christ in our lives; by our prayers we come to discern what God's mind is, and that is declared in John 17.

According to the New Testament, prayer is God's answer to our poverty, not a power we exercise to obtain an answer.

Intercession does not develop the individual who intercedes, it blesses the lives of those for whom he or she intercedes. The reason so few of us intercede is because we don't understand this.

By intercessory prayer, we can hold off Satan from other

lives and give the Holy Spirit a chance with them. No wonder Jesus put such tremendous emphasis on prayer!

If your crowd knows you as a man or a woman of prayer, they have a right to expect from you a nobler type of conduct than from others.

If I pray that someone else may be or do something that I am not and don't intend to do, my praying is paralyzed.

When you put God first you will get your times of prayer easily, because God can entrust them to the soul who won't use them in an irrational way and give an occasion to the Enemy to enter in.

Watch God's ways in your life, you will find He is developing you as He does the trees and the flowers—a deep, silent working of the God of creation.

The Enemy goes all he can against our communion with God, against our solitude with God; he tries to prevent us from drawing our breath in the fear of the Lord.

The greatest answer to prayer is that I am brought into a perfect understanding with God, and that alters my view of actual things.

We must steadfastly work out repentance in intercessory prayer.

Beware lest activity in proclaiming the truth should mean a cunning avoidance of spiritual concentration in intercession.

The lost sight of God inevitably follows spiritual teaching that has not a corresponding balance of private prayer.

See that you do not use the trick of prayer to cover up what you know you ought to do.

The meaning of prayer is that I bring power to bear upon another soul that is weak enough to yield and strong enough to resist, hence the need for strenuous intercessory prayer.

Never try to make people agree with your point of view, begin the ministry of intercession. The only Being worth agreeing with is the Lord Jesus Christ. Remember 1 John 5:16: "If anyone sees his brother sinning a sin which does not lead to death, he will ask, and He will give him life for those who commit sin not leading to death."

The prayer of the saints is never self-important but always God-important.

What happens when a saint prays is that the Paraclete's almighty power is brought to bear on the one for whom the saint is praying.

God does not give faith in answer to prayer—He reveals Himself in answer to prayer, and faith is exercised spontaneously.

Preaching

A personal testimony feeds you from hand to mouth—you must have more equipment than that if you are to preach the Gospel.

The preacher must be part of the message, must be incorporated in it. That is what the baptism of the Holy Spirit did for the disciples. When the Holy Spirit came at Pentecost, He made these people living epistles of the teaching of Jesus, not human gramophones recording the facts of His life.

If you stand true as a disciple of Jesus, He will make your preaching the kind of message that is incarnate as well as oral.

To preach the Gospel makes *you* a sacrament, but if the Word of God has not become incorporated into you, your preaching is a clanging cymbal—it has never cost you anything, never taken you through repentance and heartbreak.

We have not to explain how people come to God instead of bringing people to God—that hinders—an explanation of the Atonement never drew anyone to God, the exalting of Jesus Christ, and Him crucified, does draw people to God (see John 12:32).

Remember, you go among people as a representative of Jesus Christ.

The preacher's duty is not to convict people of sin or to make them realize how bad they are, but to bring them into contact with God until it is easy for them to believe in Him.

Nobody is ever the same after listening to the truth; you may say you pay no attention to it, you may appear to forget all about it, but at any moment the truth may spring up into your consciousness and destroy all your peace of mind.

The great snare in Christian work is this—"Do remember the people you are talking to." We have to remain true to God and His message, not to a knowledge of the people, and as we rely on the Holy Spirit we will find God works His marvels in His own way.

Live in the reality of the truth while you preach it.

Most of us prefer to live in a particular phase of the truth, and that is where we get intolerant and pigheaded, religiously determined that everyone who does not agree with us must be wrong. We preach in the name of God what He won't own!

God's denunciation will fall on us if in our preaching we tell people they must be holy and we ourselves are not holy. If we are not working out in our private lives the messages we are handing out, we will deepen the condemnation of our own souls as messengers of God.

Our message acts like a boomerang—it is dangerous if it does not.

A good, clear, emotional expression contains within it the peril of satisfactory expression while the life is miles away from the preaching. The life of a preacher speaks louder than the words.

There is no use condemning sensuality or worldly-mindedness and compromise in other people if there is the slightest inclination for these in our own souls.

It is all very well to preach, the easiest thing in the world to give people a vision of what God wants; it is another matter to come into the sordid conditions of ordinary life and make the vision real there.

Beware of hypocrisy with God, especially if you are in no danger of hypocrisy among people.

Penetration attracts hearers to God, ingenuity attracts to the preacher. Dexterity is always an indication of shallowness.

A clever exposition is never right, because the Spirit of God is not clever. Beware of cleverness, it is the great cause of hypocrisy in a preacher.

Don't be impatient with yourself, because the longer you are in satisfying yourself with an expression of the truth the better will you satisfy God.

Impressive preaching is rarely Gospel preaching: Gospel preaching is based on the great mystery of belief in the Atonement, which belief is created in others not by my impressiveness but by the insistent conviction of the Holy Spirit.

There is far more wrought by the Word of God than we will ever understand, and if I substitute anything for it—fine thinking, eloquent speech—the devil's victory is enormous, but I am of no more use than a puff of wind.

The determination to be a fool, if necessary, is the golden rule for a preacher.

We have to preach something that to the wisdom of this world is foolishness. If the wisdom of this world is right, then God is foolish; if God is wise, the wisdom of this world is foolishness (see 1 Corinthians 1:18–25). Where we go wrong is when we apologize for God.

If you are standing for the truth of God you are sure to experience reproach, and if you open your mouth to vindicate yourself you will lose what you were on the point of gaining. Let the ignominy and the shame come, be weak in Him.

Never assume anything that has not been made yours by faith and the experience of life—it is presumptuous to do so. On the other hand, be ready to pay the price of "foolishness" in proclaiming to others what is really yours.

People only want the kind of preaching that does not declare the demands of a holy God. "Tell us that God is loving, not that He is holy and that He demands we should be holy." The problem is not with the gross sinners but with the intellectual, cultured, religious-to-the-last-degree people.

All the winsome preaching of the Gospel is an insult to the cross of Christ. What is needed is the probe of the Spirit of God straight down to a person's conscience till the person's whole nature shouts at her or at him, "That is right, and *you* are wrong."

It is the preacher's contact with reality that enables the Holy Spirit to strip off the sophistries of those who listen, and when He does that, you find it is the best people who go down first under conviction.

A great psychological law too little known is that the line of appeal is conditioned by the line of attraction. If I seek to attract people, that will be the line on which my aggressive work will have to be done.

To whom is our appeal? To none but those God sends you to. You can't get people to come—nobody could get you to come until you came. "The wind blows where it wishes. . . . So is everyone who is born of the Spirit" (John 3:8).

Many of the theological terms used nowadays have no grip; we talk glibly about sin and about salvation, but let the truth be presented along the line of an individual's deep, personal need, and at once it is arresting.

Some of us are rushing on at such a headlong pace in Christian work, wanting to vindicate God in a great revival, but if God gave a revival we would be the first to forget Him and swing off on some false fire.

"Not lagging in diligence" (Romans 12:11), that is, diligent in the Lord's business. Don't exhaust yourself with other things.

Beware, as of the devil, of good taste being your standard in presenting the truth of God.

"Therefore, from now on, we regard no one according to the flesh" (2 Corinthians 5:16); that is the way we do know people—according to our commonsense estimates. We who know

God have no right to estimate other people according to our commonsense judgments, we have to bring in revelation facts that will make us a great deal more lenient in our judgments. To have a little bit, only, of God's point of view makes us immensely bitter in our judgments.

Beware lest your reserve in public has the effect of God almighty's decree to the sea: "This far you may come, but no farther" (Job 38:11). I have no business in God's service if I have any personal reserve, I am to be broken bread and poured-out wine in His hands.

If you are living a life of reckless trust in God, the impression given to your congregation is that of the reserve power of God, while personal reserve leaves the impression that you are condescending to them.

We should give instruction unconsciously; if you give instruction consciously, in a dictatorial mood, you simply flatter your own spiritual conceit.

Have you never met anyone whose religious life is so exact that you are terrified at coming near the person? Never have an exercise of religion that blots God clean out.

Remember two things: be natural yourself, and let God be naturally Himself through you. Very few of us have gotten to the place of being worthily natural, any number of us are unworthily natural—that is, we reveal the fact that we have never taken the trouble to discipline ourselves.

Don't be discouraged if you suffer from physical aphasia, the only cure for it is to go ahead, remembering that nervousness overcome is power.

Beware of being disappointed with yourself in delivery, ignore the record of your nerves.

Learn to be vicarious in public prayer. Allow two rivers to come through you: the river of God and the river of human interests. Beware of the danger of preaching in prayer, of being doctrinal.

When you preach, you speak for God and from God to the people; in prayer, you talk to God for the people, and your proper place is among the people as one of them. It is to be a vicarious relation, not the flinging of theology at their heads from the pulpit.

Always come from God to people—never be so impertinent as to come from the presence of anyone else.

How do interruptions affect you? If you allot your day and say, "I am going to give so much time to this, and so much to that," and God's providence upsets your timetable, what becomes of your spirituality? Why, it flies out of the window! It is not based on God, there is nothing spiritual about it, it is purely mechanical. The great secret is to learn how to draw on God all the time.

Whenever you are discovered as being exhausted, take a good, humiliating dose of John 21:15–17. The whole secret of shepherding is that someone else reaches the Savior through your heart as a pathway.

Beware of making God's truth simpler than He has made it Himself.

By the preaching of the Gospel, God creates what was never there before, namely, faith in Himself on the ground of the redemption.

People say, "Do preach the simple Gospel"; if they mean by "the simple Gospel" the thing we have always heard, the thing that keeps us sound asleep, then the sooner God sends a thrust through our stagnant minds the better.

If anyone's preaching does not make me brace myself up and watch my feet and my ways, one of two things is the reason—either the preacher is unreal, or I hate being better.

A joyous, humble belief in your message will compel attention.

Sermons may weary, the Gospel never does.

Preparation

It is by thinking with your pen in hand that you will get to the heart of your subject.

"The heart of the righteous studies how to answer" (Proverbs 15:28). To give your congregation extemporaneous thinking, that is, thinking without study, is an insult—ponderous nothings. Preachers should give their congregations the result of strenuous thinking in unstudied, extemporaneous speech.

Extemporaneous speech is not extemporaneous thinking, but speech that has been so studied that you are possessed unconsciously with what you are saying.

Never get a studied form; prepare yourself mentally, morally, and spiritually, and you need never fear.

The great thing is not to hunt for texts but to live in the big, comprehensive truths of the Bible, and texts will hunt you.

To talk about "getting a message," is a mistake. It is preparation of myself that is required more than of my message.

Don't go to your Bible in a yawning mood.

As a student of the Word of God, keep your mind and heart busy with the great truths concerning God, the Lord Jesus Christ, the Holy Spirit, the Atonement, sin, suffering, and the like.

Slay on the threshold of your mind the thing that makes you sit down mentally and say, "I can't." Why be saved and sanctified in a rusty, indolent case?

In impromptu speaking, begin naturally, and the secret of beginning naturally is to forget you are religious. Many wear a crushing religious garb.

Beware of detaching yourself from your theme in order to heed the way you present it. Never be afraid of expressing what is really you.

To develop your expression in public you must do a vast amount of writing in private. Write out your problems before God. Go direct to Him about everything

Time spent on the great, fundamental revelations given by the Holy Spirit is apt to be looked upon as a waste of time—"We must get to practical work."

The work we do in preparation is meant to get our minds into such order that they are at the service of God for His inspiration.

Conscious inspiration is mercifully rare, or we would make inspiration our god.

Don't chisel your subject too much. Trust the reality of your nature and the reality of your subject.

The discipline of your own powers is a very precious acquirement in the service of God; it delivers you from breathless uncertainty and possible hysterics. Learn to respect the findings of your own mind.

Always check private delight in preparation. Close your preparation with prayer and leave it with God till wanted.

When you speak, abandon yourself in confidence, don't try to recall fine points in preparation.

The burning heart while Jesus talks with us and opens up the Scriptures to us is a blessed experience, but the burning heart will die down to ashes unless we keep perennially right with God.

Spiritual insight is in accordance with the development of heart purity.

Every domain of our lives that comes under the apprehension of the Spirit of God is a call to cultivate that particular domain for Him. The trouble is that we won't break up the new soil of our lives for God.

Spiritual sloth must be the greatest grief to the Holy Spirit. Sloth has always a moral reason, not a physical one—the self-indulgent nature must be slothful.

Learn to fast over your subject in private, do the mechanical work, and trust God for the inspirational in delivery.

Don't memorize what you have to say or you will serve up *"cauld kale het"!* [Scottish phrase—kale, a strong-tasting vegetable, is almost inedible if reheated the day after it's cooked, thus, metaphorically, something reheated that should have been thrown out]

In order to expound a passage, live in it well beforehand.

Keep yourself full with reading. Reading gives you a vocabulary.

Don't read to remember, read to realize.

Speakers without notes must have two things entirely at their command—the Bible and their mother tongue.

In impromptu speaking, never try to recall, always plunge.

Let the center of your subject grip you, then you will express its heart unconsciously.

Get moved by your message, and it will move others in a corresponding way.

Watch how God by His angels elbows you out of the hour you thought you were going to get with your Bible—only you will never call them "angels" unless you are filled with the Holy Spirit. That objectionable person was really an angel of God to you, saying "Get this thing worked out."

Redemption

God does not ask us to be good men and good women, He asks us to understand that we are not good, to believe that "No one is good but One, that is, God" (Matthew 19:17), and that the grace of God was manifested in the redemption that it might cover human incompleteness.

When people experience salvation it is not their belief that saves them—teaching goes wrong when it puts a person's belief as the ground of his or her salvation. Salvation is God's "bit" entirely.

The danger is to preach a subjective theology, something that wells up on the inside. The Gospel of the New Testament is based on the absoluteness of the redemption.

The great thing about the redemption is that it deals with *sin,* that is, my claim to my right to myself, not primarily with people's sins. It is one of the most flattering things to go and rescue the degraded, one of the social passions of humankind, but not necessarily the most Christian; it is quite another thing to tell people who are among the best of society that what Jesus Christ asks of them is that they give up the right to themselves to Him.

The great thing about the Gospel is that it should be preached. Never get distressed over not seeing immediate results. No prophets of the Old Testament or apostles of the New (or saints of the present day), ever fully understood the import of what they said or did, hence to work for immediate results is to make myself a director of the Holy Spirit.

God is no respecter of persons with regard to salvation, but He has a tremendous respect for Christian character.

There are degrees in glory that are determined by our obedience.

Salvation is a free gift through the redemption; positions in the kingdom are not gifts but attainments.

There is a difference between salvation and saintliness, between being redeemed and proving myself a redeemed individual. I may live a life of sordid self-seeking on the basis of the redemption, or I may live a life that manifests the life of the Lord Jesus in my mortal flesh (see 2 Corinthians 4:11).

Jesus Christ did not send out the disciples to save souls but to make disciples, men and women who manifest lives in accordance with the life of their Redeemer.

A charge made against some methods of evangelism is that self-interest is made the basis of the whole thing: salvation is looked upon as a kind of insurance scheme whereby I am delivered from punishment and put right for heaven. But let people experience *deliverance from sin,* and their rejoicing is not in their own interests, but that they are thereby enabled to be of use to God and other people.

The bedrock, permanent thing about Christianity is the forgiveness of God, not sanctification and personal holiness—the great abiding thing underneath is infinitely more rugged than that—it is all the New Testament means by that terrific word *forgiveness.* "In Him we have redemption through His blood, the forgiveness of sins" (Ephesians 1:7).

The virtue of our redemption comes to us through the obedience of the Son of God: "though He was a Son, yet He learned obedience by the things which He suffered" (Hebrews 5:8). Our view of obedience has become so distorted through sin that we cannot understand how it could be said of Jesus that He "learned" obedience; He was the only One of whom it could be said, because He was without sin. He did not learn obedience in order *to be* a Son, He came *as* Son to redeem humankind.

Our Lord came to make atonement for the sin of the world not by any impulse of a noble nature but by the perfect, conscious Self-sacrifice whereby alone God could redeem humankind.

Beware of the craze for unity. It is God's will that all Christians should be one with Him as Jesus Christ is one with Him (see John 17:22), but that is a very different thing from the tendency abroad today toward a unity on a basis that ignores the Atonement.

Until we have become spiritual by new birth, the atonement of Jesus has no meaning for us; it only begins to get meaning when we live "in the heavenly places in Christ Jesus" (Ephesians 2:6).

Salvation is based on the *revelation* fact that God has redeemed the world from the possibility of condemnation on account of sin (see Romans 5:12, 20–21), the *experience* of salvation means that we can be regenerated, can have the disposition of the Son of God put into us, namely, the Holy Spirit.

Belief in the redemption is difficult because it needs self-surrender first.

Do I believe that everything that has been touched by the consequences of human sin is going to be put absolutely right by God through the redemption? Redemption is the reality that alters inability into ability.

The mighty redemption of God is made actual in my experience by the living efficacy of the Holy Spirit.

Sanctification

Beware of preaching sanctification without knowing Jesus—
we are saved and sanctified in order that we might know
Him.

"Of Him you are in Christ Jesus, who became for us wisdom from God—and righteousness and sanctification and
redemption" (1 Corinthians 1:30). Jesus Christ is all these,
they are not things He works out apart from Himself.

We cannot earn things from God, we can only take what
is given us. Salvation, sanctification, eternal life are all gifts
wrought out in us through the Atonement. The question is,
am I working out what God works in?

It is quite true to say, "I can't live a holy life," but you can
decide to let Jesus make you holy. "I can't do away with my
past," but you can decide to let Jesus do away with it. That is
the issue to push.

We use the word *consecration* before sanctification—it
should be used after sanctification. The fundamental meaning
of consecration is the separating of a holy thing to God, not
the separating of an unholy thing to be made holy.

"Present your bodies a living sacrifice, holy, acceptable to
God," says the apostle Paul (Romans 12:1). You cannot separate to God what God has not purified.

If I make personal holiness a cause instead of an effect, I
become shallow, no matter how profound I seem. It means I
am far more concerned about being "speckless" than about
being real, far more concerned about keeping my garments
white than about being devoted to Jesus Christ.

The idea that I grow holy as I go on is foreign to the New Testament. There must have been a place where I was identified with the death of Jesus: "I have been crucified with Christ" (Galatians 2:20). That is the meaning of sanctification. Then I grow *in* holiness.

Jesus Christ can make my disposition as pure as His own. That is the claim of the Gospel.

The saints have gone to sleep—"Thank God, I am saved and sanctified, it is all right now." You are simply in the right place to maintain the life that is going to confront the world and never be subdued by the world.

"Now I am sanctified the world has no attraction for me." But remember, the world is what the Holy Spirit sees, not what you see. It is not gross sins that are the attraction, but things that are part of God's creation, things "in the land of Canaan"; they creep in gradually and you begin to think according to pagan standards and only in a crisis realize you have not been standing with God.

God has staked His reputation on the work of Jesus Christ in the souls of the men and women whom He has saved and sanctified.

If we are to be of any use to God in facing present-day problems we must be prepared to run the sanctification-metaphysic for all it is worth.

The great fever in people's blood today is, "Do something"; "Be practical." The great need is for the one who is impractical enough to get down to the heart of the matter, namely, personal sanctification. Practical work not based on an understanding of what sanctification means is simply beating the air.

The test of sanctification is not our talk about holiness and singing pious hymns, but what are we like where no one sees us? with those who know us best?

It is perilously possible to credit God with all our mean little prejudices, even after we are sanctified.

Pious talk paralyzes the power to live piously, the energy of the life goes into the talk—sanctimonious instead of sanctified. Unless your mind is free from jealousy, envy, spite, your pious words only increase your hypocrisy.

Beware of sentimentality, it means something has been aroused in me that I don't intend to work out.

Wherever there is true teaching of the Gospel, there will be both salvation and sanctification taking place.

If you are called to preach, God will put you through "mills" that are not meant for you personally—He is making you suitable bread to nourish other lives. It is after sanctification you are put through these things.

If I exalt sanctification, I preach people into despair, but if I lift up Jesus Christ, people learn the way to be made holy. "I determined not to know anything among you except Jesus Christ and Him crucified" (1 Corinthians 2:2).

It is a great snare to think that when you are sanctified you cannot make mistakes; you can make mistakes so irreparably terrible that the only safeguard is to walk in the light, as God is in the light.

When you come under the searchlight of God after sanctification, you realize much more keenly what sin is than ever you could have done before.

The deliverances of God are not what the saints delight in, but in the fact that *God* delivered them; not in the fact that they are sanctified but that *God* sanctified them; the whole attention of their minds is on God

We are saved and sanctified, not for service, but to be absolutely Jesus Christ's; the consuming passion of the life is for Him.

Never try to build sanctification on an unconfessed sin, on a duty left undone; confess the wrong, do what you ought to have done, then God will clear away all the hyperconscientious rubbish.

In sanctification, it has to be a valediction once and for-ever to confidence in everyone and everything but God.

You can always test the worth of your sanctification. If there is the slightest trace of self-conscious superiority about it, it has never touched the fringe of the garment of Christ.

"I lay down My life," said Jesus; "I lay it down of Myself" (John 10:17–18). If you are sanctified, you will do the same. It has nothing to do with "Deeper Death to Self," it has to do with the glorious fact that I have a self, a personality, that I can sacrifice with glad alacrity to Jesus every day I live.

Sin

Sin is not humanity's problem, it is God's.

Beware of attempting to diagnose sin unless you have the inner pang that you are one of the worst sinners.

Whenever you talk about sin, it must be "my" sin. So long as you speak of "sins" you evade Jesus Christ for yourself.

Sin is the outcome of a relationship God never ordained, a relationship that maintains itself by means of a wrong disposition, namely, my claim to my right to myself. That is the essence of sin.

My right to myself is not merely something I claim, but something that continually makes me insist on my own way.

Whenever God touches sin, it is independence that is touched, and that awakens resentment in the human heart. Independence must be blasted clean out, there must be no such thing left, only freedom, which is very different. Freedom is the ability not to insist on my rights but to see that God gets His.

There are people whose actual lives shock us, and there are those whose actual lives are "speckless"—but whose ruling disposition is "my claim to my right to myself." Watch Jesus Christ with them both, and you get the attitude we have lost.

Jesus Christ never faced people as we do; you may put before Him publicans and sinners and clean-living moral people, and you find He is much sterner with the latter. To recognize this would mean a revolution in outlook.

Original sin is doing without God. That phrase covers sin in its beginning in human consciousness and its final analysis in the sight of God.

"For from within, out of the heart of men, proceed . . ." (see Mark 7:21–23). We should get into the habit of estimating ourselves by the rugged statements of our Lord.

The thing that makes me feel I am different from the common herd never came from God—I am not different. Remember, the same stuff that makes the criminal makes the saint.

A saint is a new creation, made by the Last Adam out of the progeny of the First Adam, no matter how degraded.

"Christ Jesus came into the world to save sinners" (1 Timothy 1:15). What is a sinner? Everyone who is not one with Jesus as He is one with God.

Our Lord did not scathe sin, He came to save from it.

We are apt to put the superb blessings of the Gospel as something for a special few—they are for sinners saved by grace.

People may be magnificently saved and appallingly backward in development, or they may be maturely developed saints, like the apostle Paul, but neither is more than saved by God's grace.

When Jesus Christ begins to get His way, He is merciless with the thing that is not of God.

As long as things are kept covered up we think God's judgment is severe, but let the Holy Spirit reveal the secret vileness of sin till it blazes out in a conspicuous glare, and we realize that His judgment is right.

The reason people enclose themselves away from the Gospel is that conviction of sin upsets the inner balance of mind, consequently of bodily health, but when once they are convinced that holiness is of more importance than bodily health, they let all go to get holy.

The first appeal of present-day evangelism is apt to be

not on the line of how to get rid of sin but how to be put right for heaven, consequently people are not convicted of sin but left with a feeling of something insufficient in life.

The only hope for people lies not in giving them an example of how to behave but in the preaching of Jesus Christ as the Savior from *sin*. The hearts of all get hope when they hear that.

Our Lord never sympathized with sin, He came "to proclaim liberty to the captives" (Isaiah 61:1; Luke 4:18), a very different thing. We have to see that we don't preach a theology of sympathy but the theology of a Savior from sin.

It is not our business to convict people of sin, the Holy Spirit alone convicts of sin; our duty is to lift up the One who sets free from sin. It is not a question of something being curbed or counteracted or sat on, it is a radical alteration on the inside, then I have to assimilate that alteration so that it is manifested in the practical relationships of my life.

The life of the Holy Spirit in a saint is fierce and violent against any tendency to sin.

The attitude of Jesus toward *sin* is to be our attitude toward *sins*.

When conviction of sin by the Holy Spirit comes, it gives us an understanding of the deeps of our personalities we are otherwise not conscious of (see John 16:8–11).

The forgiveness of God penetrates to the very heart of His nature and to the very heart of human nature. That is why God cannot forgive until a man or a woman realizes what sin is.

Sin is reality, sins are actuality.

Measure your growth in grace by your sensitivity to sin.

Many people get to the place where they will call themselves sinners, but they do not so readily come to the place where they say, "Against You, You only, have I sinned" (Psalm 51:4).

Salvation from sin is frequently confounded with deliverance from sins. One can deliver oneself from sins without any special work of God's grace. The bedrock of New Testament salvation is repentance, and repentance is based on relationship to a person.

A great many people are delighted to hear about the life of Jesus—its holiness and sublimity—but when the Holy Spirit begins to convict them of sin, they resent it and resent it deeply.

Conviction of sin in the beginning is child's play compared with the conviction the Holy Spirit brings to a mature saint (see 1 Timothy 1:15).

Humiliation by conviction of sin is rare today. You can never be humiliated by another human being after the conviction of sin the Holy Spirit gives.

On the threshold of the Christian life people talk a lot about sin, but there is no realization of what sin is, all that is seen is the effects of sin.

If we are ever going to come anywhere near understanding what our Lord's agony in the Garden of Gethsemane represents, we have to get beyond the small ideas of our particular religious experiences and be brought to see sin as God sees it: "For He made Him who knew no sin to be sin for us, that we might become the righteousness of God in Him" (2 Corinthians 5:21).

If we eliminate the supernatural purpose of Jesus Christ's coming, namely, to deliver us from sin, we become traitors to God's revelation.

The cross of Christ is God's last and endless Word. There the prince of this world is judged, there sin is killed and pride is done to death, there lust is frozen and self-interest slaughtered—not one can get through.

It was not social crimes but the great, primal sin of independence of God that brought the Son of God to Calvary.

Study

Study, to begin with, can never be easy, the determination to form systematic mental habits is the only secret. Don't begin anything with reluctance.

Beware of any cleverness that keeps you from working. No one is born a worker; people are born poets and artists, but we have to make ourselves "laborers."

The discipline of our minds is the one domain God has put in our keeping. It is impossible to be of any use to God if we are lazy. God won't cure laziness—we have to cure it.

More danger arises from physical laziness (which is called "brain fag") than from almost any other thing.

Inspiration won't come irrespective of study but only because of it. Don't trust to inspiration, use your own "axe" (see Psalm 74:5). Work! Think! Don't luxuriate on the mount!

The demand for inspiration is the measure of our laziness. Do the things that don't come by inspiration.

It is difficult to get yourself under control to do work you are not used to—the time spent seems wasted at first, but get at it again. The thing that hinders control is impulse.

Your mind can never be under your control unless you bring it there, there is no gift for control. You may pray till doomsday, but your brain will never concentrate if you don't make it concentrate.

In the most superficial matters put yourself under control, your own control. Be as scrupulously punctual in your private habits as you would be in a government office.

Don't insult God by telling Him He forgot to give you any brains when you were born. We all have brains—what we need is *work*.

It is better for your mental life to study several subjects at once rather than one alone. What exhausts the brain is not using it but abusing it by nervous waste in other directions. As a general rule, the brain can never do too much.

You can never work by impulse, you can only work by steady, patient plod. It is the odd five minutes that tells.

To learn a thing is different from thinking out a problem. The only way to learn a thing is to keep at it uninterruptedly, day after day, whether you feel like it or not, and you will wake up one morning and find the thing is learned.

Beware of succumbing to failure as inevitable—make it the stepping-stone to success.

In beginning to study a new subject you do it by repeated starts until you get your mind into a certain channel, after that the subject becomes full of sustained interest.

Beware of mental lounging. Whenever we see notebooks for study or work of any kind waiting to be done, we either go into dreamland or we gather everything around us in an enormously bustling style, but we never do good, solid work. It is nothing in the world but a habit of nerves, which we have to check and take time to see that we do.

A subject has never truly gripped you until you are mentally out of breath with it.

We have no business to go on impulses spiritually, we have to form "this mind . . . which was also in Christ Jesus" (Philippians 2:5). People say their impulses are their guides—"I feel impelled to do this or that"—that may be sufficient indication that they should not do it.

Remember, there must always be a mechanical outlet for spiritual inspiration.

I infect my surroundings with my own personal character. If I make my study a place of stern industry, it will act as an inspiration every time I go into it, but if I am lazy there, the place will revenge itself on me.

Note two things about your intelligence: first, when your intelligence feels numb, quit at once, and play or sleep—for the time being the brain must recuperate; second, when you feel a fidget of associated ideas, take yourself sternly in hand and say, "You shall study, so it's no use whining."

Mental stodge is different. Mental stodge is the result of one of three forms of overfeeding—too much dinner, too much reading, or too many meetings.

Irritation may be simply the result of not using your brain. Remember, the brain gets exhausted when it is not doing anything.

Beware of saying, "I haven't time to read the Bible or to pray"; say rather, "I haven't disciplined myself to do these things."

Before any habit is formed, you must put yourself under mechanical laws of obedience, and the higher the emotion started by the Spirit of God, the keener must be the determination to commit yourself.

If we have no system of work, we shall easily come to think we are working when we are only thinking of working, that we are busy when we are only engaged.

The more we talk about work, the less we work, and the same with prayer.

We must be willing to do in the spiritual domain what we have to do in the natural domain if we want to develop, namely, discipline ourselves.

Vision is an inspiration to stand us in good stead in the drudgery of discipline; the temptation is to despise the discipline.

Enchain your body to habitual obedience.

Beware of being haunted by a suppressed dissatisfaction with the arrangements of your actual life—*get* the right program! The secret of slacking is just here.

The Teaching of Jesus

Our Lord did not come to this earth to teach people to be holy, He came to make people holy, and His teaching is applicable only on the basis of experimental redemption.

The teaching of Jesus is not first; what *is* first is that He came to give us a totally new heredity, and the Sermon on the Mount describes the way that heredity will work out.

A good way to find out how much stodge there is in our spiritual lives is to read the Sermon on the Mount and see how obtuse we are to the greater part of what Jesus Christ taught.

There is a calm deliberation about the injunctions in the Sermon on the Mount, we are not asked to obey them until the Holy Spirit brings them to remembrance; when He does, the question is, will I exercise the disposition given me in regeneration and react in my actual life in accordance with the mind of Christ?

Weighing the pros and cons for and against a statement of Jesus Christ's means that for the time being I refuse to obey Him.

We are never justified in taking any line of action other than that indicated by the teaching of Jesus and made possible for us by the grace of God.

Our Lord's teaching does not mean anything to someone until it does, and then it means everything.

Make your mind sure of what our Lord taught, and then insist and reinsist on it to the best of your ability.

Distortions of belief come because principles are put in the place of Jesus Christ. I must have a personal relationship to Him first and then let the Holy Spirit apply His teaching.

Nothing must switch the disciple's loyalty to our Lord by loyalty to principles deduced from His teaching.

There are no infallible principles, only an infallible person.

All my devotion is an insult to God unless every bit of my practical life squares with Jesus Christ's demands.

Beware of being negligent in some lesser thing while being good in some spiritual thing, for example, you may be good in a prayer meeting while not good in the matter of cleaning your boots. It is a real peril and springs from selecting some one thing our Lord taught as our standard, instead of God Himself.

Matthew 5:48 is the standard for the Christian: "Therefore you shall be perfect, just as your Father in heaven is perfect." Size yourself up with a good sense of humor, "me, perfect!" That is what Jesus Christ has undertaken to do.

The religion of Jesus is morality transfigured by spirituality, we have to be moral right down to the depths of our motives.

It cannot be too often emphasized that our Lord never asks us to do other than all that good, upright people do, but He does ask that we do just those same things from an entirely different motive: "Unless your righteousness exceeds the righteousness of the scribes and Pharisees, you will by no means enter the kingdom of heaven" (Matthew 5:20).

We should make less excuse for the weakness of a Christian than for anyone else. A Christian has God's honor at stake.

When we are regenerated and bear the name of Christ, the Spirit of God will see to it that we are scrutinized by the world, and the more we are able to meet that scrutiny the healthier will we be as Christians.

Civilized organizations were never more deadly opposed to the teaching of Jesus than in the present age.

Whenever an organization begins to be conscious of itself, its spiritual power goes, because it is living for its own propaganda. Movements that were started by the Spirit of God have crystallized into something God has had to blight, because the golden rule for spiritual work has been departed from (see John 12:24).

"I did not come to destroy but to fulfill" (Matthew 5:17). Our Lord was not anti-anything, He put into existing institutions a ruling principle that, if obeyed, would reconstruct them.

If you have never been brought close enough to Jesus to realize that He teaches things that grossly offend you as a "natural man," I question whether you have ever seen Him.

As soon as you get out of touch with God, you are in a hell of chaos. That is always in the background of the teaching of Jesus (compare Matthew 5:21–26). That is why the teaching of Jesus produces such consternation in the natural man.

Whenever a truth comes home to me, my first reaction is to fling it back on you, but the Spirit of God brings it straight home: "You are the one." We always want to lash others when we are sick with our own disobedience.

The scrutiny we give other people should be for ourselves. You will never be able to cast out the plank in someone else's eye unless you have had a beam removed, or to be removed, from your own eye (see Matthew 7:3–4).

It is perilously possible to do one of two things—bind burdens on people you have no intention of helping them lift, or placidly to explain away the full purport of our Lord's teaching (see Luke 11:46).

Divorced from supernatural new birth, the teaching of Jesus has no application to me, it only results in despair.

Our Lord's teaching about the maimed life and the mature life has not been sufficiently recognized. You can never be mature unless you have been fanatical (see Matthew 5:29–30, 48).

"Whoever compels you to go one mile, go with him two" (Matthew 5:41). If you are a saint, the Lord will tax your walking capacity to the limit.

It is a slow business teaching a community living below the Christian level; I have to act according to the Christian ethic while not ignoring the fact that I am dealing with a community that lives away below it. The fact that I live with a degenerate crowd does not alter my duty, I have to behave as a disciple of Jesus.

Temptation

To be raised above temptation belongs to God only.

Wherever there is moral responsibility there is temptation, that is, the testing of what one holds in one's own person.

The old Puritan idea that the devil tempts people had this remarkable effect: it produced people of iron who fought; the modern idea of blaming people's heredity or their circumstances produces people who succumb at once.

When we say a thing is "satanic," we mean something abominable according to our standards; the Bible means something remarkably subtle and wise. Satanic temptations are not bestial—those temptations have to do with an individual's own stupidity and wrongdoing.

The Holy Spirit is the only One who can detect the temptations of Satan, neither our common sense nor our human wisdom can detect them as temptations.

Every temptation of Satan is the acme of human wisdom, but as soon as the Spirit of God is at work in someone, the hollow mockery at its heart is recognized.

Jesus Christ deals with Satan as the manifestation of something for which humanity is held responsible. Humanity is nowhere held responsible for the devil.

The temptation in Christian work today is to turn our sympathies toward human beings, "Put people's needs first." No, sympathy with God first—let Him work as He will.

If you allow human sympathy to make you susceptible to the satanic side of things, you instantly sever yourself from the susceptibility that in all temptation ought to be turned Godward.

Our Lord's words to Peter, "Get behind Me, Satan! You are an offense to Me, for you are not mindful of the things of God, but the things of men" (Matthew 16:23), crystallize for us His authoritative view of the conclusions of the human mind, when that mind has not been formed by the Holy Spirit, namely, that it is densely and satanically incapable of understanding His form of thought.

Satan does not tempt to gross sins—the one thing he tempts to is putting myself as master instead of God.

Beware of removing our Lord into a religious wardrobe where the cast-off halos of the saints are kept, but remember that "we do not have a High Priest who cannot sympathize with our weaknesses, but was in all points tempted as we are, yet without sin" (Hebrews 4:15; compare 2:11).

How are we to face the Tempter? By prayer? No. With the Word of God? No. Face the Tempter with Jesus Christ, and He will apply the Word of God to you, and the temptation will cease. "For in that He Himself has suffered, being tempted, He is able to aid those who are tempted" (2:18).

The moments of severest temptation are the moments of His most divine succor.

Testimony

It is never our testimonies that keep our experiences right—our experiences make us testify.

To testify is part of the life of every Christian, but because you have a personal testimony it does not follow that you are called to preach.

To say what God has done for you is testimony, but you have to preach more than you have experienced—more than anyone has ever experienced—you have to preach Jesus Christ. Present the object of your faith, the Lord Jesus, lift Him up, and then either give your testimony or know you have one to give.

To say a thing is the sure way to begin to believe it. That is why it is so necessary to testify to what Jesus Christ has done for you.

The false mood creeps in when you have the idea that you are to be a written epistle—of course you are! but you have not to know it.

Whenever you meet anyone who is going on with God, you find his or her testimony explains your own experience. A true testimony grips everyone who is after the truth.

It is easier to stand true to a testimony mildewed with age—because it has a dogmatic ring about it that people agree with—than to talk from your last moment of contact with God.

Am I trying to live up to a testimony, or am I abiding in the truth?

The danger of experience meetings, when they get outside the New Testament standard, is that people don't testify to anything that glorifies God but to experiences that leave you breathless and embarrassed. It is all on the illuminated line, on the verge of the hysterical.

People are precipitated into testifying before the vision they have had is made real; "Now I have had this experience," or, "Now I have become that." What we need to do after the vision is to examine ourselves before God and see if we are willing for all that must happen before it is made real in us.

When we get the vision of what God wants us to be, we are put to the blush by what we actually are, and that humiliation is the precursor of the coming reality, a heart-panging disgust at the realization of what we are. That is what the Holy Spirit works in us, a disgust that will end in nothing less than death, then God can begin to make the vision real.

Never give an educated testimony, that is, something you have taught yourself to say, wait till the elemental moves in you.

Be prepared to be unreserved in personal testimony, but remember, personal testimony must never be lowered into personal biography.

You cannot bring a knowledge of Jesus Christ to others, you can only tell them what He is to you, but until they get where you are, they will never see what you see.

If my testimony makes anyone wish to emulate me, it is a mistaken testimony, it is not a witness to Jesus.

The Holy Spirit will only witness to a testimony when Jesus Christ is exalted higher than the testimony.

Thinking

"For what man knows the things of a man except the spirit of the man which is in him?" (1 Corinthians 2:11). People discover intellectual things for themselves, but they cannot discover God by human intellect. "Even so no one knows the things of God except the Spirit of God" (verse 11).

Think of the labor and patience of people in the domain of science, and then think of our lack of patience in endeavoring to appreciate the Atonement, and you see the need there is for us to be conscientious in our thinking, basing everything on the reality of the Atonement. We prefer to be average Christians—we don't mind it having broken God's heart to save us—but we do object to having a sleepless night while we learn to say "Thank you" to God so that the angels can hear us. We need to be staggered out of our shocking indolence.

We have no business to limit God's revelations to the bias of the human mind.

"I can't alter my thinking." You can. It is actually possible to identify your mind with the highest point of view and to habituate yourself by degrees to the thinking and the living in accordance with it.

Your mental belief will show sooner or later in your practical living.

If I make my life in my intellect, I will certainly delude myself that I am as good as I think I am. "As he thinks in his heart"—that means "me," as I express my thinking in actual life, "so is he" (Proverbs 23:7).

I can think out a whole system of life, reason it all out well, but it does not necessarily make any difference to my actual life—I may think like an angel and live like a tadpole.

Note the things your thinking does not account for.

Truth is discerned by moral obedience. There are points in our thinking that remain obscure until a crisis arises in personal life where we ought to obey, as soon as we obey the intellectual difficulty alters. Whenever we have to obey it is always in something immensely practical.

Obedience is the basis of Christian thinking. Never be surprised if there are whole areas of thinking that are not clear—they never will be until you obey.

Every new domain into which your personal life is introduced necessitates a new form of responsible intelligence.

Watch what you say you don't understand—you understand only too clearly.

Learn to be glad when you feel yourself a chaos that makes you bitterly disappointed with yourself, because from that moment you will begin to understand that God alone can make you order and beauty.

Young life must be in chaos or there is no development possible.

Until you get an answer that satisfies only your best moods, don't stop thinking, keep on querying God. The answers that satisfy you go all over you, like health or fresh air.

Don't shut up any avenue of your nature, let God come into every avenue, every relationship, and you will find the nightmare curse of secular and sacred will go.

Intellectual obstinacy produces the sealed mind: "Jesus said to them, 'If you were blind, you would have no sin; but now you say, "We see." Therefore your sin remains'" (John 9:41).

There is no jump into thinking, it is only done by a steady, determined facing of the facts brought by the engineering of circumstances. God always insists that I think where I am. Beware of that abortion of providence, "If I were you, . . ."

With regard to other people's minds, take all you can get, whether those minds are in flesh-and-blood editions or in books, but remember, the best you get from another mind is not that mind's verdict but its standpoint. Note the writers who provoke you to do your best mentally.

Never cease to think until you think things home and they become character.

Very few of us are real as God is real, we are only real in spots—awake morally and spiritually and dead intellectually or, vice versa, awake intellectually and dead morally and spiritually. It takes the shaking of God's providence to awaken us up as whole beings, and when we are awakened we get growing pains in moral senses, in spiritual muscles we have never used. It is not the devil, it is God trying to make us appreciative sons and daughters of His.

Our thinking is often allowed to be anti-Christian, while our feelings are Christian. The way I think will color my attitude toward other people.

Always make a practice of provoking your mind to think about what it easily accepts. A position is not yours until you make it yours through suffering.

If you have ever done any thinking, you don't feel very complacent after it—you get your first touch of pessimism; if you don't, you have never thought clearly and truly.

An appalling thing is that people who ignore Jesus Christ have their eyes open in a way many a preacher of the Gospel has not. Ibsen, for instance, saw things clearly; he saw the inexorable results of sin but without any deliverance or forgiveness, because he saw things apart from the Atonement.

The first thing that goes when you begin to think is your theology. If you stick too long to a theological point of view you become stagnant, without vitality.

Never try to pillory incarnate reason by your own petty intelligence.

"I still have many things to say to you, but you cannot bear them now" (John 16:12). These words are true in our mental lives as well as in our spiritual lives.

Doubt is not always a sign that someone is wrong—it may be a sign that he or she is thinking.

Keep the powers of your mind going full pace, always maintaining the secret life right with God.

If you teach anything out of an idle intellect, you will have to answer to God for it.

Never be distressed at the immediate result of thinking on the deep truths of religion, because it will take years of profound familiarity with such truths before you gain an expression sufficient to satisfy you.

God never simply gives us an answer, He puts us on a line where it is possible for truth to break more and more as we go on.

Before the mind has begun to grapple with problems, it is easy to talk; when the mind has begun to grapple with problems, it is a humiliating thing to talk.

Unless you think, you will be untouched, unbroken by the truths you utter.

A logical position is satisfying to intellect, but it can never be true to life. Logic is simply the method your intellect follows in making things definable to yourself, but you can't define what is greater than yourself.

We command what we can explain, and if we bring our explanation into the spiritual domain we are in danger of explaining Jesus away, and every spirit that annuls Jesus is not of God (see 1 John 4:3). We have to be intelligently more than intelligent, intellectually more than intellectual, that is, we have to use all our wits in order not to worship our wits but be humble enough to worship God.

Don't run away with the idea that everything that runs contrary to your complacent scheme of things is of the devil.

As you go on with God, He will give you thoughts that are a bit too big for you. God will never leave servants of His with ideas they can easily express, He will always express through them more than they can grasp.

It takes a long time to get rid of atheism in thinking.

Workers For God

The worker for God must live among the commonsense facts of the natural world but must also be at home with revelation facts.

Be a worker with an equal knowledge of sin, of the human heart, and of God.

Never take it for granted, because you have been used by God to a soul, that God will always speak through you—He won't. At any second you may blunt your spiritual intuition, it is known only to God and you. Keep the intuitive, secret life clear and right with God at all costs.

Never pray for the gift of discernment, live so much in contact with God that the Holy Spirit can point out, through you, to others where they are wrong.

Our confidence is to be based on the fact that it is God who provides the issue in lives, we have to see that we give Him the opportunity of dealing with people by ceasing to be impressive individuals.

Beware of allowing the discernment of wrong in another to blind you to the fact that you are what you are by the grace of God.

How do I deal with a sinful soul? Do I remember who I am, or do I deal with that soul as if I were God?

Never say, "That truth is applicable to So-and-so," it puts you in a false position. To know that the truth is applicable to another life is a sacred trust from God to you, you must never say anything about it. Restraint in these matters is the way to maintain communion with God.

How many people have you made homesick for God?

The value of our work depends on whether we can direct people to Jesus Christ.

"'Do you love you Me?'. . . 'Feed My sheep'" (John 21:17). That means giving out my lifeblood for others, as the Son of God gave His lifeblood for me.

Christian service is not our work, loyalty to Jesus is our work.

Whenever success is made the motive of service, infidelity to our Lord is the inevitable result (compare Luke 10:20).

The curse of much modern Christian work is its determination to preserve itself.

This fundamental principle must be borne in mind that any work for God, before it fulfills its purpose, must die, otherwise it abides alone. The conception is not that of progress from a seed to full growth but of a seed dying and bringing forth what it never was. That is why Christianity is always a forlorn hope in the eyes of the world.

The element of faith that enables us to experience salvation is less than the faith required to make us workers for God. I have to bring into harmony all the strayed forces of my nature and concentrate them on the life of faith.

Beware of the temptation to compromise with the world, to put their interests, their needs, first; "They have kindly become interested in our Christian work, given so much time to it, now let us winsomely draw them in"—they will winsomely draw you away from God.

We constantly ask, "Am I of any use?" If you think you are, it is questionable whether you are being used by the Holy Spirit at all. It is the things you pay no attention to that the Holy Spirit uses.

Your dead-set determination to be of use never means half so much as the times you have not been thinking of being used—a casual conversation, an ordinary word, while your life was "hidden with Christ in God" (Colossians 3:3).

As a worker, you must know how to link yourself on to the power of God; let the one you are talking to have the best of it for a time, don't try to prove that you are in the right and she or he is in the wrong. If we battle for a doctrinal position, we will see no further spiritually.

Never interfere with God's providential dealings with other souls. Be true to God yourself and watch.

Individual responsibility for others, without becoming an amateur providence, is one of the accomplishments of the Holy Spirit in a saint.

As workers for God, feed your hearts and minds on this truth, that as individuals we are mere iotas in the great purpose of God. Every evangelical craze is an attempt to confine God to our notions, whereas the Holy Spirit constrains us to be what God wants us to be.

The greatest service you can render God is to fulfill your spiritual destiny.

Where would you be if God took away all your Christian work? Too often it is our Christian work that is worshipped and not God.

We rush through life and call ourselves practical, we mistake activity for real life; consequently when the activity stops we go out like a vapor, it has not been based on the great, fundamental energy of God.

Beware of Christian *activities* instead of Christian *being*. The reason workers come to stupendous collapses is that their work is the evidence of hearts that evade facing the truth of God for themselves—"I have no time for prayer, for Bible study, I must be always at it."

The lives that are getting stronger are lives in the desert, deep-rooted in God—they always remind you of God whenever you come in contact with them.

Never shrink from dealing with any life you are brought up against, but never go unless you are quite sure God wants you to, He will guide. God's permission means there is no shadow of doubt on the horizon of consciousness; when there is, wait. God never guides by fogs or by lightning flashes, He guides naturally.

Don't insult God by despising His ordinary ways in your life by saying, "Those things are beneath me." God has no special line, anything that is ordinary and human is His line.

Any worker following Paul's advice to Timothy, "Preach the word! Be ready in season and out of season" (2 Timothy 4:2), will be continually surprised with new discoveries of truth, and there will be a perennial freshness about the spoken word.

You cannot be too severe with self-pity in yourself or in others. Be more merciless with yourself than you are with others.

Remember, weariness in work that is attended by spiritual weakness means you have been using your vital energy without at the same time witnessing. Natural weariness in work while you witness produces steady and wonderful rejuvenescence.

If you obey God, His order may take you into a cesspool, but you will never be hurt.

If my life as a worker is right with God, I am not concerned about my public pose—using discreet terms that will impress people—my one concern in public and private is to worship God.

When a worker jealously guards his or her secret life with God, the public life will take care of itself.

Remember, in estimating other lives there is always one fact more you don't know. You don't know why some people turn to God and others don't, it is hidden in the inscrutable part of an individual's nature.

If we realize the intense sacredness of a human soul in God's sight, we will no longer romp in where angels fear to tread, we will pray and wait.

Never talk for the sake of making the other people see you are in the right; talk only that they may see the right, and when they do see it you will be so obliterated that they will forget to say "Thank you."

Notice carefully by what you are hurt and see whether it is because you are not being obeyed or whether it is because the Holy Spirit is not being obeyed. If it is because you are not being obeyed, there is something desperately wrong with you.

In the majority of cases we don't care a bit about a soul rebelling against Jesus Christ, but we do care about a soul humiliating us.

Nothing hoodwinks us more quickly than the idea that we are serving God.

The last lesson we learn is "hands off," that God's hands may be on.

When you are brought face-to-face with a case of happy indifference, pray for all you are worth, but let the person alone with your tongue—the hardest thing for an earnest Christian to do.

It is much easier to do Christian work than to be concentrated on God's point of view.

Beware lest human pity pervert the meaning of Calvary so that you have more compassion for a soul than for the Savior.

As workers together with God, we are called upon not to be ignorant of the forces of the day in which we live. God does not alter, the truths of the Bible do not alter, but the problems we have to face do alter.

Never allow people to confess to you unless it is for their own souls' sake; make them tell God. The habit of confessing tends to make one person dependent on another, and the one who confesses becomes a spiritual sponge, mopping up sympathy.

The judicious weighing of what you should allow other people to tell you and what not to allow them to tell you depends on two things: your experience of life among people, and your experience of life with God.

Never give someone the help God alone should give, hand that soul right on to God.

Keep your mind stayed on God, and I defy anyone's heart to stop at you—it will always go on to God. Our duty is to present God and never get in the way, even in thought.

My business as a worker is to see that I am living on the basis of the Atonement in my actual life.

When you come in contact with the great, destructive sins in people's lives, be reverent with what you don't understand. God says, "Leave that one to Me."

"We then, as workers together with Him" (2 Corinthians 6:1)—the One referred to is almighty God, "the Creator of the ends of the earth" (Isaiah 40:28). Think of the impregnable position it gives the feeblest saints to remember that they are coworkers with God!

Note to the Reader

The publisher invites you to share your response to the message of this book by writing Discovery House Publishers, Box 3566, Grand Rapids, MI 49501, USA. For information about other Discovery House books, music, or videos, contact us at the same address or call 1-800-653-8333. Find us on the Internet at http://www.dhp.org/ or send e-mail to books@dhp.org.